Tension in the writing.

ABBA CDDC EEFGGF (ABBA ABBA CCEDED)

Oxomoron - <u>two</u> contradectury words pushed togetha

sonnet borrowed from Italians but failed in personality.

Ambic hexsemiter - twelve syllable line
    (French)

Imagine themselves some place in Scripture then write

Petrock - courtly love.

Body, Soul, Reason
            (Rule)

Blood, Flem, Yellow Bile, Black Bile
                        (Melancholy)

Straunge - stand-offish.

Medival thought of themselves as corrupt

Luther & Calvin - Say Earth is center.

THE ELIZABETHAN CLUB SERIES 2

EUROPEAN METAPHYSICAL POETRY

by Frank J. Warnke

New Haven and London, Yale University Press

*Originally published for the Elizabethan Club
with assistance from the
foundation established in memory of
Oliver Baty Cunningham of the
Class of 1917, Yale College.*

*Library of Congress catalog card number: 61-14439.
ISBN: 0-300-01849-5 (cloth);
          0-300-01848-7 (paper).*

*Printed in the United States of America by
The Colonial Press Inc., Clinton, Mass.*

*Published in Great Britain, Europe, and Africa by
Yale University Press, Ltd., London.
Distributed in Latin America by Kaiman & Polon,
Inc., New York City; in Australasia and Southeast
Asia by John Wiley & Sons Australasia Pty. Ltd.,
Sydney; in India by UBS Publishers' Distributors Pvt.,
Ltd., Delhi; in Japan by John Weatherhill, Inc., Tokyo.*

FOR JANICE

Contents

PREFACE ix

INTRODUCTION I

FRENCH POEMS 87
 Maurice Scève 88
 Guy Le Fèvre de la Boderie 96
 Jean de la Ceppède 98
 Agrippa D'Aubigné 106
 Jean Bertaut 108
 Jean de Sponde 114
 Pierre Motin 122
 Jean-Baptiste Chassignet 126
 Etienne Durand 130
 Théophile de Viau 140
 Marc-Antoine de Saint-Amant 150
 Laurent Drelincourt 156

GERMAN POEMS 161
 Friedrich von Spee 162
 Martin Opitz 166
 Paul Fleming 170
 Andreas Gryphius 184
 Christian Hofmann von Hofmannswaldau 188
 Johann Scheffler ("Angelus Silesius") 190
 David Schirmer 194
 Catharina Regina von Greiffenberg 204
 Quirinus Kuhlmann 208

DUTCH POEMS 211
 Jacob Revius 212
 Joost van den Vondel 224

Contents

Constantijn Huygens   228
Heiman Dullaert   240
Jan Luyken   246

SPANISH POEMS   253
San Juan de la Cruz   254
Lope de Vega   256
Francisco de Quevedo   261
Sor Juana Inés de la Cruz   270

ITALIAN POEMS   277
Tommaso Campanella   278
Giambattista Marino   280
Giuseppe Artale   284

BRIEF LIVES   289

BIBLIOGRAPHY   305

INDEX TO INTRODUCTION   311

INDEX OF TITLES   315

Preface

This volume is the product of two literary interests which have absorbed me for several years—English Metaphysical poetry of the seventeenth century, and the interrelationships of the various national poetic traditions in Renaissance and late Renaissance Europe. A Morse Fellowship from Yale University in 1957–58 enabled me to do research in Europe, where the librarians of the University Library, Amsterdam, and the Bayrische Staatsbibliothek, Munich, lightened my task through their unfailing helpfulness and courtesy.

Anyone concerned with the examination of Metaphysical poetry as an international phenomenon owes a debt of gratitude to the pioneer studies of Alan Boase and Odette de Mourgues, and it is a pleasure to acknowledge that debt. I am more immediately and personally indebted to many of my colleagues at Yale: René Wellek and Eugene M. Waith, who, together with Lowry Nelson of the University of California at Los Angeles, read the manuscript of my book with care and sympathy as well as perceptiveness; Henri Peyre and Curt von Faber du Faur, who made helpful suggestions on French and German materials; Alexander M. Witherspoon, with whom I have often exchanged ideas on seventeenth-century poetry; Stanley G. Eskin, who, providentially in Paris at a time when I needed to be but wasn't, kindly checked the original editions of two French texts for me.

I owe thanks, and the memory of stimulating conversations, to N. A. Donkersloot of the University of Amsterdam and Friedhelm Kemp of the Bayrische Rundfunk, Munich. Benjamin Hunningher of Columbia University, who several years ago first introduced me to the language and literature of Holland, kindly advised me on my translations from the Dutch, and my colleague José J. Arrom assisted me with the Spanish poems.

I owe the greatest debt to my colleague and friend Louis L. Martz, who has, since the inception of this volume, helped and encouraged me with his experience, learning, and sensitivity.

I am happy to make acknowledgment to the following publishers for texts reproduced with their permission:

Oxford University Press for citations from the works of John Donne, George Herbert, Richard Crashaw, Henry Vaughan, and Andrew Marvell; Plon for a selection from the *Oeuvres* of Bertaut, ed. A. Chenevière; Laterza e figli for selections from Campanella, *Poesie*, ed. G. Gentile, and from Marino, *Poesie varie*, ed. B. Croce, and *Lirici Marinisti*, ed. Croce; Droz for selections from Chassignet, *Le Mespris de la vie*, ed. A. Müller, and Théophile de Viau, *Oeuvres poétiques*, ed. J. Streicher; Giard for a selection from D'Aubigné, *Le Printemps*, ed. F. Desonay; J. B. Wolters for selections from Huygens, *Gedichten*, ed. J. A. Worp; the Fondo de Cultura Económica for selections from Sor Juana Inés de la Cruz, *Obras completas*, ed. A. Mendez Plancarte; El Monte Carmelo for a selection from San Juan de la Cruz, *Obras*, ed. Padre Silverio de Santa Teresa; Lambert Schneider Verlag for a poem by Quirinus Kuhlmann, quoted from *Deutsche Gedichte des 16. und 17. Jahrhunderts*, ed. W. Milch; M. Aguilar for two selections from the *Lágrimas de un Penitente* of Quevedo, in their edition of the *Obras completas*, ed. L. A. Marin; Uitgevers-Maatschappij Holland for selections from Revius, *Over-Ysselsche sangen en dichten*, ed. W. A. P. Smit; Garnier Frères for selections from Scève, *Oeuvres poétiques complètes*, ed. B. Guégan; Propyläen-Verlag for selections from Angelus Silesius, *Sämtliche poetische Werke*, ed. G. Ellinger; Cailler for selections from Sponde, *Poésies*, ed. A. Boase and F. Ruchon; De Spieghel for selections from Dullaert and Luyken quoted from *Spiegel van de Nederlandsche Poezie door alle eeuwen*, ed. V. van Vriesland; Maatschappij voor Goede en

Goedkoope Lectuur for a selection from Vondel, *Werken,* ed. J. F. M. Sterck.

My translations from Marino were first published in *Studies in the Renaissance,* and are reprinted with the permission of the Renaissance Society of America. My translations from Luyken first appeared in *Comparative Literature* and are reprinted with the permission of that journal.

F. J. W.

Saybrook College
Yale University
May 1961

Introduction

Early in our century a revolution in taste restored John Donne to his position as one of the major English poets and gave to the other "metaphysical" poets—George Herbert, Richard Crashaw, Henry Vaughan, Andrew Marvell—a favored prominence which they had never before enjoyed. The revolution as such is long since over: Donne is no longer seen as a twentieth-century man before the fact, a taste for the Metaphysicals no longer makes all-out warfare on Milton and the Romantics an obligation, and familiarity with Donne is no longer the badge of an exclusive sensibility. But the rearrangement of our classics wrought by Eliot and the rest has been permanent; the Metaphysicals are now a central and important part of the heritage of the cultivated English or American reader, and there is no sign that they will cease to be such.

The rediscovery of the Metaphysical poets was an aspect of a larger movement in twentieth-century thought and taste—the revaluation of the entire literary Baroque. A definition of Baroque poetry is hard to come by; [1] practically it might be something like this: the dominant European literary style from the late 1500's to the late 1600's, characterized by a general extravagance of language, a tendency to exceed the limits of its medium, and a concern (thematic, but consistently mirrored

1. One of the most useful surveys of attempts at definition of the literary Baroque is contained in R. Wellek's "The Concept of Baroque in Literary Scholarship," *JA*, 5 (1946), 77–108. Wellek's suggestions for the literary application of the term are among the most sensible yet offered. More recently, in a book to which I shall have repeated occasion to refer (*Metaphysical, Baroque and Précieux Poetry*, Oxford, 1953), Odette de Mourgues has precisely defined the French and English literary Baroque, seeing it as a phenomenon parallel to but distinct from the Metaphysical style.

in technique) with the relations of appearance and reality. The Baroque vision, conditioned by the Reformation and Counter-Reformation quickening of the religious impulse, by the disturbing teachings of the new science, and by a consequent intensification of the conflict between humanism and religion, has as its core a systematic doubt in the validity of appearance, a doubt which expresses itself as an obsessive concern for appearance.[2] Baroque poetry cannot "imitate nature" as literally as either Renaissance or neoclassical poetry; in it the multiple realities of earthly experience are always melting together to emerge in new combination as the hard unity of art. Beneath the surprising, sometimes perverse surface of this art lie the related convictions that only the ultimate spiritual unity is real and that only the sensibility can be a source of knowledge. Thus it is that the sensuous texture of some Baroque religious poetry stands in only apparent contradiction to its spiritual concerns and that some Baroque amorous poetry celebrates physical love in the most cerebral of terms.

The concerns, emphases, and preoccupations of the Baroque poets give rise to characteristic techniques—hyperbole, startling conceit, dramatic contrast—which appear regularly throughout the period and give it a distinct identity when set against the Renaissance and the eighteenth century, with their more strict submission to the controls of decorum and common sense. But within the larger unity of any period style exist a number of alternative directions, and such "stylistic variations" are especially evident in a period of violent change like the seventeenth century. Hyperbole and conceit may be sensuous and decorative, as in Marino, or conceptualized and functional, as in Donne; the feeling for contrast may issue as

2. Although, as a matter of general discretion, I shall avoid generalizations based on parallelisms between different arts, it is illuminating in this context to note that Heinrich Wölfflin, in his influential *Kunsthistorische Grundbegriffe* (9th ed. Munich, 1948, pp. 22–23), cites the careful representation of appearances as one of the features distinguishing Baroque painting from that of the Renaissance.

antithesis, as in Gryphius, or as paradox, as in Herbert; the Baroque attempt to exceed the rational limits of its medium may take sometimes the form of an irrational confusion of the senses, sometimes the form of irony and ambiguity which involve the entire universe in the individual poem, sometimes the form of imitation of the other arts through extreme musical, painterly, or sculptural effects.

The term "baroque" is relatively new to literary history, and there is notoriously little agreement on its proper denotation. I think it can most profitably be used as a generic designation for the style of the whole period which falls between the Renaissance and the neoclassical era; most modern readers agree in finding a period quality in the literature of the late sixteenth century and the first two-thirds of the seventeenth, and "baroque" suggests this quality better than "seventeenth century" or "late Renaissance." As the designation of a period, "baroque" refers not to a precisely definable style but to a cluster of related styles. One of these is the Metaphysical; another is that curious phenomenon, as much social as artistic, known as *préciosité*. One is left with that group of poets most often called simply "baroque"—Giles Fletcher, Marino, Góngora, D'Aubigné, Gryphius, Vondel—practitioners of a style marked by sensuous imagery, exclamatory syntax, and an attempt to achieve the stupefying and marvelous, a style which is more a hyperextension of Renaissance techniques than a revolt against these techniques. Such poets adhere to a precisely definable style which is neither Metaphysical nor Précieux, and their style deserves a name. One might use the term "High Baroque." [3]

3. What I call "High Baroque" is effectively synonymous with the "Baroque" of Miss de Mourgues. In using such a term, I must cheerfully be classed with those, noted by de Mourgues, who "confess . . . that . . . there are literary manifestations which express a kind of baroque within the baroque" (p. 70 n.). My practice, incorporating R. A. Sayce's recommendation of a "hierarchy of terminologies" ("The Use of the Term Baroque in French Literary History," *Comp. Lit., 10, 1958, 246–53*),

The unity of a period style appears not in the dominance of a set of identical techniques but in the way in which differing, even contrasting techniques articulate a common group of preoccupations and emphases; an individual poet, even a school of poets, manifests only a selection of the qualities which together make up the period style.[4] The reader of Marino or Du Bartas finds something which bears a family resemblance to what he finds in Donne or Sponde, but he also finds important differences. Donne cannot properly be called "Marinistic" any more than Leopardi can be called "Wordsworthian"; yet, as Wordsworth and Leopardi are both Romantic, so Marino and Donne are both Baroque. Donne's style belongs at once to the general classification *Baroque* and to the more precisely definable classification *Metaphysical,* and both phenomena are international in scope.

The pages which follow contain a selection of Baroque poetry which is also Metaphysical. It differs from other collections of Metaphysical poetry in that the poems were written not by Englishmen but by Frenchmen, Dutchmen, and Germans, and, to a slighter degree, by Italians and Spaniards. My purpose in translating this poetry is not only to draw attention to a body of art which is, in its own terms, delightful and valuable, but also to suggest the extent to which not only the Baroque style but also its Metaphysical variation ought to be regarded as international phenomena, further manifestations of the real unity of our culture.

---

recognizes different orders of denotation in stylistic labels. Thus "Renaissance" designates a very large and varied period style, "Baroque" the smaller but still quite varied period style which follows it, and "Metaphysical," "High Baroque," and "Précieux" precisely definable styles within the Baroque.

4. Cf. René Wellek and Austin Warren, *Theory of Literature* (New York, 1949), p. 278: "It should be frankly realized that a period is not an ideal type or an abstract pattern or a series of class concepts, but a time sequence, dominated by a whole series of norms, which no work of art will ever realize in its entirety."

Before looking at these Continental poets it would be wise to glance at that English poetry which we are in the habit of calling Metaphysical. Even here a problem in definition makes itself felt at once, for, to a much greater extent than most stylistic phenomena, Metaphysical poetry is associated in the minds of its readers with the work of one man, John Donne. Yet, since every poet has his individual voice as well as his adherence to a collective style, one cannot simply make a touchstone of Donne's style in determining what poetry is Metaphysical; certain of his crucial themes, techniques, and emphases will occur in all Metaphysical poetry, but others will not. Metaphysical poetry has, when tried on the ear, a "metaphysical" sound; that is to say, it sounds significantly like the poetry of John Donne. But each Metaphysical poem has also the unique sound of the individual poet. The composition of the core of style, the shared tricks and visions which go to make up the common sound, emerges if we compare Donne and the diverse English poets who are traditionally classed as his followers.

From Dryden to the present, discussions of Donne's style have centered on his imagery. Dryden drew attention to his predecessor's curiously indecorous images, his habit of "perplex[ing] the minds of the fair sex with nice speculations of philosophy." Dr. Johnson, in his famous observations in the "Life of Cowley," gave the essential definition of the conceit as "the most heterogeneous ideas . . . yoked by violence together"; and T. S. Eliot signaled the modern revival of Donne's reputation by echoing Johnson's definition while rejecting his strictures.[5] The characteristic image of Donne's poetry is the conceit, the metaphor which elicits surprise by the apparent dissimilarity of the things compared. But Donne's conceits are susceptible of more extended definition: however surprising,

5. John Dryden, "A Discourse Concerning the Original and Progress of Satire," in *Essays of John Dryden*, ed. W. P. Ker (2 vols. Oxford, 1926), *2*, 19; Samuel Johnson, "Abraham Cowley," in *Lives of the English Poets*, Everyman's Library (2 vols. London, 1925), *1*, 11–12; T. S. Eliot, "The Metaphysical Poets," in *Selected Essays* (New York, 1950), pp. 241–50.

even perverse, they may seem on first impact, there is usually an ultimate validity in them, and it is a validity which may be perceived by the intellect as a resemblance in function or essence, thus differing from the High Baroque conceit, which is usually based on a far-fetched resemblance in appearance or in superficial value. Marino's description of his girl's breasts as "alps of ivory" is startling but not much more, however amiable the flow of the verse. Donne's famous compasses in the "Valediction: Forbidding Mourning" are equally startling, but the metaphor has an appropriateness which increases in profundity if we consider its thematic relevance to the body of Donne's love poetry. In Marino, as in the fifteenth-century Tebaldeo and Cariteo, sprightly but perverse intelligence discovers a chance physical resemblance and builds a metaphor on it. In Donne intelligence of a more serious sort discovers a real functional resemblance between the apparently dissimilar and makes a metaphor which is also an insight.

The importance of the intellectual conceit in Herbert, in Marvell, even in Crashaw suggests that it is one of the defining features of Metaphysical poetry. "Conceit," as its etymology indicates, is a figure which derives from a concept rather than an observation, and this use of the ingenious intellect to create imagery links all the Baroque styles. But the Metaphysical conceit retains its validity and its emphasis as concept, whereas the High Baroque conceit almost always shifts its emphasis to the sensuous level. The difference in nature points to an over-all difference in poetic: the Metaphysical conceit has its value to the extent that it communicates; the High Baroque conceit, even in poetry of a more serious sort than Marino's, has its value to the extent that it astonishes or overwhelms.[6]

6. Marino gives clear expression to this aim in his famous lines:

> È del poeta il fin la meraviglia
> (parlo de l'eccellente e non del goffo):
> chi non sa far stupir, vada alla striglia!
> (*Poesie Varie*, ed. B. Croce, Bari, 1913, p. 395)

Closely related to the conceit (which, in its Metaphysical form, focuses attention on the contradictory or veiled nature of experience) are the qualities of paradox and irony so marked in Donne's poetry. The manifold paradox of death as life in "The Canonization" is, like the conceit of the lovers as the world in "The Good-Morrow" and "The Sunne Rising," part of an attempt to get at a concealed truth, that truth which, as Donne says in "Satyre III," stands "On a huge hill / Cragged and steep." The paradoxes in the two "Anniversaries" are meant as serious statements of a truth beyond logic and as such differ completely from that ornamentally paradoxical line—"Bagnar coi soli e rasciugar coi fiumi" [7]—which is a crux of the Italian Baroque. The pervasive irony of the *Songs and Sonets*, which makes "The Indifferent" only semi-facetious as a hymn to the erotic impulse and gives "The Anniversarie" an almost tragic quality in its perception of the mutability of that impulse, distinguishes Donne's poetry from much High Baroque love poetry, in which irony exists in a simpler dimension, implying at most the lover's recognition of a public world whose values differ from his own.[8] Donne's rhetoric, like his imagery, is used purposefully to activate a whole vision of experience, and it suggests that the major concern of his poetry is neither the description of a world nor the expression of an isolated emotion but the desperately ultimate probing of the self-contradictory mysteries of experience.

Donne's material is that of his contemporaries and immediate predecessors—woman, death, God—but his attitudes toward his material, as readers then and now have observed, mark the advent of something new in English poetry. Sexual love inspires, in the *Songs and Sonets*, neither erotic description nor

7. In Giuseppe Artale's famous sonnet on the hair and tears of the Magdalen (*Lirici Marinisti*, ed. B. Croce, Bari, 1910, p. 453).

8. In Marino's "L'amore incostante," for example (*Poesie Varie*, pp. 55–58), the lover boasts his inconstancy with considerable complacency but in full awareness that he is the heretic in terms of society's conception of love.

neoplatonic flights; Donne is concerned rather with sex as a *coincidentia oppositorum*[9]—body and soul have their respective claims, each claim excludes the other, and yet both claims are undeniably, however mysteriously, valid. The precarious balance in "The Extasie" is no facile synthesis of sexual urge and platonic rationalization; it is an assertion of the equal truth of mutually exclusive attitudes—if one wishes, a truth of experience which flies in the face of all logic. Considered in the light of the recurrent themes of the *Songs and Sonets*, poems as different as "Womans Constancy" and "The Good-Morrow" become not so much expressions of different moods as complementary treatments of a mystery of experience which demands to be viewed from different sides. Donne explores sexual passion with a psychological profundity akin to Petrarch's, and with an even greater awareness of its complexity.

The attitudes of Donne's religious poetry are as much of a new departure as those of his love poetry. The general rejection of the customary syntax of formal address or prayer, the passionately individual utterances of the *Holy Sonnets*, the internal contemplation of the "Hymn to Christ on Last Going into Germany" all indicate the emergence of a new relation of poet to material, in short of a new basis for poetic style.[10] The connection between attitude and technique emerges most clearly in the divine poems, and it is in them that we become most sharply aware of the poet's central impulse—to view emotional experience in terms of its implicit metaphysical and theological mysteries.[11]

9. The term is Nicholas of Cusa's. Indeed, Nicholas, with his concern for the relations of unity and multiplicity and their suprarational reconciliation, is a philosopher who shows a very special kinship with the Metaphysical poets.

10. Louis L. Martz, in *The Poetry of Meditation* (New Haven, 1954), has traced the relation of this new style to the practice of formal meditation. The late Renaissance flowering of meditative practices is in itself perhaps a product of the unitive impulse which I feel to be central to the Baroque mentality.

11. James Smith, in his essay "On Metaphysical Poetry" (*Scrutiny*, 2,

> Thou lov'st not, till from loving more, thou free
> My soule: Who ever gives, takes libertie . . .

He writes in the "Hymn to Christ," and the formulation is a typical and revealing one: desiring God's grace and the consequent freedom from earthly attachments, he perceives that this freedom depends on his loss of the freedom of the will, a freedom which inevitably leads him away from God. The search for salvation is carried on as an attempt to perceive a theological mystery, and this mystery in turn is reduced to the form of a metaphysical problem. Divine truth contradicts human logic, and supernatural knowledge has the form of paradox.

As my comments on some of the *Songs and Sonets* have suggested, however, the experience of earthly love is viewed under a similar aspect. The examples cited could be multiplied many times:

> Loves riddles are, that though thy heart depart,
> It stayes at home, and thou with losing savest it:
> But wee will have a way more liberall,
> Than changing hearts, to joyne them, so wee shall
> Be one, and one anothers All.

The point is, I think, that, whatever Donne's specific subject, he is concerned most of all with the metaphysical contradictions involved in the experience of it. Even the most superficial of Donne's poems, the *Verse Letters*, show, beside conventional exercises in wit for its own sake, the restless impulse to plunge to the bottom of the most troubling of human awarenesses—that each truth has its equal and opposite truth:

No. 3, 1933, 222–39), finds the basis of the style in "an overwhelming concern . . . with problems either deriving from, or closely resembling in the nature of their difficulty, the problem of the Many and the One." The indebtedness of my general view of Metaphysical poetry to Smith's perceptions will be obvious.

> Our Soule, whose country's heaven, and God her father,
>   Into this world, corruptions sinke, is sent,
> Yet, so much in her travaile she doth gather,
>   That she returnes home, wiser then she went . . .[12]

The term "metaphysical" has a validity not fully understood by Dryden when he first applied it to Donne or by Johnson when he permanently confirmed its application.

The concern with the contradictions of experience results from the attempt to see each experience in the light of total reality. The unitary nature of ultimate reality and hence of divinity, affirmed by both Platonic tradition and Christian theology, lies behind all of Donne's paradoxes and defines his final subject as that greatest of metaphysical problems, the problem of the Many and the One.[13] His poetry does intellectually something akin to what High Baroque poetry does imagistically—it explores the diverse phenomena of existence in order to measure them against a final reality in terms of which they are mere illusion. Hence, I believe, the effect of the "unified sensibility" which Eliot's early essay established as a key term for the understanding of Metaphysical poetry. The persistent urge to unify experience explains Donne's characteristic confusion of erotic and devotional reference, as it explains the radical variety of his diction: the mixture of terms from scholastic philosophy, astronomy, alchemy, and geography with the locutions of daily speech is, like the combination of naturalistic detail with traditional love language, one of the distinguishing features of Metaphysical style.

But the unified sensibility of the poet is an index of the disunified sensibility of the man and the age, as Eliot seems to

12. "To Sir Henry Goodyere," in *The Poems of John Donne,* ed. H. J. C. Grierson (2 vols. Oxford, 1912), *1,* 183–84. My citations of the English poets are taken from the standard Oxford editions. In addition to Grierson's *Donne,* I have used Hutchinson's *Herbert,* Martin's *Crashaw* and *Vaughan,* and Margoliouth's *Marvell.*

13. Cf. Smith (above, note 11).

recognize in some of his later observations on Donne.[14] Metaphysical complexity has its connections with High Baroque grotesqueness and disjointedness.[15] The conceptions with which the Baroque poets work are not new; they are simply the whole body of values and attitudes inherited from the Middle Ages and the Renaissance. But the Baroque need to bring the philosophical assumptions out into the open, to make them the very texture of poetry, reveals a fundamental insecurity of attitude and suggests that the intellectual history of the late Renaissance may explain both the Baroque style and its Metaphysical variation.

My assumptions that Donne's style is meaningfully related to that of the Continental High Baroque poets and that it is part of a suprapersonal response to the conditions of the age are supported by the course of English poetry in the seventeenth century. Despite the currency of such terms as "School of Donne" and "Donne Tradition," [16] the major English Metaphysicals are marked by the vigorous individuality of their styles rather than by any conspicuous imitation of Donne. Only in the early, secular poetry of Vaughan do we find many direct borrowings from Donne, and only in Marvell do we find detailed resemblances which indicate influence. George Herbert

14. T. S. Eliot, "Deux Attitudes Mystiques: Dante et Donne," *Chroniques*, 3 (1927), 149–73.

15. De Mourgues finds the essential difference between Metaphysical and Baroque styles to be the difference between balance and distortion: "In metaphysical poetry we judge a poem by the art with which the poet achieves the reconciliation of clashing opposites. In baroque poetry we should judge a poem by the art with which the poet expresses the experiences of a sensibility determined to go, unchecked, to the bitter end of its reactions to the problems of the age" (p. 74).

16. George Williamson, *The Donne Tradition*, Cambridge, Mass., 1930; Joan Bennett, *Four Metaphysical Poets*, Cambridge, 1934; and, to a slighter degree, Helen C. White, *The Metaphysical Poets*, New York, 1936. All assume imitation of Donne as a major element in the formation of the style. Martz, *Poetry of Meditation*, is typical of the newer scholarship in pointing out that the tradition is not especially marked by such imitation.

shows distinct stylistic resemblance to Donne but few traces of direct influence, and both Crashaw and the Vaughan of *Silex Scintillans* look to Herbert rather than Donne as master— as spiritual rather than artistic master, for the three poets show notable individual variations from each other.[17]

Seventeenth-century England does have its "School of Donne," whose members, ranging in time from Lord Herbert of Cherbury to John Cleveland and in spirit from the ribald Carew to the contemplative King, are united by imitation of Donne rather than by any more profound psychological kinship. Its traditions are more amorous than devotional, and it numbers none of the major figures to whom the term "Metaphysical" is usually applied. To some extent the School of Donne imitated only the surface of the master's poetry, borrowing devices or even whole lines but seldom expressing the kind of vision from which those devices sprang. Cowley is at least as much pre-Augustan as late Metaphysical, and developments in his later poetry—the increasing use of allegory and simile in place of conceit, the ever-greater reliance on a kind of rationality which allows no place to paradox or to contradiction—suggest that the Metaphysical features of *The Mistress* are the result of fashion rather than shared vision. And though the mathematical imagery of Cleveland's "Mark Antony" may seem the *reductio ad absurdum* of Metaphysical style, the poem is actually a good example of that other great variation in the European Baroque—*préciosité*.

Once in a while—in Lord Herbert, in Henry King, in Carew, even occasionally in "natural, easy" Suckling—Donne's imitators view passionate experience in the light of metaphysical contradictions. Donne's influence, as is usually the way with influences, exercises itself on minds which have already some predilection toward his way of looking at things. In gen-

17. Vaughan's numerous direct echoes of Herbert are usually embedded in a poetic context which differs markedly from that of his master and hence gives the echoes themselves an original quality. Cf. below, pp. 16–17.

eral, however, to find in England Metaphysical poetry of the deepest and truest sort we must turn to that great line whose members were not so deeply influenced by Donne and were, with the exception of Marvell, dedicated to the sacred muse.

George Herbert has in profusion the Donnesque qualities of ingenuity and intellectuality, paradox and passion, but he rarely echoes Donne and seldom resembles him closely. His stock of images—the tools of daily life, musical instruments, church architecture—contrasts strongly with Donne's, and his favorite narrative forms, miniature allegories like "Redemption" and "The Pilgrimage," condensed autobiographies like "Affliction (I)," are unlike the older poet's impassioned arguments. Herbert's diction too, humbler and more concrete, is entirely his own, and his occasional didacticism gives *The Temple* a more public quality than the *Divine Poems*.

Herbert's very conception of poetry illuminates his artistic uniqueness and independence; the "simplicity" which he claims for himself in the two "Jordan" poems implies a rejection not only of Elizabethan decoration but also of the deliberate obscurity often practiced by his brother Edward, the kind of obscurity which occurs in Donne's occasional poems. His claim is justified. A poem like "Vanitie (I)" is hard, but it has none of the willful syntactical difficulty of Donne's "Elegie on the Death of Prince Henry" or Herbert of Cherbury's "Satyre I." Concerned with dismissing secular science as an exercise in vanity, the poem manages to deepen its expression through imagery which suggests equivalences between any nonreligious intellectual activity and a wide range of human pursuits—commerce, court attendance, and, most of all, sexual license. By expanding his reference thus, Herbert is able to evoke with greater profundity than otherwise the sin of misdirected love which is the true subject of his poem:

> The fleet Astronomer can bore,
> And thred the spheres with his quick-piercing minde:

He views their stations, walks from doore to doore,
  Surveys, as if he had design'd
To make a purchase there: he sees their dances,
  And knoweth long before
Both their full-ey'd aspects and secret glances.

The nimble Diver with his side
Cuts through the working waves, that he may fetch
His dearly-earned pearl, which God did hide
  On purpose from the ventrous wretch;
That he might save his life, and also hers,
  Who with excessive pride
Her own destruction and his danger wears.

  The subtil Chymick can devest
And strip the creature naked, till he finde
The callow principles within their nest:
  There he imparts to them his minde,
Admitted to their bed-chamber, before
  They appeare trim and drest
To ordinarie suitours at the doore . . .

The obliqueness of the poem's meaning derives from the pur-
poseful seriousness with which the poet uses his metaphors; his
statement is as simple as its nature will let it be, but meta-
phorical statement of this sort is never simple. "Prayer (I),"
with its string of verbless analogies (strikingly like some German Baroque poems), has a similar difficulty, one which is innate rather than sought.

Herbert's claim of simplicity is really nothing more than a
rejection of extrinsic ornament, and though the obscure pose of
Donne's verse letters (which gives rise to an ornamental wit
as extrinsic as the decorations of the Elizabethan sonneteers)
has no place in Herbert's scheme, the younger poet's functional
structure, like his use of the Metaphysical conceit, allies his
work unequivocally to Donne's more important poems. The

traditional grouping together of the two poets is justified not only by technique but also by the particular kind of awareness which creates this technique: the dynamic equilibrium of contradictory truths at the heart of Herbert's poetry is exemplified by the couplet which concludes "The Agonie":

> Love is that liquour sweet and most divine,
> Which my God feels as bloud; but I, as wine.

The contradictory vision is the bond which unites poets as diverse as Crashaw and Vaughan to both Herbert and Donne and to the whole body of Christian poetry in the Metaphysical manner. The enigmatic Crashaw is a case in point. Whereas Donne, Herbert, and, in much of his work, Marvell, favor a diction stripped almost bare of its sensuous implications, Crashaw revels in sensuous detail: a rose "sweating in a too warm bed," melting incense, precious stones, mother's milk. Whereas the central tradition of English Metaphysical poetry organizes its art around intellectual propositions which have a "tough reasonableness," [18] Crashaw uses a method which borders on that of free-association. And his slightly infantile, more than slightly perverse sexuality contrasts both with Herbert's asceticism and with Donne's and Marvell's mature understanding of sexual passion.

Crashaw has properly been recognized as one of the closest English relatives of the Continental High Baroque religious poets,[19] and yet, if we compare him to the recognized masters of that manner—to Marino, to Vondel, even to Giles Fletcher —we find him clearly Metaphysical. There is, to begin with, the colloquial, conversational manner basic to so much of his work:

18. The phrase is taken from Eliot's influential essay on Andrew Marvell, in which he defines Metaphysical wit as "a tough reasonableness beneath the slight lyric grace" (*Selected Essays*, p. 252).

19. See, for example, Mario Praz, *Secentismo e marinismo in Inghilterra*, Florence, 1925, and Austin Warren, *Richard Crashaw: A Study in Baroque Sensibility*, Baton Rouge, 1939.

> Lord, what is man? why should he coste thee
> So dear? what had his ruin lost thee?
> Lord what is man? that thou hast overbought
> So much a thing of nought?

There is, furthermore, the intellectual foundation which supports even his most profusely sensuous conceits; Giles Fletcher's comparison of Christ's cheeks to "snowy apples sopp'd in wine" differs in kind from Crashaw's comparison of the Virgin's breast to snow:

> Sweet choise, said we! no way but so
> Not to ly cold, yet sleep in snow . . .

in which the self-contradictory implications of the imagery express the theological mystery of the virgin birth. And the lines from "To the Countess of Denbigh" which apply fortress-imagery suggesting a woman's defense of her chastity to the Countess's resistance of the impulse toward religious conversion suggest the Donne of "Batter my heart, three-person'd God." Despite all his yieldings to the temptations of High Baroque decoration, Crashaw is ultimately faithful to the native Metaphysical tradition.

Henry Vaughan, unlike Donne in his use of nature, unlike Crashaw in his emotional restraint and his avoidance of sensuous excess, is unlike Herbert as well, despite his many verbal borrowings from *The Temple*. His notoriously loose logical structure has little in common with Herbert's tightly knit handiwork, and his recurrent esotericism underlines a poetic attitude which is opposed to the one outlined in the "Jordan" poems.[20] "Regeneration," the first poem in *Silex Scintillans*, has the shape of one of Herbert's miniature allegories, but the mys-

20. One important strain of this esotericism, the use of Hermetic ideas, has been examined by Elizabeth Holmes in her monograph *Henry Vaughan and the Hermetic Philosophy*, Oxford, 1932. One should, however, recognize that Vaughan's Hermeticism almost always appears within a framework of orthodox Christian reference.

terious symbols encountered by the poet in his vision find nowhere the clear and unequivocal explanation which Herbert finds in "Love unknown" or "Jesu." In the latter poem Herbert pieces together a broken word:

> When I had got these parcels, instantly
> I sat me down to spell them, and perceived
> That to my broken heart he was *I ease you*,
> And to my whole is *JESU*.

But Vaughan, in "Vanity of Spirit," having found "A peece of much antiquity, / With Hyerogliphicks quite dismembered, / And broken letters scarce remembered," finds no such practical satisfaction:

> I took them up, and (much Joy'd,) went about
> T'unite those peeces, hoping to find out
> The mystery; but this neer done,
> That little light I had was gone:
> It griev'd me much. At last, said I,
> *Since in these veyls my Ecclips'd Eye*
> *May not approach thee, (for at night*
> *Who can have commerce with the light?)*
> *I'le disapparell, and to buy*
> *But one half glaunce, most gladly dye.*

Vaughan's conception of the poet as a dealer in hidden mysteries of which he himself can never have more than a shadowy comprehension has no more in common with Donne's conception of the poet as a witty and learned gentleman writing for those of similar attainments than it does with Herbert's conception of the poet as a moral instructor, and his art, accordingly, is as different from that of his two great predecessors as theirs is from each other's. But poetic as such determines poetic style no more completely than content does. Vaughan's style is Metaphysical because his particular confrontation of experience (which relates, in his case, to the rear-guard action which mysticism fought against science in the 1650's and 60's) [21] required the Metaphysical techniques of intellectual conceit and conversational tone and the Metaphysical awareness of contradictory truths. Sometimes, as in "The Timber," Vaughan's expression can be surprisingly like that of the earlier Metaphysicals; more often he strikes his own note, as in the closing lines of "The Night," which could have been written by no other English poet: [22]

> There is in God (some say)
> A deep, but dazling darkness; As men here
> Say it is late and dusky, because they
>   See not all clear;
> O for that night! where I in him
> Might live invisible and dim.

Metaphysical poetry in England achieved its first full triumph in John Donne's intellectual probing of the mystery of his passions; [23] it continued in two different traditions: love poetry written in imitation of Donne and religious poetry written by a group of gifted and very individualistic poets

21. Cf. below, pp. 74–75.

22. The paradoxical figure (derived from Dionysius the Areopagite) which dominates the lines turns up also in Lord Herbert of Cherbury's "Sonnet of Black Beauty" (Herbert of Cherbury, *Poems,* ed. G. C. Moore Smith, Oxford, 1923, p. 38), as well as in *Paradise Lost,* III, line 380— "Dark with excessive bright thy skirts appear." However, it is worth noting that both Lord Herbert and Milton imply rational explanations of the interpenetration of brightness and black, whereas Vaughan exploits the irrationality of the figure.

23. The Metaphysical style does not, however, originate exclusively with Donne's love poetry of the 1590's. The religious sonnets of William Alabaster and much of the work of Southwell, composed during the same period, show most of the traits of the style, and some of these traits are occasionally found earlier, in Fulke Greville and even Sidney. De Mourgues, pp. 12–25, discusses Metaphysical elements in the latter two poets; Helen Gardner and G. M. Story, in their edition of Alabaster (Oxford, 1959), present him as an early Metaphysical poet; and Martz, pp. 179–210, sees in Southwell the beginnings of the "meditative" traditions of seventeenth-century poetry.

whose sensibilities, conditioned by their age, had for all their divergences enough similarity to produce a distinctive variety of poetry within the European Baroque. The pattern of English Metaphysical poetry suggests a temptingly neat hypothesis —that the Metaphysical manner itself is the result of a particular kind of late Renaissance religious sensibility found all over Europe, that only Donne turned an analogous sensibility independently to secular themes, and that other English secular poetry written in the Metaphysical manner is purely imitative and therefore casts no light on the origins of the phenomenon. Two stubborn facts, however, question this hypothesis—the considerable amount of Metaphysical love poetry written by French, German, and Dutch poets throughout the seventeenth century, and the great independent of English poetry, Andrew Marvell. Unique among the English Metaphysicals, Marvell belongs neither with the imitators of Donne, for his style is far too personal and idiosyncratic, nor with the great religious succession, for his themes are often secular and seldom specifically devotional. Sometimes his art is very close to Donne's, as in the "Definition of Love," with its extended mathematical conceit, but for the most part his small but very great body of lyric poetry is Metaphysical in a completely different way. "On a Drop of Dew," for all its learned imagery, and "The Garden," for all its philosophical depth, share with the "Mower" poems and "Bermudas" a reliance on description and sensuous imagery never found in Donne, and Marvell's passion for external nature finds a contemporary English counterpart only in Vaughan.

Although Marvell belongs unequivocally to the English Metaphysical succession,[24] his style shows the interpenetration with High Baroque qualities which is characteristic of many of the Continental Metaphysicals: "Upon Appleton House," with

24. Smith (above, note 11), p. 239, regards Donne, George Herbert, and Marvell as the *only* English poets to whom the term "metaphysical" ought properly to be applied.

its rambling descriptions and inset narratives, is in the genre of Constantijn Huygens' *Voorhout;* his pastoral dialogues have points of connection with the *canzoni* of Marino; and, most significantly, some of his best poems show the High Baroque taste for contrast and antithesis as opposed to the Metaphysical leaning toward paradox and synthesis. The uncompromising dualism of the "Dialogue between the Resolved Soul and Created Pleasure," for example, echoes the religious poets of the German Baroque with their stern rejection of the temptations of the world.

But Marvell is always a Metaphysical, though always in his own way. Even in his most extreme moods of Christian Platonism he exhibits a more puzzlingly complex set of values than, let us say, Andreas Gryphius. The "Dialogue between the Soul and the Body" opens with a stanza in which the complaint of the Soul itself implies the senses as the only vehicles of knowledge.

> O who shall, from this Dungeon, raise
> A Soul inslav'd so many wayes?
> With bolts of Bones, that fetter'd stands
> In Feet; and manacled in Hands.
> Here blinded with an Eye; and there
> Deaf with the drumming of an Ear.
> A Soul hung up, as 'twere, in Chains
> Of Nerves, and Arteries, and Veins.
> Tortur'd, besides each other part,
> In a vain Head, and double Heart.

The Soul longs to be liberated from the Body, but can visualize its freedom only in terms given by the Body; the ironic equipoise of the contradiction stamps Marvell as a Metaphysical poet in the deepest sense, and the conclusion of the same poem, in which the poet gives Body the last word, measures his distance from Gryphius or Vondel, whose dualism is always unbalanced in favor of Soul.

The descriptive, decorative, and pastoral elements in Marvell's lyrics, like the Jonsonian traits they often display, emphasize once again two important aspects of English Metaphysical poetry—the variety of personal styles which are embraced in the concept, and the fact that it is a stylistic phenomenon which is not the result of imitation. Donne, Herbert, Crashaw, Vaughan, and Marvell display differing aims and differing sensibilities; they are united by a set of shared stylistic traits—ingenious metaphor, consistent intellectuality, radically all-inclusive diction, and colloquial tone—and, ultimately, by a shared habit of vision—the tendency to view their experience in the light of total reality, with a consequent concern for metaphysical problems and contradictions.

The European poets represented in the following selection, like the English poets just discussed, show notable differences from each other in theme, attitude, and technique. But if, as I believe, the English poets traditionally classified as Metaphysical do in fact share a core of style which justifies the classification, the poets of this volume deserve, I think, a place beside them. Their resemblances to Donne are often casual or fortuitous, but no more so than those of their English counterparts. Théophile de Viau, Marc-Antoine de St.-Amant, and David Schirmer, like Marvell and Vaughan, show an enthusiasm for nature which contrasts with Donne's indifference to it, and from time to time they use mythological or pastoral references utterly alien to Donne's poetic world, but Théophile's tone of passionate conversation, Schirmer's conceptualized paradoxes, and St.-Amant's sexual realism draw our attention to their kinship with the entire Metaphysical succession. Friedrich von Spee, Heiman Dullaert, and Jean de la Ceppède, like Crashaw and the New England Metaphysical Edward Taylor, are fond of the ritual image, of mystical contemplation rooted in sense perception, but they share with Donne and Herbert, as with Chassignet, Fleming, and Revius, a witty and all-pervasive awareness of the Christian mysteries.

Donne remains the great figure of Metaphysical poetry, and defining the style in terms which do not get too hopelessly mixed up with the personal or unique qualities of his style remains a problem. I think that at least one principle emerges from a reading of the English and the Continental Metaphysicals: the positive definition of Donne's style, the things that are in his poetry, can serve as a partial definition of Metaphysical poetry as a whole; the negative definition of his style—avoidance of the mythological and the pastoral, relative unimportance of physical description, lack of interest in external Nature—cannot.

I have suggested that Metaphysical and High Baroque are aspects of a period style, alternative and to some extent parallel directions within the Baroque era. Inevitably there are interpenetrations of the two manners, and, as Crashaw's work indicates, these interpenetrations occur markedly in religious poetry. Although Reformation and Counter-Reformation did not create the Baroque styles, they did create a set of attitudes which gave especially wide scope to both the High Baroque sense of contrast and the Metaphysical sense of paradox.

The High Baroque religious lyric is characterized by a dynamic interplay between the utter rejection of all worldly experience and the systematic exploitation of that experience in its most sensuous aspects. There is no doubt a connection between the sensuous techniques of this poetry and the sacramental emphases of the Council of Trent,[25] but it is unwise to see these techniques as exclusively an expression of the Counter-Reformation. Du Bartas, D'Aubigné, Gryphius, and Giles Fletcher were all Protestants, and this fact in itself suggests that Counter-Reformation attitudes and Baroque poetic style are parallel reactions, not cause and effect. High Baroque poetry, like Metaphysical poetry, is concerned with the insoluble

25. Warren, *Richard Crashaw*, pp. 63–76, goes into the connection at some length, and his observations are illuminating.

contradictions between man as a creature of sense and man as an immortal spirit, between the aimless flux of time and the changeless moment of eternity, between the transient beauty of earth and the permanent glories of Heaven. Hence the paradoxical effect of much of Crashaw, in which the rich excess of sensuous imagery and the passionate expression of quasi-sexual emotion end in the affirmation of their opposite—the exclusive reality of the world of the spirit. Hence, too, the distinctive rhetoric of Andreas Gryphius, with its catalogues, its kaleidoscopes, its ruthless antitheses. A concern with the contradictions of experience is, of course, to be found in any age which produces great religious poetry; the religious experience itself leads inevitably to the contemplation of the self-contradictory. But the Renaissance poets—one thinks of Spenser, of Ronsard, even of Dante—see experience on two levels, the finally real level of the spirit and the provisionally real level of the flesh. They project the relationship through a poetic style which leans heavily on simile and its extension, allegory. Neither Metaphysical nor High Baroque poets can rest content with the double vision of reality; they seek neither to reconcile the two worlds nor to resolve their conflict but to reduce them to a unity. But this impulse toward unity takes different forms. For the Metaphysicals it resides in a tenuous balance of contradictions, a dramatization of the conflict between appearance and reality which requires as its instruments metaphor and conceit, paradox and irony. For the High Baroque poets it resides in the conception of art as artifact, in the subjective re-creation, in the hard, bright materials of earth, of a vision which is intransigeant in its other-worldliness. In their work there is a distorted, tortured quality which results from an innate conflict between value and experience and makes their chief instruments antithesis, catachresis, oxymoron, and a type of neo-Petrarchan conceit which differs from Donne's in that it affirms not the complexity of experience but its absurdity.

High Baroque rejects logic and reason with a good deal of violence; Metaphysical stresses logic and reason—in order ultimately to transcend them.

Many of the Continental religious poets whom I have classified as Metaphysical show an admixture of High Baroque emphases and attitudes, sometimes even within the individual poem. But the differences in effect between their poetry and Donne's are due not so much to this fact as to the very individual accent with which each of them utters his religious awareness. The Frenchman Sponde, the Dutchman Revius, the German Fleming differ from the Englishman Donne as they differ from each other—partly in the varying degrees to which High Baroque elements occur in each, partly in the varying national traditions and linguistic necessities by which each is affected, but primarily in the distinctive and personal way in which each is a Metaphysical poet. Perhaps this very quality of individuality itself ought to take its place as a final item in the definition of Metaphysical style.

The Metaphysical manner is an important variation of an international style, and the European poets, sacred and secular, collected in this volume handle it with rich diversity. The reader interested in noting, behind all differences of culture and language, the international quality of that manner ought to bear in mind Marvell as well as Donne when he reads Etienne Durand or Paul Fleming, as he ought to bear in mind Crashaw and Vaughan when he reads La Ceppède, or Johann Scheffler, or Jan Luyken. The English poets supply the definition of Metaphysical poetry, but it is a definition more evocative than dogmatic.

A number of European poets of the seventeenth century wrote love poetry which would have offended Dryden's sense of decorum—sometimes in the intrusion of "nice speculations of philosophy," sometimes in a characteristic passionate ratiocination, almost always in the emphasis laid on the contradictory aspects of emotional experience. Only one of these poets, the Dutchman Constantijn Huygens, can be shown definitely to have read any of the English Metaphysicals; he met Donne in London in the early 1620's and subsequently translated nineteen of his poems into Dutch.[26] Much of Huygens' poetry is utterly

26. The poems translated are: "The Flea," "The Apparition," "Witchcraft by a picture," "Twicknam Garden," "Song: Goe, and catche a falling starre," "The triple foole," "A Valediction: of weeping," "The Dreame," "Elegie II," "Elegie VI" (part), "The Extasie," "The Blossome," "Womans Constancy," "A Valediction: forbidding mourning," "The Sunne Rising," "Breake of Day," "Loves Deitie," "The Legacie," "Goodfriday, 1613. Riding Westward" (Huygens, *Gedichten*, ed. J.A. Worp, 8 vols. Groningen, 1894, *2*, 214–19, 255–72). Rosalie L. Colie, in *Some Thankfulness to Constantine*, The Hague, 1956 (the only full-length study in English of Huygens' life and works), examines the Donne translations in detail, finding "Goodfriday" and "The Extasie" particularly deserving of praise. The question of Donne's influence on Huygens has been one of the most vexed in Dutch literary scholarship. T. Jorissen, in "John Donne en Constantine Huiygens," *Nederland*, *3* (1870), 62–84, affirmed an influence, damning Donne for it in terms which sound absurd even in the light of late nineteenth-century taste. J. ten Brink, in his *Schets eener Geschiedenis der Nederlandsche Letterkunde* (Leeuwarden, 1867), had accepted the idea of Donne's influence, but H. J. Eymael, in "John Donne's Invloed op Constantijn Huygens," *De Gids*, 4th ser. *9* (1891), 344–66, denies such an influence categorically, on the curious grounds that Huygens was too good a Dutchman to allow himself to be influenced by a foreigner! Finally, in "De zogezegde Invloed van John Donne op Constantijn Huygens," *Album opgedragen aan Prof. Dr. J. Vercoullie* (2 vols. Brussels, 1927), *1*, 93–105, F. de Backer took the trouble to examine the poetry, as neither Jorissen nor Eymael had. Finding the Donne translations faithful and technically good, except for an occasional coarseness which is alien to Donne, de Backer points out that they are, if anything, more obscure than their originals and hence concludes that there is little or no real influence of Donne on Huygens' original compositions. Huygens' own tendencies toward obscurity and wit, it seems to me, do not invalidate the theory that he underwent Donne's influence. One is influenced, inevitably, only by that with which one already has an affinity. As Miss Colie rhetorically asks, "Who can separate in Huygens' religious poetry his borrowed metaphysical style and his own?" (p. 146). It seems to me that, although Huygens' long poems and *jeux d'esprit* are quite un-Donnesque, at least two groups of poems—the *Heilighe Daghen* and some of the courtship poems—show the effects of a reading of Donne. Huygens is a major

unlike Donne's except to the extent that it shares the general
Baroque tendencies toward contrast and surprise; the long descriptive poems—*Voorhout, Daghwerck, Hofwijck,* and the
rest—have more affinities with Sir John Denham than with
Donne and are defined most of all by elements which are
specifically Dutch: realistic, homely description, and a kind
of overt moralizing never found in Donne and seldom found in
the later English Metaphysicals. His early *Zedeprinten,* ver-
sified characters, show some resemblances to Donne's youthful
Paradoxes and Problems as well as to the earlier English char-
acter-writers, but they fit also the venerable Dutch traditions
of emblem, genre-painting, and descriptive-didactic poem.[27]

Huygens' very first poems, largely *jeux d'esprit,* show more
fondness for paradox and verbal wit than most Dutch poems of
the time, but they have no particular kinship with Donne's
work. Ingenuity and intellectuality are there in abundance,
together with the obscurity for which Huygens was noted in
his own time, but they are modified by a tone which is usually
bourgeois and sometimes gross. With none of Donne's or
Carew's elegant indecency, he tends toward a coarse humor
alien to the English poets. Again, national tradition triumphs;
one thinks of some of Jan Steen's pictures of daily life. Another
feature of Huygens' work is his fondness for word-play—puns,
multiple internal rimes, variant sound-repetitions—which con-
tinues from the first exercises of the adolescent to the poem in
English which the nonagenarian courtier sent to English-born
Queen Mary.[28] Sometimes this word-play resembles Donne's
or Herbert's, but more often it expresses a quite different aspect
of seventeenth-century sensibility—that love for trivial and
rather naive verbal juggling which turns up among poets as

---

poet and a very original one; the influence, like the others he underwent,
is absorbed into his own personality and given a new direction.

27. Colie, pp. 46–47.

28. "An Elzabeth was queen, (I'll alter but a letter).
   God give our Marie a Crown, Sh'ill proove an Elzabetter."

(Huygens, *Gedichten, 8,* 352)

varied as Marino, the *précieux*, and the members of the German *Sprachgesellschaften.*

If we leave aside Huygens' religious lyrics, in which he is unquestionably a Metaphysical poet,[29] we find only one important group of poems in which he employs the full Metaphysical manner. The sequence belongs to the period of his courtship and marriage, and one remembers that Huygens translated "The Dreame" and the "Valediction: Forbidding Mourning" as well as "The Flea" and "Womans Constancy." [30] The several poems to "Sterre" ("Star"), his name for his betrothed, Susanne van Baerle, play with the name in a manner familiar to readers of the English Metaphysicals, and other poems of the period—"Kommerlick ontwaken" and "Van d'ure dat ick waeck," for example—combine colloquial tone with an intellectual analysis of personal passion. "Kommerlick ontwaken," with its rhythmically broken opening lines and its systematically paradoxical reversal of the values of life and death, stands as a type of this aspect of Huygens' art.

When moved by intense experience of religion or sexual love, Constantijn Huygens, that serene representative of the prosperous Dutch oligarchy, expressed himself in the style of the Metaphysicals, and it is reasonable to think that some echoes of Donne found their way into that expression, although only one direct (and quite openly admitted) borrowing from Donne appears in his work.[31] These love lyrics by Huygens seem to

29. Cf. below, pp. 68–71.
30. See Colie, pp. 55–60.
31. I refer to his "Vrouwen Onstade" ("Woman's Inconstancy"), which I quote in full:

Wat zeid' hij 't na mijn' sinn een van de kloeckste Wijsen
   Ick derv geen' Vrouwen prijsen,
   De beste die ick ken
Moght licht veranderen terwijl ick besigh ben.

(quoted in *Spiegel van de Nederlandsche poëzie door alle eeuwen,* ed. V. van Vriesland, Amsterdam, 1939, p. 210)

be the only examples of secular Metaphysical poetry in seventeenth-century Holland. P. C. Hooft, whose Italianate lyrics
had introduced the Renaissance into Dutch poetry and to
whom Huygens sent his translations of Donne, admired the
Englishman's wit in extravagant terms,[32] but his own style
remained of the Renaissance, and closer to Tasso than to
Marino. G. A. Bredero, with Hooft the most gifted of Dutch
love-lyrists of the time, continued to write during his short
life poems which have a folklike simplicity equally far from
Metaphysical and High Baroque manners. And Joost van den
Vondel, the greatest of all Dutch poets, expressed his snorting
distaste for all Metaphysical obscurity in lines addressed to
Tesselschade Visscher, a gifted and charming bluestocking of
the Hooft circle, who had urged Huygens to continue his
translations:

> De Britse Donn',
> Die duistre zon,
> Schijnt niet voor ieders ogen,
> Zeit Huygens, ongelogen.
> (The British Donne,
> That darken'd sun,
> Shines not for every eye,
> Says Huygens—It's no lie.)

Ironically, the great Joost himself could, in the presence of
religious mysteries, turn stanzas of an unmistakable "Metaphysical" cast,[33] and we shall see that seventeenth-century

---

> With the words of that wise man agree I must:
> I'll never woman trust;
> The best I know, 'tis said,
> May change the moment that I turn my head.

The wise man is surely John Donne, and he made his statement in
"Goe, and catche a falling starre."

32. Hooft's judgment is cited in Colie, p. 61.
33. Cf. below, pp. 57–58.

Holland offers a body of religious Metaphysical poetry second only to that of England.

Religious poetry with a Metaphysical accent occurred widely all over northern and western Europe in the seventeenth century. The distribution of amorous poetry written in a comparable style is more puzzling: in England the work of Donne and his imitators and Marvell; in Holland some of the lyrics of Huygens; in Germany the poetry of a small and ill-defined group and of a few peripheral and isolated later practitioners; in Italy and Spain an occasional lyric. Outside of England, only France boasts an important and varied tradition of secular Metaphysical verse, a tradition which begins in the middle of the sixteenth century, follows a number of different directions, and dies out almost completely before 1650.

Maurice Scève (1504–1564), the author of the sequence of *dizains* called *Délie*, defies classification. There is some justification for seeing in him the earliest Metaphysical poet, but such a description will require at least some modification. In its thoroughgoing deification of the lady, as in its unvarying formality of diction and rhythm, *Délie* is closely related to the work of the Italian *stilnovisti* of the late thirteenth century, and it seems likely that their influence, in addition to the unquestionable influence of Petrarch, worked on Scève and the other poets of his native Lyon. Stilnovist poetry itself, intellectual in structure, philosophical in vocabulary, conceptual in imagery, is something like Metaphysical poetry, but in Scève these qualities are reinforced by other traits which ally him still more closely to the English poets of the following century. His habit of expressing an insight through its embodiment in a strikingly concrete image leads to a type of condensed conceit fully typical of the later Metaphysical poets:

> Tu me seras la Myrrhe incorruptible
> Contre les vers de ma mortalité,

or

> Tu m'es le Cedre encontre le venin
> De ce Serpent en moy continuel.

His tendency to mingle the experiences of physical passion and intellectual perception, constant in *Délie,* is nowhere more strongly marked than in the beautiful dizain which begins "Asses plus long, qu'un Siècle Platonique," in which the lover's soul can experience the spiritual virtues of the loved one only when the lover's body feels the embrace of her arms. The paradoxical implications of this dizain typify another aspect of Scève's work, a concern for the contradictory, especially as he perceives it in the experience of a love which is at once totally spiritualized and insistently physical. In dizain CCCLXXII his lady's rigor purifies him even as her beauty inflames him, both actions occurring simultaneously and plunging the poet into a kind of double fire.[34]

Scève's unique genius founded no school. Louise Labé and Pernette du Guillet, the learned ladies who were the other major ornaments of poetry in Lyon (the latter was the original of Scève's Délie), had some of his intellect and much of his understanding of passion, but they never blended them in his characteristically ambiguous way. To find the next traces in France of something like the Metaphysical style one must turn to Agrippa D'Aubigné. Generally described[35] as the chief French exponent of Baroque poetry, D'Aubigné is usually committed, especially in his masterpiece, *Les Tragiques,* to a manner which is High Baroque in the extreme. In the love poetry of his earlier period, however, his distraught and violent visions assume both philosophical complication and colloquial immediacy. The lyrics of *Le Printemps* are in the Petrarchan tradi-

34. De Mourgues, pp. 17–22, makes illuminating comments on three of the four poems by Scève included in my translations.

35. Ibid., pp. 88–93. See also Imbrie Buffum, *Agrippa D'Aubigné's Les Tragiques: A Study of the Baroque Style in Poetry,* New Haven, 1951. Alan Boase, "Poètes anglais et français de l'époque baroque," *Revue des sciences humaines,* new ser. 55–56 (1949), 155–84, maintains that D'Aubigné is occasionally Baroque in the manner of Donne and Herbert.

tion, but D'Aubigné modifies his Petrarchanism through psychological violence as Scève had modified his through intellectual complexity. The one poem by D'Aubigné included in the following selection is like much of his love poetry in its perilous approach to the ridiculous, but his imagery of blood and fire and wounded entrails takes on a demonic force through its very extremeness, and in stanzas 3 and 4 the qualifying presence of wit lends the force of irony to his compulsive symbols. D'Aubigné is not a Metaphysical poet, but he deserves a place on the periphery of that style.

Jean de Sponde, more important for his religious verse,[36] shows in his few secular poems an analogous kind of violence, combined with an even more markedly conversational tone. But in these poems Sponde seldom views his emotional experience in terms of philosophical or theological speculation; this essential feature of the Metaphysical style, prominent in Scève, appears again first in the love lyrics of Jean Bertaut and Pierre Motin. Written around the same time as Donne's earlier poems,[37] they display a surprisingly similar way of grasping experience and stand out against the more standard French love poetry of the 1590's much as Donne's stands out against the work of the sonneteers. French poetry at the close of the sixteenth century presents a pattern of stylistic disintegration followed by complex and varied attempts at reintegration, much as English poetry of the early 1600's does. The smoothness, clarity, and grace of Ronsard developed, on the one hand, into the delicate *préciosité* of Desportes, on the other into something very much like its own opposite—the tortured metaphors and wrenched logic of D'Aubigné. The enrichment of the French language by borrowings from Latin and Greek, so favored by the Pléiade, fell into disrepute and was replaced,

36. Cf. below, pp. 64–66.
37. Both poets are represented in *recueils* of 1597, 1598, and 1599. Bertaut's collected works were first published in 1601. See *Le Préclassicisme Français*, ed. J. Tortel (Paris, 1952), pp. 227–28, 233.

for some poets, by the kind of word-coinage indulged in by Du Bartas. Mythological reference itself, so sturdy a rafter in the structure of French Renaissance poetry, became progressively weaker.

A new kind of classical synthesis began its slow but steady movement toward stylistic dominance when Malherbe abandoned the High Baroque style of his "Larmes de St. Pierre" for a type of poetry in which reason, common sense and decorum played a more important role.[38] This burgeoning classicism exerted a growing influence on the major currents in French poetry of the first half of the seventeenth century— the High Baroque, the Précieux, and the Metaphysical. In the early years of the century, however, French Metaphysical poetry showed little of this modifying influence and assumed a shape much like that of its English counterpart.[39]

The *Stances* of Jean Bertaut are set in the Petrarchan mould of adoration for a distant and cold mistress, but, in their rigidly intellectual form and their substitution of dialectic for description,[40] they have little in common with the Petrarchan poetry of his countrymen—Ronsard, Desportes, or even D'Aubigné. In one passage, for example, Bertaut compares his love to flame and then, to praise the celestial quality of his mistress, exploits the fact that the natural quality of flame is to ascend:

38. Malherbe's role in French literary history is analogous to Ben Jonson's in English. The triumph of Malherbe's principles was more rapid, partly because the Metaphysical style constituted less of a challenge in France, partly because the authoritarian ideals of the French court found in his principles a more complete embodiment. I later suggest (below, pp. 81–82) that the two considerations are related.

39. See de Mourgues' discussion of La Ceppède and Sponde (pp. 49–66). I cannot agree with her assertion (p. 64) that no Metaphysical aspect may be found in the French love poetry of the period.

40. Jean Tortel writes in "Quelques constantes du lyrisme préclassique" (*Le Préclassicisme Français*, p. 132): "Il ne faut pas chercher la grandeur d'un Bertaut dans son inspiration, car à vrai dire il n'exprime que des poncifs, mais dans le sens qu'il a, le premier peut-être, et plus que tout autre depuis Scève en tout cas, de la dialectique poétique. En fait, sa poésie . . . ne cesse d'argumenter, un peu à la manière de Donne."

32

Ne vous offensez point, belle ame de mon ame,
De voir qu'en vous aymant j'ose plus qu'il ne faut:
C'est bien trop haut voller, mais estant tout de flame
Ce n'est rien de nouveau si je m'éleve en haut.

The comparison of the poet's passion to flame, in itself conventionally Petrarchan, receives a Metaphysical treatment which is carried on in the lines which follow, intellectual and learned in their diction:

Comme l'on voit qu'au ciel le feu tend et s'élance,
Au ciel de vos beautez, je tens pareillement:
Mais luy c'est par nature, et moy par cognoissance;
Luy par necessité, moy volontairement.

Another of the *Stances* is shaped by the same fondness for exploring the manifold implications of a single metaphor: his mistress's beauty is like the sea in comparison with that of her rivals; she absorbs them as the sea absorbs tributary rivers. Following the figure, the beloved becomes for the lover a perilous sea in which he is adrift and drowned, with no light of hope to serve him as guide or savior (the poem makes an interesting comparison with Marino's "Mentre la sua donna si pettina," which has such a very different effect). By an ironical twist, however, the lover's "flame" makes him a lighthouse to other lovers adrift on the sea of passion, and through a final irony he perceives that his power of illumination comes from the reflection of the sun-like beauty of his beloved:

Car ténébreux de moi je n'ai point de clarté
Qu'autant que m'en départ ta divine beauté,
Comme fait le Soleil au globe de la Lune . . .

Bertaut's Metaphysical flavor here comes not only from his handling of image for intellectual or functional significance rather than for descriptive capacities but also from the self-contradictory imagery applied to the beloved: at once sea and sun, she is equated with elements which are opposite as well as cosmic. Here, as in Donne's "Valediction: Of Weeping" or in Carew's "A Beautiful Mistress," logic arrives at an insight which defies logic (in contrast to much High Baroque poetry, which eschews logic in expressing its supralogical insights).

Akin to Donne's poetry, Bertaut's is not altogether analogous, for it shows neither the cynicism and brutal realism of some of Donne's amorous verse nor the abrupt, conversational tone and varied diction so typical of the entire English Metaphysical group; his structure and imagery seem sometimes at variance with his tone. But in other French poets of the time we find the conversational note too; Pierre Motin's sonnets to Mademoiselle La Croix assume in their tone of voice and manner of address that the loved one is an untidy complex of tissue, desire, and spirit rather than a goddess or a cosmic principle. More exactly, Motin implies that she is all these things simultaneously, and thereby achieves a typical complexity. He is especially fond of a playfully blasphemous juxtaposition of the experiences of sexual love and religious devotion, and the punning potentialities of his beloved's name give him ample occasion to indulge this taste.

The Metaphysical strain which appears in Bertaut and Motin is not an isolated phenomenon in late-Renaissance France. We find it to an intense degree in the work of the so-called *libertin* poets—Etienne Durand, Théophile de Viau, Marc-Antoine de St.-Amant, Tristan l'Hermite—who were active from 1610 to 1650.[41] Durand, broken on the wheel and burned to death at the age of 28 for the crime of *lèse-majesté*, symbolizes the coming of a new era almost as dramatically as Giordano Bruno. The brash daring which led him, in 1618, to

41. Théophile, Tristan, and St.-Amant make up the acknowledged core of the *libertin* movement (see Antoine Adam, *Théophile de Viau et la libre pensée française en 1620*, Paris, 1935). I include Durand in the group on the basis of the implications of his poetry, implications which lead Jean Tardieu (in "Etienne Durand, poète supplicié," *Le Préclassicisme Français*, p. 193) to the same conclusion.

libel Louis XIII permeates his single volume of love lyrics, the *Méditations* of 1610. The title itself, with its devotional implications, predicts the mixture of passion and intellectuality which one finds in the volume, and his most important poem, the "Stances à l'Inconstance," is an achieved triumph of the Metaphysical style. Its theme is that of "The Indifferent," "Confined Love," and "Elegie III"—change is all-pervasive and constant, the very principle upon which the universe is built. Durand's treatment, too, evokes Donne; the goddess of inconstancy addressed in the poem has something of the function of Venus in "The Indifferent," and the hymn opens with a blasphemous application of Eucharistic imagery which recalls the Christian references of "Elegie XIX":

> Recoy ces vers sacrez à ta seule puissance
> Aussi bien que mon âme autrefois te receut.

Durand's vision is both intellectual and cosmic; Inconstancy is to the world a "seconde essence," a goddess who abides "partout et nulle part." The entire poem seems almost an extension and intensification of Donne's suggestion that change is a cosmic principle, and the English poet's rhetorical question:

> Are Sunne, Moone, or Starres by law forbidden,
> To smile where they list, or lend away their light?
> Are birds divorc'd, or are they chidden
> If they leave their mate, or lie abroad a night? [42]

receives, as it were, a scholarly answer from Durand:

> Si la terre pesante en sa base est contrainte
> C'est par le mouvement des atosmes divers,
> Sur le dos de Neptun ta puissance est dépeinte,
> Et les saisons font voir que ta Majesté saincte
> Est l'âme qui soutient le corps de l'Univers.

42. *Poems of John Donne*, 1, 36.

But Durand does not confine himself to generalized observations. The last four stanzas introduce his mistress, a further manifestation of inconstancy but also a being of flesh and blood, whose appearance lends to the poem a final tortured ambiguity; Durand's image of himself as a faithful priest serving at the altar of his mistress in the temple of Inconstancy could serve as a symbol for those vital polarities which the *Songs and Sonets* weld into a mysterious unity.

Paradoxically faithful in his infidelity, bizarrely religious in his libertinism, curiously intellectual in his passion, Durand evinces a profound awareness of the contradictions of experience. Furthermore, although he expresses himself in the conventional lyric forms of the high Renaissance—"stances," sonnet, ode—and although he enriches his imagery with classical references and personifications, he is capable of striking the note of colloquial urgency characteristic of his English contemporaries: "Je te fais un présent des restes de ma perte," or "Depuis si J'ay vescu, J'ay vescu par miracle," or "Si vous estes mon coeur, si vous estes mon âme / Comment puis-je estre en vie et séparé de vous?" [43]

The voice of a man speaking, the effect of an intense private conversation unexpectedly overheard, are also among the striking qualities in much of the work of Théophile de Viau, whose present popularity after three centuries of relative neglect is rapidly giving him his position as a major French poet. Born in 1590, the same year as Durand, he resembles him in his naturalism, his intellectuality, and his complexity of vision.[44] Although the weirdly distorted and richly colored visions of his later poetry have justly led many of his admirers to see him

43. Tardieu, pp. 192, 195, cites these passages as typical of the personal, confessional element in Durand's genius.

44. The peculiarly despicable poem in which Théophile rejoices at the execution of Durand should not be taken as evidence to the contrary; Adam (p. 92) ascribes the poem to Théophile's duties as the protégé of the Comte de Candale, a supporter of the court favorite Luynes.

as one of the chief French exponents of High Baroque style, Théophile displays in the elegies and sonnets of his middle period a sensibility akin to that of the English Metaphysicals, though refracted through a highly individual personality.[45] His sonnet "Au moins ay-je songé que je vous ay baisee" begins with a conversational abruptness, his "Stances à Cloris" open directly on an interior monologue seized in a moment of the greatest intimacy, and the long and beautiful "Élégie à Cloris" evokes the Metaphysical *frisson* with terrifying skill. If lines of this last-mentioned poem sound like Donne or Scève in their succinct incorporation of body and spirit—"Aussi bien faudrat-il qu'une vieillesse infame / Nous gele dans le sang les mouvemens de l'ame"—other lines sound like Marvell in their ironic but desperate understatement:

> Ceux qui jurent d'avoir l'ame encore assez forte
> Pour vivre dans les yeux d'une Maistresse morte
> N'ont pas pris le loisir de voir tous les efforts
> Que fait la mort hideuse à consumer un corps . . .

Théophile may, I think, be classified as a Metaphysical poet, but he is one in very much his own manner, expressing his contradictory vision in language of the greatest clarity and precision.

The alert, experimental way in which Théophile confronts the experiences of love and death, like so many of the qualities of his poetry, may possibly be traced to the overt naturalism which he espouses in his critical utterances and which kept him in almost constant danger of meeting Etienne Durand's fate.[46] The principle expounded in his *Fragments d'une Histoire Co-*

45. Boase, "Poètes anglais et français," p. 177, makes a similar observation: "le ton familier et mâle et quelquefois le tour d'esprit nous rappelle la manière anglaise."

46. An account of the famous "Affaire Théophile," dealing with the accusation of atheism against the poet and his subsequent exile, condemnation in absentia, and imprisonment, may be found in Adam, pp. 161–89, 333–404.

mique—"Il faut écrire à la moderne"—underlines his stylistic innovations as it does those of his contemporary and friend, Marc-Antoine de St.-Amant.[47]

One of St.-Amant's unique features, if we compare him to other poets of his day and nation, is a brutal realism in speech and imagery:

> Entrer dans le bordel d'une démarche grave,
> Comme un Coq qui s'apreste a jouer de l'ergot;
> Demander Janneton, faire chercher Margot
> Ou la jeune Bourgeoise, à cause qu'elle est brave . . .

In this, as in some other of his lighter poems, coarse language and barnyard metaphor represent one of the directions taken by late Renaissance naturalism. The mood is that of the more cynical of Donne's *Elegies*,[48] and in other respects too St.-Amant resembles the early Donne—in his coolly insolent wit, his offhand tone, his sexual imagery. One of his sonnets concludes with an intricate exercise in insult (which exploits, one may note in passing, Donne's recurrent image of eyes as mirrors):

> Pour me donner un nom qui me soit convenable,
> Cloris, ton jugement est plus que raisonnable,
> Quand tu viens m'appeler un miroir à Putains.
>
> Je n'en refuse point le titre ny l'usage:
> Il est vray, je le suis, tes propos sont certains,
> Car tu t'es bien souvent mirée en mon visage.

---

47. The passage is quoted in *Le Préclassicisme Français*, pp. 264–65. The same work (pp. 267–68) quotes St.-Amant's introduction to the first edition of his poems, in which he boasts of his small Latin and less Greek.

48. The relation of Donne's *Elegies* to the body of doctrine which the Renaissance knew as "naturalism" is examined by L. I. Bredvold in "The Naturalism of Donne in Relation to Some Renaissance Traditions," *JEGP*, *22* (1923), 471–502.

In general, St.-Amant's amorous poems are more concerned with perceiving witty correspondences than with painting libidinous scenes; the sonnet "Je viens de recevoir une belle missive," opening with a swift and personal directness, proceeds to characterize the speaker's mistress first as a trapper and then as someone who stamps her "image lascive" on the heart of her lover. Both conceits function as expressions of the relation between the lovers rather than as descriptions of the beloved. The concluding lines have a clear phallic relevance, but even this remains almost abstract:

> . . . puis que j'ay le mot justement à six heures,
> Amour, conduis l'aiguille au milieu du Cadran.

But St.-Amant's style is not always, or even usually, Metaphysical. Some of his best-known poems—"La Solitude," for example, and "Le Contemplateur"—are written in a quite different manner, discursive, descriptive, in an ultimate sense sentimental. Only in his lighter pieces, when he is espousing the claims of natural impulse, does St.-Amant assume the voice of a Metaphysical poet. This fact in itself might lead one to postulate some kind of connection between Metaphysical style and libertine beliefs, to assume that self-conscious modernism, belief in nature, and a notably cool attitude toward Christianity underlie the style, at least in its French manifestation. Such an idea would be even more misleading than the idea, previously rejected, that a specific kind of religious awareness creates the style. There is, to begin with, the whole body of religious poetry in the Metaphysical manner; [49] there is the secular poetry of Bertaut and Motin, neither of whom is in any respect a *libertin* (Bertaut, as a matter of fact, was a bishop); there is, finally, the poetry of Andrew Marvell, neither free-thinker nor radical and yet, even more than Donne, the closest English relative of the French *libertins*.[50]

49. Cf. below, pp. 54–76.
50. Ruth Wallerstein, in *Studies in Seventeenth-Century Poetic* (Madi-

Marvell's treatment of nature underlines emphatically his affinities with the *libertins*. Like many of Théophile's poems, "The Garden" and "The Nymph Complaining" bring flowers and rivers and rising suns, the whole observed world in its cyclic renewal, into the range of the Metaphysical sensibility. Again like Théophile, Marvell sees his eternal-seeming passion in the light of the relentless changes of time; he is aware that the beauty of nature, which seems an obbligato to his own fragile love, will pursue its course when he and his mistress are dust. His recurrent "green"—color of nature, color of hope, color of the puzzling unity from which all the diversity of life rises and to which it returns—might symbolize as well the nature of Théophile and St.-Amant.

Marvell's enthusiasm for "nature" implies perhaps a kind of "naturalism" in his beliefs, but, although his specific philosophic ideas remain masked behind the ambiguities of his poetry, there are enough Christian affirmations throughout it to discourage any assumption that he was a follower of naturalism in the late-Renaissance meaning of that term.[51] The philosophic naturalism of Théophile and the young Donne ought not, then, to be seen as a "cause" of Metaphysical poetry. No one thing really is. Metaphysical poetry, like any other stylistic phenomenon, is not "caused" by any particular ideology, but it does flourish in certain kinds of climate; there are preconditions to the writing of such poetry, but they are of various sorts. One sort of precondition, perhaps the most important in general European terms, is a heightened religious awareness in an age of sword-sharp theological controversy. Another, in contrast to it but essentially subsisting with it, is the profession of a naturalistic, materialistic value-system in the heart of a culture which officially and rather violently supports a religious *Weltanschauung,* and in this condition the *libertin* poets lived.

---

son, Wisconsin, 1950), pp. 276–77, 306–17, comments on *libertin* resemblances to Marvell.

51. See Bredvold (above, note 48).

Perforce they were rendered unusually sensitive to the complexities of life and thought, and their world-view, with its emphasis on the desirability of earthly felicity, departed so radically from the accepted values of Christian Europe that they were bound to develop a taste for paradox and indirection.

But libertine naturalism was not a very strong foundation for poetic style. Unlike the English Metaphysicals in the religious succession, whose style remained adequate to their theme throughout their careers, Théophile and St.-Amant both concluded with extreme High Baroque phases, as did their fellow Tristan l'Hermite, whose earlier style, though predominantly précieux, shows some Metaphysical affinities in its conceits and its psychological realism. In general, for the French poets, Metaphysical poetry was a stage, a temporary equilibrium, before plunging into the fully dislocated universe of the High Baroque.[52]

Metaphysical poetry, which may be rooted in a certain kind of religious perception or in an individual world-view which implicitly contradicts that of the culture in which the poet lives, may also have its foundation in less clearly definable attitudes and circumstances. Such elements, I think, form the basis of the Metaphysical secular lyrics of seventeenth-century Germany. German lyric poetry of the 1600's is preeminently Baroque,[53] and its style, by and large, has the qualities of the general European High Baroque. To some extent this fact is due to imitation on the part of the Germans, but among the better poets of the century it is due to the persistence of a native tradition which in many respects corresponds to the wider currents of the European Baroque.

52. The sort of universe described in de Mourgues, pp. 88–99.

53. The dominance of the term in contemporary German scholarship is partially explained by the consistent temper of seventeenth-century German poetry. There are, as I hope to demonstrate, Metaphysical elements in German *Barockdichtung,* but there is not, as in England, France, and Holland, a clear Metaphysical line as distinct from High Baroque.

Even before the Thirty Years' War destroyed the conditions of earlier German culture, the German poet was faced with the necessity of reintegrating his art. The tradition of the *Minnesinger* was dead with the feudalism which had sustained it; the bourgeois tradition of the *Meistersinger*, already decadent, had barely survived the sixteenth-century commercial decline of the German cities.[54] While the religious poets were able to restate, with considerable vigor, a tradition of devotional verse which goes back to the medieval hymn, the secular poets, in the tenuous security of provincial court or free city, created an art of almost Byzantine impersonality. Poetry of the senses, it has its connections with Marino and the Italians, but it frequently takes its conceits with a dreadful seriousness; largely the poetry of a limited social group, it has connections too with French *préciosité*, but it lacks the sophistication and finish evident in Voiture and Tristan.

The ravages of war and the chaos of politics undoubtedly have something to do with the unequal quality of German poetry in the late Renaissance. Like the English civil wars of the fifteenth century, the conflict which raged on German soil from 1618 to 1648 tended to strangle artistic and intellectual activity, disrupting life in court, university, and town. Unlike the fifteenth-century English, the seventeenth-century Germans produced an enormous quantity of art-verse, but the importance assumed by foreign travel in the formation of so many German poets of the time argues a certain bankruptcy in the native culture as eloquently as do the lifeless imported shepherdesses who adorn their fancy.[55] And yet the *Barock-*

---

54. C. V. Wedgewood, *The Thirty Years War* (London, 1957), pp. 47–49, relates the cultural decline of Germany in the early 1600's to its economic dilemmas.

55. Of the German poets represented in this volume, no fewer than six—Opitz, Fleming, Gryphius, Hofmannswaldau, Scheffler, and Kuhlmann—studied at one time or another at Leiden in Holland. In addition, Scheffler studied at Padua, Gryphius traveled extensively in France and Italy, and Hofmannswaldau traveled in France, Italy, and England. The

lyrik has its treasures, and they are not stolen treasures. Andreas Gryphius, the greatest German poet of the century, has a splendid, dark vigor which allies him to Dürer; Friedrich von Spee, despite imagery which recalls Crashaw and pastoral devices like Guarini's, has his deepest affinities with the *Volkslied;* and even the most unlikely court poet has an occasional lyric which still evokes delight.

Religious feeling produced the best German poetry of the period, as well as most of the German poetry which can be called Metaphysical, but amid the mass of secular lyrists a few love poets stand out for the intensity and individuality which they bring to the fashionable style. Significantly in the context of this book, the direction which their individuality takes is often that of Donne or Marvell or Théophile.

The first of this group in which the Metaphysical accent may be heard is Martin Opitz, lawgiver of German Baroque poetry, whose *Buch von der Deutschen Poeterey* dominates the theory of the age as completely as his introduction of the alexandrine meter from France dominates its practice. Opitz is full of contradictions: the *Buch von der Deutschen Poeterey*, most important for establishing the accentual principle in German metrics, is in its poetics largely a paraphrase of Ronsard's *Abrégé de l'art poetique*, a set of prescriptions for writing poems in the high Renaissance style. The author's departures from his source, however, adumbrate an utterly different poetic, one which gives ample play to the Baroque taste for contrast and surprise as well as recommending a conscious verbal ambiguity entirely at variance with Ronsard and his fellows.[56]

Opitz' poetry supplies examples of each of the three kinds of

cosmopolitanism of these men saved the German lyric from complete disintegration, but at a certain cost in spontaneity and naturalness.

56. See K. Borinski, *Die Poetik der Renaissance und die Anfänge der Literarischen Kritik in Deutschland* (Berlin, 1886), pp. 71–75, and G. Fricke, *Die Bildlichkeit in der Dichtung des Andreas Gryphius* (Berlin, 1933), p. 14.

art which his theory, in its confusing way, at different times seems to support. "Ich empfinde fast ein Grauen," the best known of his lyrics and the one by which he holds fast to the meager immortality of the anthologies, is a good example of Renaissance *carpe diem* verse, with connections not only to Ronsard but also to Goliardic verse and ultimately to Catullus. More frequent in his work are poems which in their love of the bizarre, the surprising, and the ornamental justify the customary classification of Opitz as the leading poet of the "Frühbarock." In some other poems, and they are among his best, a Metaphysical coloration flickers briefly. "Ach Liebste, lass uns eilen," another *carpe diem* poem, is made up of the familiar catalogue of earthly beauties which must fade:

> Das Mündlein von Corallen
> Wird ungestalt,
> Die Händ' als Schnee verfallen
> Und du wirst alt.

But in the last stanza, although the songlike meter remains unchanged, the statement becomes more equivocal:

> Wo du dich selber liebest,
> So liebe mich,
> Gieb mir, dass, wenn du giebest,
> Verlier auch ich.

The "Wo" is multisignificant, referring simultaneously to the degree of love the poet demands and to the self-interest on which he bases his appeal—"Love me *as* you love yourself," but also "Love me *if* you love yourself"; the last two lines, with or without their sexual implication, suggest, as nothing earlier in the poem has, the mystery of the love experience, the loss of identity inseparable from the assertion of identity implicit in the lover's reaching his goal. It is the mood of Donne's "We're tapers too, and at our owne cost die."

Another lyric, "Kompt, lasst uns ausspazieren," is for its first five stanzas a familiar celebration of the beauties of spring and nature and the songs of birds, but its last stanza again introduces a puzzling note; addressing the birds, the poet says:

> Ihr könnt noch Mittel finden,
>   Entfliehen aus der Pein;
> Sie muss noch mehr mich binden,
>   Soll ich erlöset seyn!

The combination of sexual symbolism ("binden") and paradox deepens and darkens the poem's effect.

The twist which Opitz gives to the endings of these two conventional poems indicates pretty clearly that one small corner of the learned literary dictator's personality was in conflict with the artistic aims which he had borrowed from his models. But one should not overstress this element in his work. He is fond of paradox, and occasionally he uses the Metaphysical conceit, but on the whole his poems are simple continuations of Renaissance lyric tradition, modified somewhat by Baroque grotesqueness, and even those which show a Metaphysical tendency are expressed in a static rhetoric of formal appeal or apostrophe which has little of the dramatic effect of true Metaphysical poetry. Sometimes he can start a poem with memorable abruptness—"Ich will dies halbe Mich, was wir den Körper nennen, / Dies mein geringstes Teil verzehren durch die Glut . . ." [57]—and he can evoke the interaction of microcosm and macrocosm with a cosmic gusto which recalls Herbert's "Providence." But his wit takes more often the way of Marino than the way of Donne, and his hyperboles usually have more in common with the pretty archness of Herrick's "How Roses Came Red" than with the transfigured illumination of Carew's "A Beautiful Mistress."

57. The opening lines of a sonnet exalting the spirit over the body. See also his "Spiegel der Welt."

Paul Fleming, long regarded as the most "natural" of German Baroque poets,[58] was an avowed follower of Opitz, but his compulsion to view love in the light of the metaphysical problems of duration and identity owes more to his own nature than to the influence of the older poet. Typical of this aspect of Fleming's art is "Auff ihr Abwesen," with its Donnesque concern for the lover's loss of identity in the beloved:

> Ich irrte hin und her, und suchte mich in mir,
> Und wuste dieses nicht, das ich gantz war in dir . . .

The manner, if we compare it to Donne's "The Legacie," is a bit heavy-handed; Fleming dwells lovingly on his paradox instead of capping it, as Donne might have, with either a witty development or a further set of paradoxes, but the Metaphysical quality of the poem remains evident.

As a love poet Fleming is only sporadically a Metaphysical. The theme of the redemption informs almost all his devotional verse with a specifically Metaphysical vision,[59] but his love poems include as many conventional Petrarchan lyrics and High Baroque descriptive pieces as Metaphysical poems. Indeed, only one complex of emotions seems to have moved Fleming to Metaphysical manners of expression in his secular verse: that experienced by the lover who feels that he has lost his identity in the loved one. The paradox in the situation is intensified and complicated by several developments in the narrative outlined by Fleming's love lyrics. At first, the lady's Laura-like disdain moves him to perplexed wonder that the possessor of his soul can scorn him ("Ist's müglich, dass sie mich auch kann im Schlafe höhnen?"); later, when his beloved has become betrothed to him, his departure on a journey to Persia leads him to the insoluble question of how the exchange of

58. Curt von Faber du Faur's brief description of Fleming in his recent *German Baroque Literature* (New Haven, 1958), pp. 81–82, properly repeats this traditional estimate.

59. Cf. below, pp. 71–72.

souls can defy physical separation ("An Basilenen"); finally, when he returns to find that she has forgotten him and accepted another suitor, his recognition that his soul is still in her power leads him to an outburst full of unresolved intellectual tensions ("Ein Kaufmann, der sein Gut nur einem Schiff' vertraut").

His use of paradox, then, makes Fleming a Metaphysical poet, and other features of the style sometimes appear in his work: Metaphysical conceit dominates "Ein Kaufmann," colloquial turns of expression articulate "Ist's müglich, dass sie mich," and a deliberate syntactical complexity is found in several other poems. But, more often than not, his conceits are Marinistic and his tone formal. It is only in a younger poet of the Opitz school, the Saxon David Schirmer, that we find the conversational manner associated with a style marked by intellectual conceit and extended paradox.

Schirmer is one of the more interesting and vital of German Baroque poets, and the fact that he is one of the least well known suggests the role played by chance in the making of literary reputations. For it is precisely the fact that Schirmer is such a consistent exponent of the Metaphysical style that explains the neglect which he has suffered. In England the Metaphysical style was established in the secular genres by a very great poet, who promptly received the compliment of imitation; in France, secular Metaphysical poetry was written, to some extent, by a distinct group of poets, the *libertins*, who almost constituted a movement; in Germany despite the existence of a considerable body of religious Metaphysical poetry, most secular verse was High Baroque or Précieux in style, and even Opitz and Fleming wrote only a part of their verse in a style approaching that of their English Metaphysical contemporaries. Schirmer is not a great poet; he can in no way be compared to Donne or Théophile. He is a good minor poet who developed a highly individual style with coincidental affinities to that of Donne and Marvell, and, since his practice differed markedly from that of more important German poets of the period, most scholars have ignored him.[60] The major poet can afford to be original; the minor poet is safer in following paths which will allow posterity to pigeon-hole him.

Even in the more conventional of Schirmer's love lyrics, the familiar complaint of the amorous shepherd has a personal freshness which communicates to the modern reader immediately, despite the stiff archaism of its mode. The dire Petrarchan predictions of "Sie quället ihn" are modified by an endearingly brisk facetiousness of tone as well as by gemlike bits of nature description which recall Carew. "Er hat sich in ihr verloren" is built around Fleming's favorite paradox, but its abrupt opening line and its colloquially broken rhythms recall Donne as well.

The most Metaphysical of Schirmer's poems are found in the long sequence of sonnets to "Marnia" with which he capped his poetic work. The story of the sequence is unusual in both its honesty and its complexity: the poet, a young man of highly susceptible but more than somewhat shallow feelings, meets the beautiful and witty Marnia. After inflicting the usual torments for a while, she grants him her love and then, with a terrible swiftness, dies. He mourns her in the most extreme terms and vows never to love again, but the reader, by this point familiar with Schirmer's personality, is not surprised when the poet, without waiting too long, meets a new girl and promptly falls just as much in love. The emotional and moral complications of this experience provide the material for the last poems of the sequence: Schirmer solves his problem by seeing the new love as a reincarnation of Marnia, and that lady herself finally appears in a vision to set her seal of approval on the new liaison. Throughout these poems Schirmer puzzles over questions of identity and relationship, and his language assumes the in-

60. The only published study of Schirmer in our century is W. Sonnenberg's dissertation, *Studien zur Lyrik David Schirmers*, Göttingen, 1932.

tricacy and ingenuity of the Metaphysical style to an even greater degree than in his earlier poems. The sequence, which has not been reprinted in full since the seventeenth century and which can be represented here only by a few selections, does not deserve oblivion.

Secular Metaphysical poetry, then, is not as conspicuous in Germany as in England and France. The political and social chaos of the Thirty Years' War fostered the ornamental escapism of High Baroque love poetry more than the analytic realism of Metaphysical love poetry. In fact, the small group of love poets just discussed as Metaphysical ought really to be seen as a school. Opitz, who in both theory and practice introduced Metaphysical elements into German poetry, was the friend of both Fleming and the literary theorist August Buchner, who, as professor of literature at Wittenberg, developed Opitz' theories with their intellectual emphasis and their advocacy of extreme metaphor.[61] Buchner, in turn, was the teacher of Schirmer and other Saxon poets who stand in the Opitz-Fleming tradition, the tradition of the intellectual love lyric.

The Metaphysical current in secular poetry, though weak, can be traced further through seventeenth-century Germany. The short-lived Sybilla Schwartz, one of the infrequent woman poets of the time, has a few lyrics which, like Fleming's, examine love in terms of the problem of identity; Hofmann von Hofmannswaldau, though primarily Marinistic in manner, occasionally writes a passage of colloquial immediacy; and some of the poems of Johann Christian Günther carry German Metaphysical style into the rococo age.

Secular Metaphysical poetry flourished in seventeenth-century England and France; in a more restricted way, analo-

61. For some account of Buchner and his influence see R. Newald, *Die Deutsche Literatur vom Späthumanismus bis zur Empfindsamkeit*, Vol. 5 of H. De Boor and R. Newald, *Geschichte der Deutschen Literatur* (6 vols. Munich, 1957), pp. 179–82. See also Fricke, pp. 5–12.

gous poetry existed in Germany; and at least one representative of the style can be found in Holland. Curiously, Italy and Spain, normally so active in poetic innovation, have relatively little love poetry which can be called Metaphysical. Giambattista Marino, frequently mentioned in these pages, is in many ways a key figure for the understanding of seventeenth-century literature. A superb poetic technician, he had almost no artistic conscience, and his art, free of any impurities such as thought or morality, is a kind of improbable laboratory in which the poetic style inherited from the previous century undergoes its bizarre but logical transformations. There is an unbroken continuity between the great monuments of Italian Renaissance poetry and Marino's work; palpable and concrete imagery, quasi-musical exploitation of the potentialities of the medium, an imagination which thinks exclusively in terms of figure—all these things link Marino to his great predecessors. But he has neither the wise humanity of Ariosto nor the ethical seriousness of Tasso nor the bitter-sweet sensitivity of Poliziano. The Renaissance poets created textures of surpassing richness, but always over an intense vision of one sort or another. For Marino the texture is all, and, since it was impossible to make poetry richer or more musical than Tasso had made it, Marino intensified the effect of richness by introducing the new and the startling.[62] After the languors of Tasso, the Italian poet, it seems, had only two choices—to revert to a more chastened but strangely inconclusive classicism, in the manner of Gabriele Chiabrera, or, as it were, to cry for madder music, stronger wine—"Chi non sa far stupir, vada alla striglia." [63]

Marino and the poets who, in following him, gave seventeenth-century Italian poetry its characteristic shape chose the latter way, and in their work Baroque appears as overblown

62. Cf. Francesco de Sanctis, *Storia della Letteratura Italiana* (5 vols. Milan, 1950), 5, 18–45. It seems to me that de Sanctis' classic analysis of *secentismo* retains most of its validity, despite the century which has passed since it first appeared.

63. Cf. above, p. 6, note 6.

Renaissance. In their secular verse as in their religious verse, in *Adone* as in *La Strage degli Innocenti*, the aim is a rarefied sweetness made sweeter by the occasional intrusion of horror, an enticing sexuality made more enticing by a touch of perversity, a facile religiosity made more facile by sensuality.

But Marino is a key figure in seventeenth-century literature not only because of his enormous influence all over Europe [64] but because his work shares in so many different currents of that complex age. His poetry is High Baroque in its sensuousness, its artificiality, its reliance on surprise, but it is very untypical in its determined triviality. High Baroque poets like D'Aubigné, or Góngora, or Vondel present a disjointed world because that is the way they see it; Marino presents a disjointed world deliberately because that is his way of perking up a jaded appetite.[65] This motive gives to his work a family relationship, although only a distant one, to both the French *précieux* and those poor relations of préciosité, the members of the German *Sprachgesellschaften*. The seventeenth-century *précieux* derives his style from the fact that he attempts to say, for the delectation of a narrowly defined social group, something completely conventional in a completely surprising way;[66] the difference between the French *précieux* and the so-called "Nürnberger Zunft" is finally not much more than the difference between sophisticated, cosmopolitan Paris and provincial, war-isolated Nuremberg. Although Marino did not employ coterie terms and cannot really be seen as a précieux, his ornate expression of trivial thought frequently brings his style close to theirs.

As his determined and ingenious search for novelty some-

64. See my article "Marino and the English Metaphysicals," *Studies in the Renaissance*, 2 (1955), 160–75.

65. De Mourgues, pp. 88–93, investigates the compulsive nature of D'Aubigné's world.

66. Both de Mourgues (pp. 103–17) and G. Mongrédien ("La Préciosité" in *Le Préclassicisme Français*, pp. 162–74) agree in defining préciosité largely in terms of social function.

times gives a quasi-précieux turn to his verse, so too does it sometimes lead to the formulation of a *pointe* or the introduction of a mundane metaphor which lend him a superficial similarity to the Metaphysicals. His recognized influence on St.-Amant [67] has to do not only with extended nature description but also with the unusual possibilities of witty metaphor. For these reasons, two of Marino's sonnets have found their way into this volume, as have two sonnets by Giuseppe Artale, the most nearly Metaphysical of his followers. They define one segment of the Metaphysical periphery as D'Aubigné's *stances* define another.

At least one other figure of the Italian *seicento* deserves mention in this context—the philosopher Tommaso Campanella, whose intellectual seriousness and abstract diction contrast strikingly with the techniques of the *marinisti*. But Campanella, every inch a "metaphysical" poet, is in no sense a Metaphysical poet. He is concerned not with dramatizing the conflicts and mysteries of passionate experience but with presenting philosophical truth. For him intellectual analysis is not a technique of poetry but the aim of poetry, and his closest English affinities are with Chapman rather than with Donne.

The Spanish lyric in the late Renaissance is a vigorous and varied genre, ranging in its effects from folk-song simplicity to the Baroque complexity of Góngora's *Soledades*, but the Metaphysical combination of conceit, colloquialism, and paradox, markedly present in the devotional poetry of Lope de Vega and Quevedo, seems largely absent from Spanish love poetry. The one important exception to this generalization is Francisco de Quevedo, many of whose amorous lyrics combine concrete particularity and intellectual complexity in a manner fully characteristic of the Metaphysical style. The final style of Luis de Góngora is famous as an extreme example of poetic complexity and obscurity, but, with its deliberate intricacy, its Latinate syntax, and its rich allusiveness, it suggests Milton

67. See Adam (above, note 41), pp. 443-54.

more readily than Donne to the English-speaking reader. Of the two literary movements which made themselves felt in early seventeenth-century Spain, the *culteranismo* of Góngora, enormously important in its own terms, has little significant connection to the Metaphysical current in European poetry. The rival *conceptismo*, epitomized in Quevedo, has, as its name implies, such a connection, but, apart from the work of Quevedo himself, the movement produced little Metaphysical poetry on secular themes. The conceit in Spanish *conceptismo* is more often Marinistic than Donnesque.[68]

Spanish America, however, offers at least one additional practitioner of the Metaphysical style—the Mexican nun Sor Juana Inés de la Cruz. Despite her vocation she is at her best as an analyst of human passion, and from this preoccupation derive her most typical qualities—consistent intellectuality, paradox, and a striking immediacy of tone. Like the New England devotional poet Edward Taylor, she shows that the Metaphysical style could flourish in the new world as well as in the old.

Secular Metaphysical poetry thus displays an irregular and perplexing pattern of distribution, but one perceives a definite

---

68. E. R. Curtius writes in *European Literature and the Latin Middle Ages*, Bollingen Series, *36* (New York, 1953), p. 294: "There have been frequent attempts to separate Cultism and Conceptism, but they cannot be separated." He is, of course, correct to the extent that the two phenomena are not mutually exclusive and that they often imply one another, but I think his suggestion that they are merely aspects of the same phenomenon is misleading. The hostility which Góngora and Quevedo felt toward each other's work, together with the distinctive quality of conceptistic religious verse, would tend to support the traditional view of *conceptismo* as dealing with thoughts and *culteranismo* as dealing with words. Gerald Brenan, *The Literature of the Spanish People* (New York, 1957), p. 252, writes: "It is the opposition between Donne on the one hand and Milton on the other: between poetry for the eye and poetry for the ear: between poetry that takes in the contemporary scene and poetry that uses the poetic material of the past as a sounding-board to give a greater richness of meaning: between *Prufrock* and *Finnegans Wake*."

concentration in the countries of the north—England, France, Germany, and Holland. Religious Metaphysical poetry, a more extensive and in some ways more important body of work, shows a similar though less intense concentration, and some consideration of it may help to uncover the common roots of the style.

All Christian poetry shows a family likeness, the belief from which it springs enforcing inevitably a certain unity of style. But the religious poetry of the seventeenth century has qualities which distinguish it from that of other ages, both in its choice of genre and in its handling of that genre. Various types of religious verse continue, of course, throughout the century. Narrative poetry on religious themes, a genre represented historically by poems as important and diverse as the *Divina Commedia* and D'Aubigné's *Les Tragiques*, reaches one of its peaks in *Paradise Lost* and falls into various pits in Cowley's *Davideis*, Marino's *Strage degli Innocenti*, and St.-Amant's *Moïse Sauvé*. The laudatory and hortatory genres, poems of praise and edification, continue in full force, numerically if not qualitatively; the endless *recueils* of religious verse in France, emblem books like those of Quarles in England and Jacob Cats in Holland, the spiritual pastorals so popular in Germany—all belong to one or both of these categories, as do the more public poems of Herbert and Vaughan—"The Church Porch" and "Rules and Lessons." But most characteristic of the religious poetry of the seventeenth century is the tremendous importance assumed by the devotional lyric, the religious poem in which an individual relationship to God is expressed, debated, or described with great personal emotion and much intellectual energy.

Devotional poetry as a mode of private communication with or contemplation of the deity is not an invention of the seventeenth century; one need only summon up the names of Juan de la Cruz or Iacopone da Todi. But surely no other century has seen so many poets of major or near-major importance devote themselves to this genre, and when seventeenth-century religious poetry is mentioned, it is of the devotional poets that we think. There is a further distinction in the practice of these poets: whereas Iacopone, Juan, the Dutch nun Hadewych, and other privately oriented religious poets of earlier centuries are all either technically mystics or very nearly so, few of the seventeenth-century group are. Crashaw and Vaughan, in their different ways, are fond of the language of mysticism, and Donne is fascinated by the idea,[69] but essentially these poets are concerned less with the mystical experience than with the analytic assessment of their personal relation to God. They often seek a union with divinity; they never express such a union.

The specifically devotional quality of the religious poetry of this period seems certainly related to the great development, in the Baroque age, of such private religious exercises as the formal meditation. In a recent study[70] Louis L. Martz has argued that "meditation" is one of the major sources of the poetic style which we call "metaphysical"; and, indeed, many of the features which define the style can be paralleled in the late Renaissance works of systematic devotion and in the theoretical principles which underlie them. Concreteness of imagery, colloquial immediacy of tone, and the tendency toward intellectual conceit are all perhaps implicit in the "composition" which is the first stage of a meditation, and, even more significantly, the "fusion of thought and feeling" which our century has found central to Metaphysical poetry seems un-

69. Donne's "Hymne to Christ, at the Authors last going into Germany," the most mystical of his works, is a poem *about* the mystical experience, but it does not even attempt to embody the experience. Crashaw's "The Flaming Heart" and Vaughan's "The World" perhaps do, but neither poem is wholly typical of its author.

70. *The Poetry of Meditation.*

doubtedly connected to the aim and method of meditation, which "begins in the understanding, endeth in the affection." [71] The argumentative structure of much Metaphysical poetry also has its counterpart in the firm intellectual movement of the formal meditation.[72]

The devotional or meditative lyrics of the seventeenth century divide naturally into High Baroque and Metaphysical types, both subject to important historical development in the course of the century. To an even greater extent than in the secular lyric, the two types interpenetrate and modify each other: such High Baroque poets as Gryphius, Vondel, and Southwell have their Metaphysical traits, and Donne's religious poems show occasional High Baroque features.

Poets like Gryphius and Spee in Germany, Chassignet in France, and Vondel in Holland normally typify High Baroque devotional verse in its purest form. The somber sonnets in

71. Joseph Hall, *The Arte of Divine Meditation*, quoted in Martz, p. 25.

72. Despite these very real connections, I would not agree with Martz' suggestion (p. 4) that "meditative" is a better term than "Metaphysical" for the description of this sort of poetry. It seems to me that such a terminological replacement would involve an untidy confusion of genre and style. For the meditation is a genre—one which recurs at intervals in our history and which, in the sixteenth and seventeenth centuries, assumed a special importance. Metaphysical poetry is a particular style, an historically limited manner of writing in various genres. At the same time, one must recognize the important relationship which this genre and this style bear to one another. The great age of meditation is the age of Metaphysical poetry; other ages in which formal meditation or something like it makes its appearance are also ages which encourage styles akin to the Metaphysical. But I think we ought to regard formal meditation and Metaphysical poetry in the late Renaissance as standing in a parallel rather than a causal relationship. (This is not to deny the fact of influence by formal meditation on certain individual Metaphysical poets—Donne, Herbert, and La Ceppède most notably.) Some of the other points of contact noted by Martz—the impulse toward the reconciliation of opposites, the desire to merge one's self with the Absolute, the habit of self-analysis, the creation of the self as a dramatic character (pp. 118–24, 135, 211, 321–24)—are probably more rooted in the spirit of the age than in the principles of meditation *per se*.

which Gryphius alternately rejects the seductions of the world
and celebrates the mysteries of the redemption are among the
great achievements of Baroque poetry; the heaping up of
varied and startling metaphors, the mixture of cosmic and
artificial imagery, and an over-all effect of distortion and im-
balance point up relations to D'Aubigné, Marino, and the early
Malherbe. The recurrence in his work of the theme of the
world as illusion, often expressed in the metaphor of the theater, shows that the stylistic resemblance has a contentual basis.[73]

Gryphius's fairly frequent modulations from the High Baroque style typical of him into something akin to the Metaphysical style occur almost always as a result of his contemplation of the Christian mysteries. Sometimes, as in his poem
"Über die Geburt Jesu," the modulation is almost complete; at
other times his mode of expression vacillates between the
Metaphysical fusion of opposites through paradox and the
High Baroque separation of opposites through antithesis, but
even these poems have a fine intellectuality of structure which
makes them unlike more conventional High Baroque religious
lyrics.

Several other religious poets of the age show, like Gryphius,
occasional tendencies toward Metaphysical speech and form.
Jean-Baptiste Chassignet seems in some of his poems to be a
French counterpart to Gryphius, but in other poems ("Assies
toy sur le bort," "Tout le cour de nos jours") he is even closer
to the manner and the tone of the great English Metaphysicals.
Dramatic immediacy and a kind of cosmic irony give his
verse its distinctive flavor.

Joost van den Vondel is one of the major poets of the High

73. Imbrie Buffum, *Studies in the Baroque from Montaigne to Rotrou*
(New Haven, 1957), examines Baroque "theatricality" in relation to the
period's concern with the theme of illusion. Especially illuminating is
his analysis of Jean de Rotrou's Christian tragedy *Saint Genest* (1646),
with its extensive and subtle exploitation of the play-within-a-play
device (pp. 212–39). Calderón's *La Vida es Sueño* is also relevant in this
context.

Baroque style; even in his poems on the Nativity, the Crucifixion, and the mysteries of the Catholic sacraments he inclines more toward the sensuous, pictorial, and expansive than toward the intellectual, dramatic, and condensed. In fact, Vondel seems, like Crashaw and Giles Fletcher, to be one of the most Italianate of the northern Baroque poets. But such is the strength of the Metaphysical current in seventeenth-century devotional poetry that even he on a few occasions writes poems which remind us of Donne or of Vaughan—the "Uitvaert van Maria van den Vondel," for example, with its mundane conceits and its effectively understated tone, or the great chorus from the first act of *Lucifer,* with its blinding vision of deity outside the limitations of space or time.

Vondel's Italianate qualities bring up the larger question of Italian influence on the forging of the general European Baroque style. It seems to me that in many ways the Italianism of the great Dutch poet is, like that of Crashaw, not so much a matter of imitation as a matter of temperamental sympathy partly conditioned by religious affiliation. Neither Vondel nor Crashaw is really much like Marino or Achillini; in fact, in their philosophical seriousness and their passionate involvement they are both far more like Gryphius. Possibly we may posit two great subdivisions in Baroque poetry, a northern and a southern (in addition to the initial distinction of High Baroque, Metaphysical, and Précieux manners within the period style). Southern Baroque, if we take Marino as the standard, is a hyperdevelopment of certain qualities in the great and moribund Renaissance style. Its achievement in devotional verse is often vitiated by either sentimentality or sensationalism. Northern Baroque, whether we take Gryphius or Vondel or La Ceppède as the standard, is not so much a development from Renaissance style as a turning away from it, a rejection of the centuries-old habit of Italian imitation in favor of an unconscious revival of native tradition—the tradition of medieval religious poetry, with its personal fervor and its imaginative abundance.

"Italian Baroque" is perhaps a better word than "southern Baroque" for the opposed phenomenon. It is true that much of the poetry of southern Germany (unlike that of Silesia, Saxony, and the North) shares with Marinism the quality which I have described as overripe Renaissance, but the poetry of Spain in the late sixteenth and early seventeenth centuries shows none of the decline in quality which afflicts Italian poetry after Tasso. We have seen that the love lyrics of Quevedo have much of the dramatic intensity and intellectual control of northern Metaphysical poetry; at the same time the age of Philip II and his successors was able to boast the unique achievement of Góngora as well as a body of fresh lyrics rising directly from the folk tradition. In sacred poetry the Spaniards of the Baroque age made an especially important contribution, and a considerable portion of that sacred poetry was Metaphysical in style, as one might expect from the central role which Spain played in the development of the practices of formal meditation.[74]

Neither Luis de León nor San Juan de la Cruz—the two towering figures in Spanish religious poetry—is, properly speaking, a Metaphysical poet. Luis de León is a Renaissance poet who patterns himself directly on the Latin classics; Juan de la Cruz, in the intensely individual nature of his expression, largely defies stylistic categorization. Nevertheless, Juan's impassioned experience of the Absolute sometimes expresses itself in the characteristic Metaphysical blend of paradox and colloquialism, and such a poem as "O llama de amor viva" gives him a place within the Metaphysical style beside such poets as Spee and Kuhlmann. (Indeed, Kuhlmann's "In einer dunkler Nachte" is largely a paraphrase of Juan's "En una noche oscura," with the addition of other passages from the Spanish poet.) [75]

74. See Martz, pp. 4–8.
75. See Friedhelm Kemp, ed., *Deutsche Geistliche Dichtung aus Tausend Jahren* (Munich, 1958), p. 517.

Several other Spanish poets occasionally recall the Metaphysical manner, but the sacred parodies [76] of José de Valdivielso's *Romancero Espiritual* lack intellectual complexity and the religious sonnets of Bartolomé de Argensola rely on a type of ornamental conceit which makes them essentially High Baroque. However, the Metaphysical style emerges in complete form in the devotional poems of Quevedo and Lope de Vega. Quevedo, in particular, recalls Donne as well as Fleming and Huygens not only in the wittily developed conceit of such a poem as "Pues hoy pretendo ser tu monumento" but also in the tone of strident appeal and impassioned argument which is felt in almost all the poems contained in his *Lágrimas de un Penitente*. Lope, in his parodistic "Pastor que con tus silbos amorosos" and "Que tengo yo que mi amistad procuras," suggests Herbert rather than Donne, but his Metaphysical quality is equally unmistakable. [77]

Spanish poetry of the *siglo de oro* derives both its variety and its distinctive qualities from the unbroken national tradition of which it is the supreme flowering. Standing somewhat apart from the culture of the rest of western Europe, and preserving its particular variety of medievalism, [78] Spain needed only to learn from Italy the lesson of poetic form in order to be kindled into artistic greatness. The response of Spanish poets to the religious milieu of the late Renaissance took sometimes the direction of Baroque ornateness, sometimes that of Metaphysical intricacy, but it never took that of a Renaissance richness

76. I use the term in the sense employed by Martz, p. 186.

77. E. M. Wilson, "Spanish and English Religious Poetry of the Seventeenth Century," *Journ. Eccl. Hist.*, 9 (1958), 38–53, examines in detail some of the similarities between Spanish and English poetry of the Baroque age, giving particular attention to the occurrence of conceits and sacred parody and analyzing Lope's "Pastor que con tus silbos amorosos" as an example of the latter. In a subsequent article, "A Key to Calderón's *Psalle et Sile*," *Hispanic Studies in Honour of I. González Llubera* (Oxford, 1959), the same writer demonstrates Calderón's use of meditative structure.

78. See Curtius (above, note 68), pp. 541–43.

which had lost, as in Italy, both its *raison d'être* and its sense of proportion.

Similarly, the Baroque poetry of Germany, Holland, France, and England is, in its most important aspects, a native product. Its resemblances to Italian Baroque poetry are in part the result of imitation, but to a greater extent they are accidental. The dying Italian Renaissance and the burgeoning cultures of northern and western Europe created forms of art which are superficially similar but basically very different.

The poetry of the German Jesuit priest Friedrich von Spee is illuminating in this context. Spee's lyrics are almost all in the genre of the sacred pastoral, but they manage usually to avoid the mawkishness which so often afflicts that genre. Spee has been compared to Crashaw,[79] and his imagery has much of the extremeness and reliance on surprise which are customarily labeled *marinismo*. It would be easy, on first consideration, to see his work as a typical product of the impact of Marinistic fashion on a native tradition of devotional verse, but such a description would be inaccurate as well as inadequate, for the essential qualities of Spee's poetry—a childlike innocence of surface achieved through ballad meter and simple diction, joining with devious theological awareness to bring about a complex, almost discordant effect—are the reverse of Marinistic. These qualities, indeed, suggest Southwell more strongly than they do either Crashaw or Marino, and the fact that both Spee and Southwell were Jesuits no doubt explains the similarity to some extent. At the same time, the motive which their poems share—the seemingly naive expression of theologically profound insights—is essentially the result of an individually felt need to find a new and more immediate poetic form for devotional experience.

The point is, I think, that Spee's poetry, like that of Southwell in England and Gryphius and Fleming in Germany, is a

79. Edmund Gosse, for example, makes the comparison in *Seventeenth Century Studies* (4th ed. London, 1913), pp. 171–73.

part of a flowering of native tradition only tangentially related to that of Italy (in marked contrast to much German amorous poetry, with its strong reliance on foreign models). One sees, dotted all over the countryside of Austria and Bavaria, the little churches of the native Baroque. Their gaudy and touching beauty, their extremeness of statement, their barbaric piety, indicate a relationship to the splendors of Rome and Vienna, but the relationship is not primarily one of influence. The simple mountain people who painted the domes and adorned the graveyards with suffering Christs and gentle Virgins had never seen Gesù or the Karlskirche, any more than they had read the *Strage degli Innocenti* or the *Pastor Fido*. German Baroque poetry reaches one of its fullest expressions in Friedrich von Spee, and here, like German Baroque architecture, although it owes something to foreign influence, it owes more to its own internal impulse.

The best Baroque poetry of German- and Dutch-speaking Europe is by no means, however, a simple resurgence of folk art. Gryphius, for all his Christian melancholy, was an ardent student and supporter of the new science, and he wrote a poem of praise to Copernicus;[80] Spee was a learned man who wrote a tract against the persecution of alleged witches; Vondel was a leading citizen of Amsterdam, one of the most cosmopolitan cities of the seventeenth century, and it shows in every line he wrote. But their poetry, like that of the French, Spanish, and English and unlike that of the Italians of the age, never loses touch with the *Volkstümliche;* Spee's rhythms, Gryphius's diction, Chassignet's imagery, like the conversational tone of Donne's poetry, bear witness to that continuing contact.[81]

The religious poetry of northern Europe in the seventeenth

80. Gryphius, *Carolus Stuardus*, ed. Hugh Powell (Leicester, Eng., 1955), intro. pp. xli–xlv. See also Robert T. Clark, "Gryphius and the Night of Time," in *Wächter und Hüter: Festschrift für Hermann Weigand*, ed. C. von Faber du Faur, K. Reichardt, and H. Bluhm (New Haven, 1957), p. 57.

81. The sense of alienation from, and superiority to, the *profanum vulgus* remains clearly marked in Donne's *Songs and Sonets* and *Verse*

century is a resurgence of traditional piety in an ambience of new philosophical and scientific thought and new artistic fashion. From this fact comes its greatness as well as its variety.

If native piety and self-aware intellectuality combine in the High Baroque poets who show occasional Metaphysical tendencies, they combine more strikingly in those poets whose work is a consistent fusion of High Baroque and Metaphysical tendencies and in those who can be unequivocally described as Continental Metaphysicals. The Frenchman Jean de la Ceppède and the Dutchman Heiman Dullaert have much in common, especially their habit of combining Metaphysical and High Baroque elements. La Ceppède's "Voicy-l'Homme," like Dullaert's "Christus stervende," is High Baroque both in its extensive descriptive detail and in its emphasis on Christ's physical beauty; it is reminiscent, in fact, of Giles Fletcher. But the theological mystery of the Incarnation rather than religious emotionalism lies at the heart of La Ceppède's sonnet; it is centered not so much on the pity of Christ's sufferings as on the ugliness into which His divine beauty is changed by His sacrifice of love.[82] The tone of the poem is one of puzzled and disturbed awe that the divine attributes of perfect beauty and omnipotence have been transformed, by love, into their opposites:

> Ces yeux (tantost si beaus) rébatus, r'enfoncez,
> Ressalis, sont hélas! deux Soleils éclipsez,
> Le coral de sa bouche est ores jaune-pasle.

Letters, as it does in the work of Scève, Huygens, and others. The conscious poetic of the Metaphysicals is in some cases directed toward obscurity, but a stronger element in it—the impulse toward the unification or speculative thought and passionate feeling—leads in almost all cases to the presence of qualities which evoke common human experience.

82. One might compare La Ceppède's poem with Paul Gerhardt's familiar hymn "O Haupt voll Blut und Wunden," in which the figure of the crucified Christ is admired for its beauty with a straightforward—and unsophisticated—piety.

In this context the opening phrase of the poem becomes more than an apt allusion to the words of Pilate; it becomes the expression of a shatteringly final irony.

Heiman Dullaert's sonnet "Christus stervende" is an even more complete example of the fusion of High Baroque and Metaphysical elements. The octave sets up a series of Gryphius-like antitheses between Christ's divine attributes and His shameful death, but the sestet moves rapidly to a statement, in the condensed language of the Metaphysical manner, of the Christian paradox:

> O hooge wonderen! wat geest is zoo bedreven,
> Die vat hoe zoo veel sterkte uit zoo veel zwakheid groeit,
> En hoe het leven sterft om dooden te doen leven?

The special affinity between La Ceppède and Dullaert emerges very clearly in their respective poems on the repentant thief, both of which depend on the same witty reference to "stealing" heaven.[83] If these poems show just how strikingly these poets of the mixed style could resemble the English Metaphysicals in treatment of image, La Ceppède's "Soit que je vous reçoive" and Dullaert's "Aen myne uitbrandende kaerse," in quite different ways, manifest the "passionate ratiocination" of Metaphysical poetry.

Jean de Sponde, whose compelling poetic meditations on death have been recovered in our own time from three centuries of total obscurity, has often been regarded as a European

---

83. Boase, "Poètes anglais et français," p. 171, cites the La Ceppède passage as representing a Metaphysical tendency. It is, actually, a witty observation which had a wide currency in the seventeenth century: Giles Fletcher, in *Christ's Victory and Triumph,* writes:

> And with him stood the happy theefe, that stole
> By night his owne salvation . . .

(Giles and Phineas Fletcher, *Poetical Works,* ed. F. S. Boas, 2 vols. Cambridge, 1908, *1,* 71). One of the sonnets by Artale included in this volume utilizes the same conceit. Further examples may be found in Quevedo and Lope de Vega.

Metaphysical.[84] He differs from Dullaert and La Ceppède, as he differs from Crashaw, in his complete lack of interest in the ornamental detail of the High Baroque style, that rich embroidery of conventional signs which clothes so much religious poetry of the period. On the contrary, his stripped-down diction, familiar tone, and conversational rhythms announce a kinship to Donne and George Herbert:

> Mais quoy? je n'entends point quelqu'un de vous qui die:
> Je veux me despestrer de ces fascheux destours . . .

or:

> Ces desirs orgeuilleux pesle mesle entassez,
> Ce coeur outrecuidé que vostre bras implore,
> Cest indomptable bras que vostre coeur adore,
> La Mort les met en geine, et leur fait le procez.

But in another sense Sponde, as much as La Ceppède and Dullaert, ought to be regarded as a poet of the mixed style. His effective restriction to the single theme of death gives him a narrower range than any other of the poets whom we have been considering as Metaphysical, and such a poem as his justly admired "Mais si faut-il mourir" is wholly devoid of Metaphysical ingenuity and obscurity.[85] Sponde uses an occasional conceit or paradox, but he seldom or never aims at that equilibrium of the contradictory which is to Metaphysical attitude what the fusion of thought and emotion is to Metaphysical tone. In the dramatic opposition of Christian and worldly attitudes toward death, Sponde deals with an ultimate contradic-

---

84. See de Mourgues, pp. 56–62, and Boase, "Poètes anglais et français," pp. 168–71. See also the two articles in which Boase introduced the conception of "metaphysical poetry" into French studies: "Then Malherbe Came," *Criterion*, *10* (1931), 287–306; and "Jean de Sponde, un poète inconnu," *Mesures*, *5* (1939), 129–51.

85. De Mourgues, pp. 57–58, finds the poem's Metaphysical flavor not in any complexity of theme but in the qualities of immediacy, concreteness, and irony brought together by the imagery.

tion,[86] and his "Stances de la Mort" reiterate that longing to be absorbed in the divine unity of all things which is common to almost all Baroque religious poetry, but finally he lacks the quality of sophistication in both thought and technique which links poets as different as Donne and Dullaert.

If by the Metaphysical style we mean a whole broad current in European Baroque poetry, an international manner which, around a core of very real similarities, includes important variations resulting from national tradition, linguistic necessity, and individual vision, then Jean de Sponde is properly classified as an exponent of that style. "Mais si faut-il mourir," with its immediate dramatic impact, "Hélas! contez vos jours," with its conception of time as a philosophical impossibility, and "Tout le monde se plaint de la cruelle envie," with its passionate attempt to prove to the unwilling flesh the desirability of death, are enough to justify the classification. But Sponde must also, I think,[87] be seen as an isolated descendant of those fifteenth-century poets who, like him, were obsessed by the double image of death and found no great intellectual ingenuity necessary to the voicing of that obsession. He is, in many ways, closer to Villon than he is to Donne or Herbert or Vaughan— or than he is to the Dutchmen Revius and Huygens, the German Fleming, the Spaniard Quevedo, and his own younger compatriot Laurent Drelincourt, the Continental religious poets most closely related to the English Metaphysicals.

Jacob Revius sounds a good deal like George Herbert. His work never has the personal, confessional quality of much of Herbert's, and his persona is that of the preacher rather than that of the average Christian; hence, though his poems often remind us of "Man" or "Providence" or "The Water-Course," they never remind us of "The Collar" or "The Pilgrimage" or "Affliction." Within these limitations, however, the resemblance

---

86. Ibid., pp. 60–61.

87. In this respect I agree completely with Miss de Mourgues, pp. 59–60.

in style is striking: in familiar tone and diction, homely imagery, and epigrammatic tendencies, the Calvinist preacher of Deventer is a brother to the country parson of Bemerton. Like Herbert, Revius is capable of giving dramatic particularity to both theological explanation and moral instruction. Again like Herbert, he is intellectual and ingenious without ever being deliberately obscure; he seizes from his daily life objects, relationships, and events which strike him as emblematic of spiritual or moral truth, and any difficulty his poetry offers is the result of inevitable difficulty of thought rather than of the fashion of obscurity. His stock of images, with its figures of coinage and gardening and musical instruments, is very much like Herbert's; and certain areas of imagery alien to Herbert—images taken from the art of painting, or, even more, the ever-present imagery of water—may be traced to the poet's Dutch environment and to his Herbertesque fondness for utilizing the familiar.

Revius uses paradox as a formal rhetorical device surprisingly seldom, in light of the strictly Metaphysical features which his style shows in almost every other respect. But something of the vision of paradox emerges from his obsession with relations, correspondences, and hierarchies. In "Vader der Lichten," for example, he describes what amounts to a series of relative light intensities: the bright stars are made invisible by the moon, the moon in turn by the sun, the sun by the human reason, until, finally, all are darkened by the light of God. Noteworthy is the abrupt and unprepared change from material to spiritual entities within the series—a manifestation, perhaps, of that melting or fusing effect characteristic of so much Baroque poetry. Noteworthy too is the implication of the final lines: that an absolute barrier exists between human understanding and the divine nature. An overt statement to the same effect occurs in "God een Geest" ("God a Spirit"), with its denial that God has human faculties. Since Revius's poetic work is given over to the attempt to make the divine

67

nature comprehensible to human understanding, something very like paradox hovers over all that work.

Any consideration of the Metaphysical style in its European compass shows that the style does not depend on specific ideological orientation;[88] the religious Metaphysicals show this diversity of doctrinal adherence even more graphically: La Ceppède, Sponde, and Quevedo were Catholics; Drelincourt was a Huguenot; Revius, Huygens, and Dullaert were Calvinists; Fleming was a Lutheran, Jan Luyken an Anabaptist, and Quirinus Kuhlmann a complicated private kind of heretic. If no specific religious affiliation is uncongenial to the practice of the Metaphysical style, by the same token religious affiliation seems to have no determinant effect on the tone of voice, the individual pitch, with which the style is used. Thus while the Dutch Calvinist Revius is Metaphysical in the manner of Herbert, the Dutch Calvinist Huygens is Metaphysical in the manner of Donne. In the work of the latter poet, homely imagery, didactic tone, and clarity of expression are replaced by learned imagery, personal tone, and a willful obscurity of expression, this last feature being achieved not only through formal paradox but also through a heavy use of pun and wordplay—devices wholly alien to the poetic world of Revius. Wit and conceit, conversational tone and metaphysical theme ally the two Dutch poets, but in most other respects they stand at opposite ends of the spectrum of Metaphysical poetry.

"Sondagh" (Sunday), part of a sequence of nine sonnets called the *Heilighe Daghen* ("Holy Days"), will expitomize Huygens' practice as a devotional poet. It begins with a line of colloquial abruptness and irregular rhythm—"Is't Sabbath dagh, mijn ziel, of Sondagh? geen van tween"—and goes on, after a reference to the superseding of the Hebrew Sabbath by the new law, to draw a contrast between the earthly sun, which is no different on Sunday from what it always is, and the Son of God, whose redemption of man is commemorated on Sun-

88. Cf. above, pp. 19, 39–41.

day. The rest of the octave is taken up by the development of the pun and by a feverish examination of the poet's personal relationship to Christ, which hovers between an inability to see Him because of his sins and an illumination granted by the sacrifice on the cross. In the sestet Huygens complicates the word-play of "Sunday–Son-day" by the addition of "Soendagh" (Dutch for "Reconciliation-day") and, finally, "Sin-day," achieving in the final couplet an intricately ironic structure of sound and meaning:

Hoe langhe lydt ghij, Heer, dijn' Soondagh, Soendagh, Sondagh
Ondanckbaerlick verspilt, verspeelt, verspelt in Sond-dagh?

In general, the *Heilighe Daghen* abound in paradox, wit, and conceit, and many of them have the form of intimate conversation with the deity, that form which is familiar to all readers of the *Holy Sonnets* and "Goodfriday: Riding Westward." The latter poem, actually, was translated into Dutch by Huygens, and the fact suggests once again the possibility of a continuing influence of the English poet on his Dutch contemporary.[89]

If Huygens' religious poetry betrays a very special kinship, perhaps even a special debt, to English Metaphysical poetry, it also shows signs of contact or at least affinity with other currents of the wider stream of European Metaphysical poetry. His sonnet on Easter ("Paeschen") is Donnesque in its concise paradox as well as in its urgently imperative tone toward the deity, but it is more suggestive of La Ceppède in its over-all structure. This structure comes from a learned and witty observation of correspondences between the Passover and Easter, the whole series being in turn applied dramatically to the predicament of the individual soul; Huygens begins by evoking

---

89. Cf. above, p. 25, note 26. Rosalie Colie, in "Constantijn Huygens and the Metaphysical Mode," *Germanic Review*, 34 (1959), 59–73, presents a detailed discussion of the *Heilighe Daghen* as Metaphysical poems.

the night of the first Passover, when the angel sent by God to destroy the first-born of Egypt passed by the doors of the Israelites, seeing them marked with the blood of the lamb. The blood of the lamb corresponds to the blood of Christ, shed to save sinners from eternal death. The Passover associations lead, in the second quatrain, to a reference to the death of Pharaoh in the Red Sea, and the imagistic associations of the Red Sea give form to the sestet, with its picture of man overwhelmed by the billows of his own blood, this latter image exploiting the contemporary connotations of "blood" as lust and passion. This part of the poem is enriched by the image of the angel of death coming again with "flaming sword"; the allusion to the banishment from Eden reinforces one of the poem's major meanings, that the death feared is the eternal death due to original sin.

The treatment of the blood image throughout has been paradoxical: it is the symbol of human lust and sinfulness, and its shedding represents the justice of God, but at the same time it is the mark on the doors of the Israelites and its shedding on the part of Christ constitutes the ransom of humanity. This complex of contradictions is underscored finally by the closing couplet, which appeals to God in his double character as the lion and the lamb, the eternal might who sends forth the angel of death and the lamb whose blood on the door bids the angel pass by:

Merckt onser herten deur, O Leeuw van Judas Stamm,
En Leert ons tydelijk verschricken voor een Lam.

The ingenuity with which the poet manages his material is clearly Metaphysical, but this particular kind of structure— the dramatic and highly emotional application to personal life of a series of parallels between separate Scriptural passages— is relatively rare among the English Metaphysicals. We find it occasionally in George Herbert and in Edward Taylor, but it is perhaps more typical of the more Metaphysical of the *Théorèmes* of La Ceppède. "Cette rouge sueur," for example, forges a correspondence between a miracle wrought by Christ and the greater miracle of His sacrifice for man, as prefigured by the agony in the garden, and "Soit que je vo' reçoive" makes a personal parable of Christ's meeting with the disciples after His resurrection. The psychological and artistic similarities between the Dutch Calvinist and the French Catholic underline once again the fact that the Metaphysical habit of mind is not the product of any particular variety of religious sensibility.

In turning from Huygens and La Ceppède to the German Lutheran Paul Fleming, we come to a poet of analogous gifts but of more limited range and less intellectual power. Most of Fleming's religious poetry, like some of his love poetry,[90] is Metaphysical, shaped by his obsession with a few constantly-repeated themes: the shifting meanings of life and death as seen by a Christian ("Ich lebe, doch nicht ich"); the mystery of the Redemption ("Auf meinen Erlöser"); the unreality of time ("Ihr lebet in der Zeit"). Fleming revels in paradox and is particularly fond of closing his poems with lines which exploit the device in an extreme form—"Dein Tod hat meinen Tod, du Todes Tod, getötet," or "Ich will nicht meine sein. Nimm mich nur, gib dich mir!" The qualities of paradox, conceit, and ingenuity are joined in his religious verse by qualities notably absent from even the more Metaphysical of his love poems—intimacy of address, familiarity of diction, and irregularity of rhythm.

Like Donne, perhaps even more like Huygens, is the word play which the Fleming of the religious poems indulges in (it is a trick of style almost never found in his secular work). "Ihr lebet in der Zeit" has, even more than Huygens' "Sondagh," an intricately punning texture impossible to render fully in translation. In certain other respects, especially the trick of double Biblical allusion, Fleming is closer to some of the other Continental Metaphysicals than to their English counterparts;

90. Cf. above, p. 46.

"An meinen Erlöser" makes use of the correspondence between the Paschal blood smeared on the Israelites' doors and the blood shed by Christ on the cross, although in a more incidental and less structural way than Huygens' "Paeschen."

Of the important religious poets of seventeenth-century Germany, Spee is almost a Metaphysical poet, Gryphius is occasionally one, and Fleming is usually one. With the exception of their work and that of a few others later in the century, most notably the Austrian noblewoman Catharina Regina von Greiffenberg, one finds only fragmentary or incomplete manifestations of the style; there is nothing like the rich outpouring of Metaphysical devotional verse to be found in England, Holland, or France. German poetry of the Baroque age, as I have pointed out earlier, hovers perilously between the artificial and the folksy, the sophisticated and the naive. There are occasional triumphs in the extremes of manner—some poems by Spee or Gerhardt in the naive manner, some by Hofmannswaldau in the sophisticated—but in general the finest German poetry of the period achieves an individual resolution of the extremes. Thus Fleming and Gryphius in sacred poetry, like Opitz and Schirmer in secular poetry, reconcile complex thought and intricate technique with homely diction and conversational rhythm, and in so doing achieve something like the effect of their English contemporaries. That there was so little other achievement in this direction may possibly be the result of the Thirty Years' War, with its disruption of normal contact among separate classes of society as well as among adherents to separate faiths.

Perhaps it was the social conditions in Germany which favored the development of a genre of quasi-Metaphysical poetry not, so far as I know, to be found elsewhere in seventeenth-century Europe—the philosophical-devotional epigram, as practiced by Johann Scheffler (better known under his pseudonym, "Angelus Silesius") and Daniel von Czepko, who require separate classification in any examination of Metaphysical poetry in Europe. A ruptured society breeds exhortation perhaps more readily than it does drama. In any case, the spiritual epigrams of Czepko and Scheffler embody features of the Metaphysical style—paradox, colloquialism, preoccupation with ultimate philosophical contradictions—in a rigidly unvarying form and a hortatory syntax completely foreign to the major exponents of the style. This kind of poetry is represented in this volume by Scheffler, who is, in his insistent confrontation of man's relation to God, more consistently the Metaphysical poet than is Czepko. Furthermore, the element of mysticism in his vision, like his passion for external nature, allies him specifically to the younger generation of English Metaphysical poets, the generation of Vaughan and Traherne.

For the most part, the religious Metaphysical poets active during the second half of the seventeenth century constitute an independent category within the over-all stylistic movement. In their work a philosophically expressed concern with the mysteries of theology tends to yield to a suprarational attempt to seize the awareness of God through the mystical contemplation of external nature or through the individual intuition. One important exception is the Huguenot pastor Laurent Drelincourt, whose concrete and emblematic metaphors, argumentative structure, and learned diction recall the French meditative poets of the turn of the century—not only Sponde and La Ceppède, but also Jacques Grévin and Guy Le Fèvre de la Boderie, whose scattered poems distinctly show these Metaphysical features.[91] Drelincourt's "Sur les Pierres précieuses" is an admirable example of the continuation of the earlier Metaphysical sensibility.

But his contemporaries in England, Holland, and Germany show more strikingly the turn taken by the last phase of the style. Vaughan, Traherne, and, in some ways, Marvell, find

91. Boase, "Poètes anglais et français," p. 172, discusses Drelincourt as a Metaphysical poet. De Mourgues, pp. 48–49, regards Grévin and Le Fèvre de la Boderie as precursors of the style.

European counterparts in Scheffler and, to a much greater extent, in the Dutchman Jan Luyken and the German Quirinus Kuhlmann. Although Luyken bears affinities to the whole English Metaphysical succession, his closest bond, in both technique and spirit, is with Henry Vaughan, whom he resembles in his love of nature, his esotericism, and his thirst for the Absolute.[92] In the work of the Dutch poet, however, religious belief is clearly the source of the poetic technique. Whereas Vaughan's early secular verse is obviously influenced by Donne and is hence Metaphysical, the amorous lyrics of Luyken's early *Duytse Lier* are in the Italianate tradition of Hooft; unquestionably, the full-blown Metaphysical style of his first religious volumes, *Jesus en de Ziel* and *Voncken der Liefde Jesu*, is the result of his religious conversion. It is his religious sensibility which first brings him to the confrontation of the mysteries of experience, and it works a total transformation in his poetic style.

Like Vaughan and Traherne, and like Donne, Herbert, and Crashaw before them, Luyken explores the central paradoxes of existence in terms of the problem of the One and the Many,[93] but he is like the later English generation in the detail of his vision. The earlier poets had expressed themselves in a figuration based on traditional astronomy, cosmology, logic, and physics; the later Metaphysicals lean heavily on observed nature read as a set of meaningful hieroglyphics.[94] The shift in source of imagery, related to a shift in structure from the argumentative to the partially descriptive, is the major historical development within the Metaphysical movement, and it has its cause, I suspect, in the changing intellectual climate

92. See my article "Jan Luyken: a Dutch Metaphysical Poet," *Comp. Lit.*, *10* (1958), 45–54.

93. Although I agree with Smith (above, note 11) in finding a concern with this problem central to Donne, Herbert, and Marvell, I feel further that Crashaw, Vaughan, and Traherne, in their differing ways, manifest the same concern.

94. Cf. above, pp. 17–18.

of seventeenth-century Europe. For Donne and Herbert the traditional world-view—Aristotelian, Ptolemaic, Galenic—is still tenable, although the challenge of the "new Philosophy" lends still another source of tension and wit to these poets.[95] But by the time of Vaughan and Luyken the new philosophy has triumphed, and the older view has become merely quaint.

The later Metaphysicals are thus driven to two expedients for the maintenance of their vision. One is esoteric, "magical" lore; the other is the mystical apprehension of observed nature. Usually the two interact, as is the case with Vaughan, whose Hermeticism and neo-Platonism combine with his personal feeling for landscape, and usually also the personal, private vision of experience assumes more importance than in the work of the earlier Metaphysicals. The search for some sort of all-embracing system which will give at once a sanction to moral behavior and an affirmation to human value leads Luyken and Vaughan, in an age whose thought was becoming every year more coldly mechanistic and more puzzlingly abstract, to sources of magical and unprovable knowledge—to the Hermetic books, to the Cabbala, to the alchemists, and to that heterodox and mystical philosopher Jacob Boehme.[96] They are the last poets of the dying Renaissance, living in a world which has already become the world we know. It is not surprising that their search for a foundation for poetry should resemble in some ways the search carried on in our own time by William Butler Yeats.

The doctrine of "inner light" is implicit in Vaughan and explicit in the best of Luyken—in, for example, "De Ziele

95. Cf. Douglas Bush, *English Literature in the Earlier Seventeenth Century* (Oxford, 1945), pp. 37–38.

96. For Vaughan's relation to the Hermeticists and Boehme see E. Holmes (above, note 20). For Boehme's influence on Luyken and Kuhlmann respectively see A. C. M. Meeuwesse, *Jan Luyken als Dichter van de Duytse Lier* (Groningen, 1952), pp. 1–42, and C. V. Bock, *Quirinus Kuhlmann als Dichter* (Basel, 1957), passim. For a general account of Boehme's impact on English letters see W. Struck, *Der Einfluss Jacob Boehmens auf die Englische Literatur des 17. Jahrhunderts*, Berlin, 1936.

betracht de nabijheid Gods," and "De Ziel betracht den Schepper uyt de Schepselen," and its theological justification is probably to be found in the writings of Boehme.[97] In the poems of their slightly younger contemporaries, the Englishman Thomas Traherne and the German Quirinus Kuhlmann, even this justification tends to disappear, and we encounter a more personal, less doctrinal treatment of nature and God. Only that root sentiment of all Metaphysical poetry, the awareness of the self-contradictory nature of truth, keeps them within the limits of the style.

In the individualistic arrogance of their frontal attack on eternal felicity, as in such qualities as their common habit of listing impressions of experience in pell-mell disorder, Traherne and Kuhlmann are akin, and both are at the absolute periphery of Metaphysical style. But, despite the heretical novelty which blazes in Traherne's treatment of the theme of innocence or in Kuhlmann's ambition to found a world-wide religious community based on the idea of man's brotherhood in God,[98] both poets are ultimately shaped by the age which they conclude. Kuhlmann's poems are dominated by the recurrent paradox of night as day, as Traherne's are by the complex identifications of inner world with outer world, of restriction with release, of multiplicity with unity. The last voices of Baroque devotion are also the last echoes of the Metaphysical awareness.

For the literary historian all ages are ages of transition, but some ages are, as it were, more transitional than others— capable, in the inconclusive equality of historical time, of defining their personalities with a more than usual vividness. From their century's argument with itself, the poets of the Baroque

97. Especially Boehme's *Aurora oder Morgenröte* and *De Signatura Rerum.*

98. Such a poem as Kuhlmann's "75e Kühlpsalm" shows the clear influence of Boehme (especially of the *Mysterium Magnum*). The poet's intellectual background and political ideas are examined in Bock.

period made a kind of poetry which stands out with extraordinary distinctness, with something one might almost call uniqueness. Almost, not quite. The kind of poetry which I have described as "High Baroque"—sensuous, startling, concrete, ritualistic, exclamatory—finds analogues in many other periods of history. I need mention only the work of some of the fifteenth-century Italians and some of the late nineteenth-century poets in several countries.[99] The kind of poetry which I call "Metaphysical" and some of which I try to render in the following pages is roughly analogous with kinds of poetry found in at least two other eras of European history. The poetry of the Italian *stilnovisti* of the late thirteenth century and that of Baudelaire and the French symbolists in the late nineteenth century show similarities to the Metaphysical style which ought not to be overlooked.[100]

If obscurity is one of the defining features of Metaphysical poetry, the *stilnovisti* ought surely to qualify as early practitioners of the style. Cavalcanti's famous *canzone* "Donna mi prega ch'io voglio dire" is realized wholly in terms of a philosophical vocabulary and a conceptualized imagery, and Cino da Pistoia's deification of his lady leads to a type of intellectual hyperbole which at times suggests the Donne of the *Anniversaries*. Nevertheless, in its total effect the *dolce stil novo* is something quite different from the Metaphysical style: the praise of the divine beloved is never modified, as in Donne or Scève, by the contradictory awareness of her humanity, and, even more significantly, philosophical doctrine is the subject rather than the method of *stilnovist* poetry. The Metaphysicals

99. Tebaldeo, Cariteo, and Serafino Aquilano in the fifteenth century; Swinburne, D'Annunzio, Rubén Darío, in their different ways, in the nineteenth.

100. Eliot's criticism frequently implies these kinships (see, for example, *Selected Essays*, pp. 248–50), and Mario Praz, expanding Eliot's insight, posits three separate periods of Metaphysical poetry—a medieval, a baroque, and a modern ("Poesia metafisica inglese del seicento," *Poesia*, 3–4 (1946), 232–312.

77

use philosophical language as one of several instruments for exploring their emotional experience of love and God; the *stilnovisti* use their amorous emotions as an occasion for enunciating a philosophical position. Guido Guinicelli's famous "Al cor gentil ripara sempre amore" has more in common with Campanella than with the work of the true Metaphysicals.

In tone also these thirteenth-century Italians contrast with the seventeenth-century Englishmen, Frenchmen, Germans, Dutchmen, Spaniards, and Italians who are the subject of this volume. Not only the given attitude which underlies the *stil novo* but even the nuances of its imagery partake of a consistent dignity, formality, and elevation. Nowhere do we find the distinctive blend of intellectual speculation and conversational immediacy which defines the art of the seventeenth-century Metaphysicals. In Baudelaire, to an even greater extent in Jules Laforgue, we do find such a blend, but there can be little doubt that they are practicing a style intrinsically different from the Metaphysical. As in the work of several twentieth-century poets who are often called "Metaphysical" —Rilke, Eliot, Wallace Stevens—we are aware of the presence of the post-Romantic sensibility—in the importance assumed by the immediate, sensuous evocation of objects and events; in a confrontation of experience which is, despite any attempts to the contrary, ineffably private; in an implicit conception of art as the imposition of order rather than as the reflection of existing order. Several different periods in European history, under the impetus of comparable stimuli, have brought forth great flowerings of the intellectual lyric, but, if one is interested in accuracy, it is wise to restrict the term "Metaphysical poetry" to a certain kind of poetry written in the sixteenth and seventeenth centuries.[101]

101. I would similarly restrict the application of the term "Baroque." The persistent recurrence, perhaps even the regular alternation, of two polarly opposed stylistic tendencies seems to be a phenomenon of European literary history, but one should not allow the fact of resemblance between styles of different periods to blur one's recognition of the in-

This kind of poetry constitutes, I have suggested earlier, an identifiable stylistic variation within a larger period style, the Baroque. Earlier parts of this essay have pointed out the differences between the Metaphysical variation and the more widely disseminated style which I have called "High Baroque." If the poems of Donne and Durand, Schirmer and Quevedo, on secular themes and those of Herbert and La Ceppède, Fleming and Huygens, on sacred themes, to select a few characteristic figures of this volume, can be taken as representing a definite stylistic phenomenon, it may be useful to consider the particular environments in which that phenomenon occurred. Such a consideration cannot follow the relatively easy lines of point-for-point parallelism between stylistic traits and allegiance to any given religious system or any particular linguistic determination. Metaphysical poetry, as we have seen, occurs in England, France, Holland, Germany, Spain, and, to some extent, Italy; it is confined to no particular religious confession. Its distribution is more limited than that of High Baroque poetry, and its pattern may reward some examination.

England, France, Holland, Germany, and Spain. In an incomplete way, Italy. Isolated representatives in New England and Mexico. The pattern is suggestive. If there is no validity

---

dividual qualities of any given historical style. Such a blurring occurs, I think, in René Bray's conception of "Préciosité" as a literary constant (*La Préciosité et les précieux, de Thibaut de Champagne à Jean Giraudoux*, Paris, 1948), as in Eugenio d'Ors similar conception of Baroque (*Du Baroque*, version française de Mme. Agathe Rouardt-Valéry, Paris, 1936). Curtius, in his demonstration of the essential unity of European literature, assumes the existence of two opposed traditions, which he labels "Classicism" and "Mannerism" and which he sees as making their first appearance in the "Atticism" and "Asianism" of ancient oratory (pp. 67–68, 273–74). His distinctions are more discreet and sophisticated, and hence more useful, than those of Bray or d'Ors, but he, too, tends to minimize the fact of historical uniqueness. The Baroque style and its Metaphysical variant may employ devices found in antiquity or in the Latin Middle Ages, but form and diction, tone and attitude combine with these devices to produce a total effect not to be duplicated outside of the historical moment of the Baroque.

in positing an association between specific religious faith and this sort of poetry, there may be some value in considering the differing socio-political circumstances which modified both religious and artistic attitudes in sixteenth- and seventeenth-century Europe. With one important exception, Metaphysical poetry flourished in those climates in which a certain degree of doctrinal diversity was tolerated, in which speculation and the free exchange of ideas were at least possible, if not exactly encouraged. Holland was, par excellence, the country of religious tolerance; [102] England was, for the first two-thirds of the seventeenth century, agitated by the controversy over correct dogma and proper church government; France was, until the 1620's, the breeding ground of new and heterodox ideas; Germany was split among the varied forces which caused its ultimate political tragedy. In all these countries, diversity was in the air, and it may well have nourished the Metaphysical insight—the awareness of the equal claims of opposites, in terms either of philosophical perception or of emotional experience.

The exception I have referred to is, of course, Spain, which allowed even less diversity of opinion in religious and political matters than did Counter-Reformation Italy, but which produced, nevertheless, an important body of poetry in the Metaphysical style. The limited survival, in the Spain of Philip II and Philip III, of the Erasmian humanism which had flourished there during the reign of Charles V [103] can scarcely have been enough to supply a relatively free intellectual atmosphere comparable to that of the northern countries. The implication, then, may be that, though religious tolerance and the habit of speculation *encouraged* Metaphysical poetry, they did not *cause* it. The case of Spain suggests that we turn to literary history itself for a fuller explanation of the scarcity of Metaphysical poetry in Italy.

102. See J. Huizinga, *Nederland's Beschaving in de 17de Eeuw* (2d ed. Haarlem, 1956), pp. 55, 66–74.

103. Brenan (above, note 68), pp. 146–47, stresses the continuing influence of this humanism on the literature of the *siglo de oro*.

The decadence of Italian poetry in the seventeenth century ought not, I think, to be seen wholly as a reflex of Italy's political decline and its repressive intellectual atmosphere. The general vigor of Italian culture during this period displayed itself amply in the music of Monteverdi, the sculpture of Bernini, the painting of Caravaggio, and the thought of Galileo and Campanella. If the poets of the age did not show themselves capable, like their contemporaries in other nations, of forging a new style to express a sensibility formed by an age of violent change, the reason may be found simply in the fact of their carrying too heavy a load of solidified poetic tradition— the very tradition which, running from Dante to Tasso, had enabled Italian poetry to dominate European literature for close to three centuries. The hyperdevelopment of Renaissance traits which characterizes Italian Baroque poetry lends support to the theory that tradition itself denied to the poets of the *seicento* the vigor necessary to effect a change in poetic style.

Nevertheless, if the existence of a climate of diversity cannot fully explain the distribution of Metaphysical poetry, it can, I believe, throw some light on its historical development. In England and Holland the style runs its full course throughout the seventeenth century, from the art of Donne, Herbert, Revius, and Huygens, rooted in traditional theological conceptions, to the art of Vaughan, Traherne, and Luyken, which takes its being in more radically individualistic and irrational preoccupations. In both countries the style is exhausted only when an utterly new set of assumptions has triumphed in European thought and ushered in a completely different period style. In Germany the style expresses itself in fragmentary manifestations which accurately mirror the confusions of the life of the period. In Spain not only Metaphysical poetry but all poetry falls into decline after Quevedo and Calderón.[104] In France the important age of Metaphysical poetry extends

104. Calderón and Sor Juana may be considered the last important poets of Spain's great age.

from the reign of Henry IV to the assumption of power by Richelieu; the great cardinal's attack on the rights of the Huguenots, like the centralization of absolute power which he represented, seems to coincide with the end of French Metaphysical poetry, and the imprisonment of the free-thinking Théophile (1624) may be taken as the symbolic date for its cessation.[105] Richelieu's France, like Louis XIV's, supplied in its political absolutism and its enforced religious orthodoxy a fertile soil for neoclassical poetry but one which discouraged the troubling individualism of Metaphysical poetry.

It is precisely in its individualism that Metaphysical poetry contrasts most strikingly with High Baroque poetry. It is, of course, unwise to make a simple identification of the speaker in the *Songs and Sonets* or the love elegies with the actual John Donne (the female speaker in "Breake of Day" is enough to warn us from this mistake); pre-Romantic art usually expresses private emotion only through a consciously created persona. The important thing is that a persona does emerge. In Donne's poetry a clearly delineated protagonist with perceptible traits of character confronts the complexities of experience, and such a protagonist appears, I believe, in all Metaphysical poetry—in Herbert's *Temple* as in Théophile's elegies, in Sponde's *Sonnets de la Mort* as in Schirmer's sonnets to Marnia or Revius's study of God. In High Baroque poetry, if we except such an anomalous figure as D'Aubigné, character as such is purified almost out of existence. The ritual worshiper at the center of Crashaw's poetry has almost no outline of personality, and this fact largely explains why we consider Crashaw the least typical of the English Metaphysicals.

Of the manifold tensions which give Metaphysical poetry its character, the basic one is that which exists between such a

105. Richelieu's interest in literary questions strengthens the claims of a theory which would find a connection between his coming to power and the triumph of the Classical ideal. Fully aware of the influence which literature may have on society, he crushed libertinism as a source of danger to the state. See Adam, pp. 401–4, 430–34.

full-blooded conception of character and the recurrent theme of so much poetry of the Baroque age—the soul's desire to lose its identity in some all-embracing unity, whether the unity of sexual love or that of God. From the hard and disturbing interplay of self-awareness and aspiration this poetry derives both its dialectic and its enduring value.

In the prominence which it gives to the individual accent, Metaphysical poetry is a specifically European kind of art. Its champions during the first half of our century have been in the habit of positing a tradition of which it is an important part and from which Milton and the Romantics are reprehensible deviations.[106] Now that the excesses of a dilute and dying Romanticism no longer menace the work of our poets, the modern reader ought to be able, I think, to correct the over-statements which accompanied the revival of the Metaphysical poets. He ought to be able to perceive, in addition to the very real differences between Metaphysical and Elizabethan, or between Metaphysical and Romantic, the very real and perhaps more important similarities. Metaphysical poetry is a central part of the deepest tradition in European art and thought, but that tradition is wide and deep enough to include not only Dante and Donne and Baudelaire but also Tasso and Goethe and Shelley and Leopardi. For the tradition is rooted simply in the tireless and heroic investigation of the individual self, the awareness of which is the final distinguishing feature of our civilization.

The Translations

A poem, if it is alive, expresses not only its paraphraseable content but also the genius of the language, the spirit of the age, and the personality of the individual poet. It is, in a very deep sense, untranslatable. Any responsible translator's knowl-

---

106. F. R. Leavis' *Revaluation* (Cambridge, 1936) is typical of much of the criticism of the 1920's and 30's, both in its sensitive understanding of certain kinds of poetry and in its narrow insensitivity to others.

edge of this fact makes him aware at once of the two extreme but reasonable approaches to the problem of translation—the literal prose rendering designed to be read in connection with the original text and by a reader with an at least rudimentary knowledge of the language of the original, and the free composition of an independent poem inspired by the original text. Either approach may lead to good and valuable work, but the nature of this volume precludes both approaches. On the one hand, my translations exist to illustrate a thesis, the international nature of the poetic style which we know as "Metaphysical." Accordingly, real and precise accuracy must be a necessary part of my aim; a free rendering, a new poem suggested by the original, will not do at all. On the other hand, my purpose is to draw to the attention of Anglo-American readers a number of largely unfamiliar but very good poets who wrote in French, German, Dutch, Italian, and Spanish. I can scarcely expect the nonspecialist reader to have competence in Dutch, and even the poets writing in the more familiar languages employ a style which nourishes obscurity and is embedded in archaic forms of the languages. If I am to make these poets known to a relatively wide audience, I must try to render in English not only the meaning but also, as fully as I can, the poetic quality of the original.

My problem, then, is to convey at least part of the spirit of the language, the time, and the poet in each of the poems I have attempted to reproduce in our language. But at the same time, if these poets are to have any immediacy, I must restate them in terms of living poetry; that is to say, my translations must have something of the spirit of the English language, something of the twentieth-century manner, and something of my own personality.

This multiple aim is obviously impossible to achieve, but I can hope perhaps for a partial success. Even that, however, requires the adoption of two kinds of license, an ancient and a modern. Ancient freedom allows an unabashed use of special diction, archaisms, and inversions which are alien to the modern idiom; modern freedom allows metrical irregularities and approximate rhymes which would shock the authors of the original poems. But by being thoroughly licentious I may hope to reproduce both the form and the meaning of these late Renaissance lyrics without losing all connection with the poetic manner of our own time.

I realize that, in adopting both kinds of freedom simultaneously, I expose myself to the charge Ben Jonson leveled against Spenser, that of "writing no language," especially since I have exercised a similar freedom in the combination of Renaissance and modern diction. True. But I have perhaps presented to the modern reader, in a form which is almost poetry, poems which are reasonably close to those of their original authors. To convey the quality of the original, and of the original *as poetry*, even if only partially, is what I have aimed at.

In translating Continental Metaphysical poetry I have been faced with a number of more specific problems. Insofar as possible, I have retained the original meters and stanza forms, but the English language itself has enforced certain modifications. In most of the sonnets, for example, the paucity of English rhyme has obliged me to modify the straight Petrarchan octave employed by most Continental poets, and I have not scrupled to substitute an *abba cddc* scheme for the conventional Petrarchan double envelope form. A graver problem has been the alexandrine line favored by so many French poets and, through their influence, by so many German and Dutch poets. The French alexandrine is lighter, swifter, and more flexible than its heavily weighted English counterpart. It is true that Dutch and, to an even greater degree, German, have the heavy stress accent of English, but literary tradition itself, from the Renaissance on, accustomed Dutch and German ears to the length of the alexandrine. Such an acclimatization did not occur in English. As a general rule I have therefore rendered the Continental alexandrine as the

English pentameter, feeling, for example, that such a poem as Théophile's "Élégie à Cloris" cries out for the heroic couplet as its normal English clothing. Only in something like Scheffler's epigrams from *Der Cherubinische Wandersmann*, with their heavy reliance on balance, antithesis, and the marked caesura, have I carried the alexandrine over into English.

Metaphysical poetry, with its fondness for pun and word play, poses problems all its own for the translator. Such a *tour de force* as Huygens' "Sondagh," with its multiple puns accumulating throughout the poem, can only be suggested by translation, and Paul Fleming's intricate "Ihr lebet in der Zeit" has completely resisted my most persistent efforts. In dealing with the Metaphysical poets one must face with special humility the recognition that a translation, even if both faithful and poetic, can be only a cracked mirror. But a cracked mirror is better than none.

FRENCH POEMS

Maurice Scève, dizain: "Le jour passé de ta doulce presence"

Le jour passé de ta doulce presence
Fust un serain en hyver tenebreux,
Qui fait prouver la nuict de ton absence
A l'oeil de l'ame estre un temps plus umbreux,
Que n'est au Corps ce mien vivre encombreux,
Qui maintenant me fait de soy refus.
Car dès le poinct, que partie tu fus,
Comme le Lievre accropy en son giste,
Je tendz l'oreille, oyant un bruyt confus,
Tout esperdu aux tenebres d'Egypte.

Maurice Scève, Delie: dizain CXXIX

The day I spent within your presence sweet
A shining was in shadowy winter's night,
And proves the night of absence more complete,
A darker weather to the spirit's sight
Than to my Body life's encumber'd plight
Which now itself to me seeks to deny,
For since the moment that you went away,
Like the rabbit in his den amid the glades
I turn my head, and hear a muffled cry,
Completely lost in the Egyptian shades.

Maurice Scève, dizain:
"Asses plus long, qu'un Siecle Platonique"

Asses plus long, qu'un Siecle Platonique,
Me fut le moys, que sans toy suis esté:
Mais quand ton front je revy pacifique,
Sejour treshault de toute honnesteté,
Ou l'empire est du conseil arresté
Mes songes lors je creus estre devins.
Car en mon corps: mon Ame, tu revins,
Sentant ses mains, mains celestement blanches,
Avec leurs bras mortellement divins
L'un coronner mon col, l'aultre mes hanches.

Maurice Scève, Delie: dizain CCCLXVII

Long enough, as long as Plato's year,
The month I had to spend without your sight;
But when I saw your peaceful brow appear
With dignity and graciousness alight,
That empire where wise counsel holds the right,
I knew my dreams did prophecy design.
For to my body, Soul, you did return,
Feeling her hands, with white celestial tips,
And feeling those arms so mortally divine,
One crown my neck, the other twine my hips.

Maurice Scève, dizain:
"Tu m'es le Cedre encontre le venin"

Tu m'es le Cedre encontre le venin
De ce Serpent en moy continuel,
Comme ton oeil cruellement benin
Me vivifie au feu perpetuel,
Alors qu'Amour par effect mutuel
T'ouvre la bouche, et en tire a voix plaine
Celle doulceur celestement humaine,
Qui m'est souvent peu moins, que rigoureuse,
Dont spire (ô Dieux) trop plus suave alaine,
Que n'est Zephire en l'Arabie heureuse.

Maurice Scève, Delie: dizain CCLXXII

You are the Cedar against the poison dire
Of this constant Serpent which is lodg'd in me,
As your eye yet quickens me in steady fire,
Benignant even in its cruelty,
When Love whose mutual effects do so decree
Opens your mouth and draws from it a strain
Of sweetness which is humanly divine,
And being most often rigorous to my quest,
Yet breathes (O Gods) a breath more pure and fine
Than Zephyr is in Araby the Blest.

Maurice Scève, dizain:
"La blanche Aurore a peine finyssoit"

La blanche Aurore a peine finyssoit
D'orner son chef d'or luisant, et de roses,
Quand mon Esprit, qui du tout perissoit
Au fons confus de tant diverses choses,
Revint a moy soubz les Custodes closes
Pour plus me rendre envers Mort invincible.
Mais toy, qui as (toy seule) le possible
De donner heur a ma fatalité,
Tu me seras la Myrrhe incorruptible
Contre les vers de ma mortalité.

Maurice Scève, Delie: dizain CCCLXXVIII

With shining gold and rose Aurora white
Had scarcely finish'd crowning her fair head,
When my spirit, which had laps'd and perished quite
At the tangled source where diverse things are led,
Return'd to me across the curtain'd bed
To render me against my Death secure.
But you, who (you alone) have power sure
To put an end to my fatality,
Shall be to me the uncorrupted Myrrh
Against the worms of my mortality.

Guy Le Fèvre de la Boderie,
"Aus naturalistes et mécreans"

Comme le beau Soleil de sourgeon pérennel
Dardant son ray sutil pénetre une verrière
Sans le verre casser, et sans que sa lumière
Il retranche d'avec son pur rayon isnel:

Ainsi nous envoya Dieu le Pere eternel
Son Verbe et sa splendeur dedans la Vierge entière,
Sans fendre son christal ni rompre sa barrière,
Et sans se séparer du sourgeon paternel.

Vous qui ne donnez foy à la sainte écriture,
Remerquez ce mystère au livre de Nature;
Ouvrez les yeux de l'Ame afin d'apercévoir
Le Soleil du soleil qui dans les coeurs veut naistre:
Et n'attribuez plus au serviteur qu'au maistre:
Puissant doit estre cil qui donne à tous pouvoir.

Guy Le Fèvre de la Boderie,
"To Materialists and Unbelievers"

Just as the beauteous Sun with constant ray
Doth subtly through a window pierce and pass,
But neither cracks nor breaks the pane of glass
Nor is itself divided any way;

Just so did God the eternal Father send
His word in splendour to us in the Maid,
But did not break her crystal nor divide
Her barrier, nor his unity suspend.

You who believe not in the holy Book,
At Nature's mysteries cast a single look,
Open your Souls' eyes that you may perceive
The Sun of Suns, which in our hearts would shine.
No more to servant than to lord assign:
Mighty is he in whom all power doth live.

Jean de la Ceppède, "Cette rouge sueur"

Cette rouge sueur goutte à goutte roulante
Du corps de cet Athlete en ce rude combat,
Peut estre comparée à cette eau douce et lente,
Qui la sainte montagne en silence rebat.

L'aveugle-nay (qui mit tous les siens en debat
Pour ses yeux) fut lavé de cette eau doux-coulante,
Et dans le chaud lavoir de cette onde sanglante
Toute l'aveugle race en liberté s'esbat.

Et l'un, et l'autre bain ont redonné la veuë.
Siloé du pouvoir dont le Christ la pourveuë:
Et cettuy-cy de sang de son propre pouvoir.
Aussi ce rare sang est la substance mesme
De son coeur, qui pour faire à nuict ce cher lavoir
Fond comme cire au feu de son amour extreme.

Jean de la Ceppède, "This Red Sweat Slowly Falling"

This red sweat slowly falling drop by drop
From the body, locked in strife, of this Athlete,
Could be compared to the water slow and sweet   *simile*
That silently flowed from the sacred mountain's slope.

The man born blind who put his goods at stake
To gain his eyes, was washed in that sweet flood,
And in the warm bath of this wave of blood
The blinded race its comfort free doth take.
                                                    (Humanity)
Both this and the other bath have given sight:
Siloam indeed from Christ hath borrow'd might,
But this bath of blood of his own power doth heal.
Thus is this blood the very substance rare
Of his heart, which all night long this bath to fill   *Hyperbally*
Melts like wax in his love's surpassing fire.   *Simile*

Jean de la Ceppède, "Voicy-l'Homme"

Voicy-l'Homme, ô mes yeux, quel object deplorable
La honte, le veiller, la faute d'aliment,
Les douleurs, et le sang perdu si largement
L'ont bien tant déformé qu'il n'est plus desirable.

Ces cheveux (l'ornement de son chef venerable)
Sanglantez, herissez, par ce couronnement,
Embroüillez dans ces joncs, servent indignement
A son test ulceré d'une haye execrable.

Ces yeux (tantost si beaux) rébatus, r'enfoncez,
Ressalis, sont hélas! deux Soleils éclipsez,
Le coral de sa bouche est ores jaune-pasle.
Les roses, et les lys de son teint sont flétris:
Le reste de son Corps est de couleur d'Opale,
Tant de la teste aux pieds ses membres sont meurtris.

Jean de la Ceppède: "Ecce Homo"

Behold the Man, my eyes, what sight of woe!
Whom hunger, shame, the watches of the night,
And loss of blood, and sorrow's endless plight
Have so deform'd his beauty doth not show.

This hair, the glory of his reverend head,
Is drench'd in blood and in the shameful crown
So tangl'd, bristles and doth rest upon
His batter'd visage like a fence of red.

These eyes are sunken which were once so fair,
Alas, and like two eclips'd suns appear;
The coral of his mouth is palely faded.
The roses and the lilies now are fled,
And all his body like an opal dead,
From head to toe his limbs are so abraded.

Jean de la Ceppède, "Soit que je vo' reçoive"

Soit que je vo' reçoive en cète riche table,
Où vous mesme en vos mains vous portastes jadis:
Soit, ô Christ, qu'en mon coeur, de vostre Paradis
Vous fondiez, je vous suis un hoste insuportable.

Car au lieu (pour me rendre un sejour delectable)
De ranger mes desirs sous vos loix arrondis,
A pis faire tousjours méchant je me roidis,
Et vous force à quitter ce logis detestable.

Revenez y, Seigneur, non comme passager
Mais bien comme habitant: et pour n'en déloger
Randez mon ame à vous doucement asservie.
Demeurez avec elle, et l'allez possedant.
Hastez vous; car déja le Soleil de ma vie
Lassé de tant courir, penche à son Occident.

Jean de la Ceppède, "Grant that I May Receive Thee"

Grant that I may receive thee at this table
Where formerly thyself thou did'st bestow;
Allow me, Christ, thy Paradise to know,
Though to be a worthy host I am not able.

Instead of fitting will to thy decrees
(And making thus myself a worthy inn),
My harden'd heart initiates worse sin,
And drives thee from this house that does not please.

Return, O Lord, not as a passing guest,
But as a dweller: here take up thy rest;
Compel into thy bondage sweet my soul.
Live with it, keep it ever as thy own,
And hasten, for already my life's sun,
Weary with running, toward its West doth fall.

Jean de la Ceppède, "Mais, ô combien, mon Christ, peut sur vous la doleur"

Mais, ô combien, mon Christ, peut sur vous la doleur
D'une ame repentente: en vostre mort amere
Vous donnez un Disciple à vostre triste Mere:
Et vous donnez vous-mesme à ce contrit Voleur.

Voleur, dont aujourd'huy l'invincible valeur,
Le Christ mesme a volé, t'a rendu tributaire
Le Cocyte, et du Ciel fait nouveau feudataire
Fay moy part, je te pri', de ton heureux mal-heur.

Qu'à ta Croix j'aye part, et qu'ainsi je partage
Fidele et penitent avec toy l'heritage
Du Sauveur, que tu viens maintenant de voler.
Mais c'est à vous, Seigneur, de me rendre capable
D'avoir part en vos biens: car mon ame coulpable
Ne sçauroit sans vostre aide, à vous s'en revoler.

Jean de la Ceppède,
"How Much Can Touch thy Heart, O Christ"

How much can touch thy heart, O Christ, the grief
Of a soul contrite: in this thy bitter death,
To thy sad mother thou dost John bequeath,
And thou giv'st thyself to this repentant thief.

O thief whose unexampl'd boldness rare
Hath stolen Christ himself, hath vanquish'd Hell,
And won a place in Heaven's citadel,
Thy fortunate misfortune let me share!

O let me share thy cross and let me taste,
Like thee contrite and faithful, the bequest
Of the Saviour thou hast stolen valiantly.
But, Lord, 'tis thou alone can make me whole
And let me share thy gifts: my guilty soul
Without thy aid cannot return to thee.

Agrippa D'Aubigné,
"J'ouvre mon estommac, une tumbe sanglante"

J'ouvre mon estommac, une tumbe sanglante
De maux enseveliz: pour Dieu, tourne tes yeux,
Diane, et voy au fons mon cueur party en deux
Et mes poumons gravez d'une ardeur viollente.

Voy mon sang escumeux tout noircy par la flamme,
Mes os secz de langeurs en pitoiable point
Mais considere aussi ce que tu ne vois point,
Le reste des malheurs qui sacagent mon ame.

Tu me brusle et au four de ma flame meurtriere
Tu chauffes ta froideur: tes delicates mains
Atizent mon brazier et tes yeux inhumains
Pleurent, non de pitié, mais flambantz de cholere.

A ce feu devorant de ton yre alumée
Ton oeil enflé gemist, tu pleures à ma mort,
Mais ce n'est pas mon mal qui te deplaist si fort:
Rien n'attendrit tes yeux que mon aigre fumée.

Au moins après ma fin que ton ame apaisée
Bruslant le cueur, le cors, hostie à ton courroux,
Prenne sur mon esprit un suplice plus doux,
Estant d'yre en ma vie en un coup espuisée.

Agrippa D'Aubigné, "Stanzas To Diane"

I open here my breast, a bloody tomb
Of lurid woes: for God's sake, turn your eyes,
Diane, and see my cleft heart where it lies
And see my lungs engrav'd with passion's doom.

My frothing blood all blacken'd with the flame,
My wretched bones dried out with my despair;
But also what invisibly is there:
The torments which ransack my spirit's frame.

You burn me, and at the furnace of desire
You warm your icy hands; in careful wise
You stir my coals, and your inhuman eyes
Weep not with pity but with burning ire.

In the fire of the fury I provoke
Your eyes swell up with pain and overflow,
But 'tis not the unhappiness I owe—
Your eyes are troubled by my bitter smoke.

At least my death may please your greedy soul,
Burning the heart and body of your slave;
May then my spirit sweeter torture have,
In dying thus your rage exhausting whole.

Jean Bertaut, "Ne vous offensez point,
belle ame de mon ame"

Ne vous offensez point, belle ame de mon ame,
De voir qu'en vous aymant j'ose plus qu'il ne faut:
C'est bien trop haut voller, mais estant tout de flame
Ce n'est rien de nouveau si je m'éleve en haut.

Comme l'on voit qu'au ciel le feu tend et s'elance,
Au ciel de vos beautez, je tens pareillement:
Mais luy c'est par nature, et moy par cognoissance;
Luy par necessité, moy volontairement.

Aussi suis-je content que le sort adversaire
Darde sur mon amour quelque trait orageux,
Pourveu que l'accusant ainsi que temeraire,
Quelqu'un aussi le loüe ainsi que courageux.

Car il me reste assez gravé dans la memoire,
Que voulant m'approcher d'un celeste flambeau,
La mort en ceste audace est conjointe à la gloire,
Et que sous ce trophee est basty mon tombeau.

Mais puis qu'en mon amour il faut que je m'égare,
Du vol de mes desirs déreglant la hauteur,
De quel plus beau Soleil pourroy'je estre l'Icare,
Moy qui veux consoler ma mort par son autheur?

L'homme est bien malheureux, de qui l'ame indiscrette
Peut ailleurs qu'en vos mains sa franchise enfermer:
C'est ou n'avoir point d'yeux pour vous voir si parfaite,
Ou n'avoir point de coeur pour vous oser aimer.

Jean Bertaut, "Stanzas"

Soul of my soul, take no offense that I,
In loving you, beyond my due aspire:
'Tis nothing new that I should rise too high,
For fire ascends, and I am all of fire.

We see that toward the heavens fire tends,
And toward your beauty's heaven soar I still;
What Nature gives to him, my knowledge lends;
'Tis his necessity, but 'tis my will.

And thus I am content that hostile fate
Should dart his stormy lightnings on my love,
As long as my accuser must admit
That bravery my boldness doth approve.

For knowledge clear is written in my mind:
That in this flame divine I meet my doom;
In this attempt is death with glory join'd;
Beneath this monument is built my tomb.

But since in love I must so madly run,
Raising desire so far above its station,
What Icarus could find a fairer Sun,
At once for me both death and consolation?

That man is wretched whose unseeing soul
Can vow his love to any other fair:
For either he is blind to beauty's whole,
Or is afraid to love perfection rare.

Quant à moy, je plaindrois et ma peine et mes larmes,
Si je les despendois pour de moindres beautez.
Car je hay qu'un autre oeil m'enchante de ses charmes,
Que celui qui rendroit les dieux mesme enchantez.

Non, sçachant que ma flamme est celeste et divine,
Je ne puis rien aimer s'il n'est esgal aux dieux:
Je veux qu'un bel oser honore ma ruine;
Et puis qu'il faut tomber, je veux tomber des cieux.

Arriere ces desirs rempants dessus la terre:
J'aime mieux, en soucis et pensers eslevez,
Estre un aigle abattu d'un grand coup de tonnerre,
Qu'un cygne vieillissant és jardins cultivez.

Non, en volant si haut je ne crains point l'orage,
Et l'effroy du peril ne m'en retire point:
Ce qui sert d'une bride aux esprits sans courage,
Est un vif esperon dont le mien est espoint.

J'aime qu'à mes desseins la fortune s'oppose:
Car la peine de vaincre en accroist le plaisir.
Pouvoir facilement obtenir quelque chose,
M'est assez de sujet d'en perdre le desir.

Advienne seulement que mon ame embrasee
Du desir d'acquerir ceste riche toison,
Trouve la seule peine à mes voeux opposee,
Afin que de ce monstre elle soit le Jason,

Mais helas! je crains fort qu'un malheur invincible
Transforme tellement l'heur à qui je m'attends,
Qu'au lieu de difficile il le rende impossible,
Et joigne à mes travaux la perte de mon temps.

Were I to spend them on a beauty less
Than yours, I should regret my tears and pain;
No eye could captivate my soul unless
'Twere that which could the gods themselves enchain.

No, since my flame is of celestial heat,
I love one who the very gods outvies:
A bold attempt must honour my defeat;
If fall I must, I would fall from the skies.

Away with base desires which crawl below!
I would, with thoughts and cares of higher worth,
Be sooner an eagle struck by thunder's blow
Than a swan grown old in gardens of the earth.

No, in soaring so high I fear no storm,
And danger can no way my will deter:
That which a bridle is to those less firm
Is nothing to me but a lively spur.

I would that Fortune should oppose my quest:
The pains of conquest but increase my fire.
To have with ease is far from being best;
For me it is enough to kill desire.

O may it happen that my fiery soul,
Covetous of this rich and priceless fleece,
Find only Difficulty in my role,
That Jason-like I may the monster face.

But O, alas, I fear Calamity
Will quite transform the hour I await,
And Hardship make Impossibility,
And all my woes to loss of time translate.

Dementez cette crainte, ô beauté qui convie
Aux erreurs de l'Amour les plus sages esprits:
Suffise a vos rigeurs qu'il me couste la vie,
Sans que j'en perde encor et l'attente et le prix.

Ainsi de vostre teint l'immortelle jeunesse
Ne soit jamais sujette à l'empire des ans:
Ny ne puissent jamais les traits de la vieillesse
Vous rendre les miroirs des objets mal-plaisans.

Ainsi la libre voix des belles de cest âge,
Vous puisse declarer Roine de la Beauté;
Et tout ce qui dédaigne à vous en faire hommage,
Criminel envers vous de leze Majesté.

Belie this fear, O Beauty who dost sway
To amorous folly even the most wise:
Content yourself my life to take away,
Do not deny as well my waiting's prize.

Thus the immortal youth of your fair charms
Shall not grow subject to time's monarchy,
Nor shall old age with devastating harms
Make you find mirrors objects you would flee.

Thus Queen of Love and Beauty shall you name
The Beauties of our age in due array,
And any who deny your rightful claim
Shall be convicted of lèse-majesté.

Jean de Sponde, "Si c'est dessus les eaux"

Si c'est dessus les eaux que la terre est pressée,
Comment se soustient-elle encor si fermement?
Et si c'est sur les vents qu'elle a son fondement,
Qui la peut conserver sans estre renversée?

Ces justes contrepoids qui nous l'ont balancée,
Ne panchent-ils jamais d'un divers branslement?
Et qui nous fait solide ainsi cet Element,
Qui trouve autour de luy l'inconstance amassée?

Il est ainsi: ce corps se va tout souslevant
Sans jamais s'esbranler parmi l'onde et le vent.
Miracle nompareil! Si mon amour extresme,
Voyant ces maux coulans, soufflans de tous costez,
Ne trouvoit tous les jours par example de mesme
Sa constance au milieu de ces legeretez.

Jean de Sponde,
"If on the Waters Earth Hath its Support"

If on the waters earth hath its support,
How is it that so firmly 'tis sustain'd?
And if upon the winds it is maintain'd,
How is't not overthrown and cast athwart?

Do not the counterweights so delicate
Which balance us the world not swing askew?
Who makes this element so firm and true,
Amid surrounding chaos inviolate?

'Tis thus: earth's body can sustain the all,
And never midst the winds and waters fall.
Wonder unparallel'd! Did not my love,
By woes surrounded, blown from every side,
Example from the earth itself receive
And constant mid inconstancies abide.

Mais si faut-il mourir: et la vie orgueilleuse,
Qui brave de la mort, sentira des fureurs;
Les Soleils haleront ces journalieres fleurs,
Et le temps crevera ceste ampoule venteuse.

Ce beau flambeau qui lance une flamme fumeuse,
Sur le verd de la cire esteindra ses ardeurs;
L'huile de ce Tableau ternira ses couleurs,
Et ces flots se rompront à la rive escumeuse.

J'ay veu ces clairs esclairs passer devant mes yeux,
Et le tonnerre encor qui gronde dans les Cieux.
Ou d'une ou d'autre part esclatera l'orage.
J'ay veu fondre la neige, et ces torrens tarir,
Ces lyons rugissans, je les ay veu sans rage.
Vivez, hommes, vivez, mais si faut-il mourir.

Jean de Sponde, "Yes, So We All Must Die"

Yes, so we all must die, and proud life all,
Defying death, must one day feel its powers,
Incessant suns will scorch these transient flowers,
And time explode this vain inflated ball.

This fair torch which casts its smoky flame
Will gutter in its wax and die away,
The colours of this picture will decay,
These waves will break against the shore in foam.

I've seen the lightning flash before my eyes,
And heard the thunder growling in the skies,
When from every side the mounting storm doth hurry;
I've seen the snow melt and its torrents dry,
And seen these roaring lions without fury,
Live on, O men, but so we all must die.

Jean de Sponde, "Helas! contez vos jours"

Helas! contez vos jours: les jours qui sont passez
Sont desja morts pour vous, ceux qui viennent encore
Mourront tous sur le point de leur naissante Aurore,
Et moitié de la vie est moitié due decez.

Ces desirs orgueilleux pesle mesle entassez,
Ce coeur outrecuidé que vostre bras implore,
Cest indomptable bras que vostre coeur adore,
La Mort les met en geine, et leur fait le procez.

Mille flots, mille escueils, font teste à vostre route,
Vous rompez à travers, mais à la fin, sans doute,
Vous serez le butin des escueils, et des flots.
Une heure vous attend, un moment vous espie,
Bourreaux desnaturez de vostre propre vie,
Qui vit avec la peine, et meurt sans le repos.

Jean de Sponde, "Alas, but Count Your Days"

Alas, but count your days: those which are gone
Are already dead for you, and those which come
With every waking dawn to death succumb;
With half of life the half of death is shown.

These vain desires in disorder'd pile,
This heart so prideful which your arm implores,
This arm unconquer'd which your heart adores—
Death doth arrest and summon all to trial.

A thousand waves, a thousand reefs attend;
You have surviv'd them all but in the end
You'll be the spoil of reef and wave at last.
One moment waits for you, one hour arrives,
Executioners perverse of your own lives,
Living in pain and dying without rest.

Jean de Sponde,
"Tout le monde se plaint de la cruelle envie"

Tout le monde se plaint de la cruelle envie
Que la Nature porte aux longeurs de nos jours:
Hommes, vous vous trompez, ils ne sont pas trop cours,
Si vous vous mesurez au pied de vostre vie.

Mais quoy? je n'entens point quelqu'un de vous qui die:
Je veux me despestrer de ces fascheux destours,
Il faut que je revole à ces plus beaux sejours,
Où sejourne des Temps l'entresuite infinie.

Beaux sejours, loin de l'oeil, pres de l'entendement,
Au prix de qui ce Temps ne monte qu'un moment,
Au prix de qui le jour est un ombrage sombre,
Vous estes mon desir: et ce jour, et ce Temps,
Où le monde s'aveugle et prend son passetemps,
Ne me seront jamais qu'un moment et qu'une Ombre.

Jean de Sponde, "All Do Protest The Cruel Enmity"

All do protest the cruel enmity
Which Nature bears longevity of days:
Men, you deceive yourselves, just are her ways,
If measur'd to your life yourselves you see.

But what? I hear not one of you who says:
"I would be free of troublesome detours,
I must return where beauty still endures,
Where Time its infinite extension has.

Fair dwellings, far from the eye but near the mind,
Compar'd to which Time doth brief triumph find,
Compar'd to which day is a shadow made,
You are my goal: and this day and this Time,
Where the world its blind diversions doth esteem,
Shall be for me a moment and a Shade."

Lorsque, fâché, ta cruaulté j'accuse,
Et que je viens hardy te demander
Cela de quoy tu ne me veulx ayder,
Et si ne veulx permettre que j'en use,

Tu me respons d'une subtille ruze:
"Il fault, Motin, encore retarder!
Prenez ma foy que je vous veulx garder.
Je vous la donne!" O la gentille excuse!

Tousjours, tousjours tu me presches ta foy;
Et, sans tirer aultre chose de toy,
Tu veule sans plus que ta foy je retienne.
Que sert la foy sans aultre plus grand bien?
Pere Bernard prêchant a Saint-Estienne
Dit que la foy sans les oeuvres n'est rien.

Pierre Motin, "Whenever I Rage And Blame Your Cruelty"

Whenever I rage, and blame your cruelty,
And boldly beg that you'll your favour show
And grant me that felicity to know,
That succour you have still refused me,

You make an answer subtle, wise and fine:
"My dear Motin, you must be patient still!
Accept my faith and be content until
I give it you!" O that's a pretty line!

Always, always, 'tis faith I hear you preach;
Nothing of greater moment can I reach;
I'm granted faith, who other joys have sought.
But what is faith unmatch'd by higher gain?
Père Bernard preaching at St. Étienne
Tells us that faith without good works is nought.

Pierre Motin,
"O Croix, qui de la croix ton beau surnom retire"

O Croix, qui de la croix ton beau surnom retire,
De la croix qui n'est rien que suplice et tourment,
Ton nom, comme ton coeur, ne propose en t'aimant
Que martire et rigueur, que rigueur et martire.

J'adore cependant ton bel oeil qui me tire
Mille traitz qui me vont les veines allumant:
Je suis traistre à moy mesme, allant hastivement
Au danger assuré où ce bel oeil m'attire.

Je faux, o belle Croix: vostre oeil et vostre nom
Courtois, doux et piteux, ne promettent sinon
Qu'une heureuse faveur à mon mal salutaire.
Car, si la croix jadis empescha de perir
Nos esprits demy-morts, vouldriez-vous, temeraire,
Trahir vostre beau nom et nous faire mourir?

Pierre Motin, "Sonnet to Mlle. La Croix"

O Cross, who from the cross dost take thy name,
From the cross which figures torment dire and sorrow,
Thy name, thy heart, alike afflict, I borrow
But martyrdom and torture from my flame.

And yet I love that fair eye which doth drive
A thousand desires coursing through my veins,
And traitor to myself I feed my pains,
And rush to meet the dangers which there live.

I lie, O lovely Cross, thy name, thine eye,
So gentle, sweet and kind, must promise me
Favour, grace and solace for my woe.
For if the Cross of old did so restore
Our dying spirits, would'st thou, bold one, dare
Betray thy beauteous name and death bestow?

Jean-Baptiste Chassignet,
"Assies toy sur le bort d'une ondante riviere"

Assies toy sur le bort d'une ondante riviere,
Tu la verras fluer d'un perpetuel cours,
Et flots sur flots roulant en mille et mille tours
Descharger par les prez son humide carriere;

Mais tu ne verras rien de ceste onde premiere
Qui n'aguiere couloit, l'eau change tous les jours,
Tous les jours elle passe, et la nommons tousjours
Mesme fleuve et mesme eau, d'une mesme maniere.

Ainsi l'homme varie, et ne sera demain
Telle comme aujour-d'huy du pauvre corps humain
La force que le tems abbrevie, et consomme:
Le nom sans varier nous suit jusqu'au trespas,
Et combien qu'aujour-d'huy celuy ne sois je pas
Qui vivois hier passé, tousjours mesme on me nomme.

Jean-Baptiste Chassignet, "Beside A Flowing River"

Beside a flowing river sit and gaze,
And see how it perpetually runs
In wave on wave, in many thousand turns,
As through the fields it takes its fluid ways.

Thou'lt never see again the wave which first
Flow'd by thee; water never is the same;
It passes day by day, although the name
Of water and of river doth persist.

So changes man, and will not be tomorrow
That which he is today, he cannot borrow
That strength which time doth alter and consume:
Until our death one name do we retain;
Although today no parcel doth remain
Of what I was, the name I still assume.

Jean-Baptiste Chassignet,
"Tout le cour de nos jours au service est semblable"

Tout le cour de nos jours au service est semblable
Et faut s'accoustumer à sa complexion,
Ou bien si tu te plains de ta condition,
Tu rendras de tes jours le pois insupportable.

Tout ce que ceste vie a de plus convenable
Embrasse le, et le gouste; il n'est affliction
Qui n'ait au mesme instant sa consolation,
Ainsi des ronces sort la rose delectable.

Tu sçais que le logis où nature t'a mis
A mille changemens à toute heure est soubmis,
Hautain, sedicieus, impudent et rebelle:
Par ainsi, prens exemple aus forçats prisonniers,
Qui chantent maintefois sur les bancs mariniers
Bien que leur mal soit grand, et leur prison cruelle.

Jean-Baptiste Chassignet,
"Our Life One May to Servitude Compare"

Our life one may to servitude compare,
And one must grow accustom'd to its ways,
For if you do of life complain, your days
Become a weight which too much is to bear.

Embrace and taste what little life supplies
Of comfort, for there is no sorrow known
Which hath not its own consolation;
Thus from its thorns the lovely rose doth rise.

You know that in a lodging you are plac'd
Which ever subject is to change and waste,
Proud and seditious, insolent, insane:
From wretched galley slaves example take,
Who on their benches sing and merry make,
Though great is their misfortune, cruel their chain.

Etienne Durand,
"Le feu devers le Ciel s'eslève incessament"

Le feu devers le Ciel s'eslève incessament,
Les eaux courent au sein de la mer poissonière,
Et sans fin dessus nous la Lune avec son frère
Reversent l'eau qu'ils ont tiré subtilement.

Les arbres qui de terre ont leur accroissement
Par le temps ou par feu retournent en poussière:
Et mesme ce grand Tout fait d'un rien seulement
Ne sera plus qu'un rien en son heure dernière.

Enfin tout icy bas retourne dont il vient,
Et par ce seul retour le monde s'entretient:
C'est donc avec raison, ma cruelle Uranie,
Tes yeux ayant causé mes ardeurs peu à peu,
Que mes vers provenus des ardeurs de mon feu
Retournent à tes yeux, dont ils ont pris la vie.

Etienne Durand, "The Fire Rises Ever To The Sky"

The fire rises ever to the sky,
The waters flow to ocean's fruitful breast,
And the moon above us labours without rest
The tides to ebb and then to raise on high;

The trees which push out from their native earth
In time or fire to their dust return:
And this great All, of Nothing made, shall turn
At last to Nothing just as ere its birth.

We see that all returns to whence it came,
Is in all flux eternally the same:
'Tis all too just, Urania, that my sighs
Should touch in verse the source of their desire,
And burning with my love's unceasing fire,
Return to whence they take their life, thine eyes.

Etienne Durand, "Quel lieu vous tient cachez"

Quel lieu vous tient cachez, nourrissons de ma flame
Cependant qu'aveuglé je m'esgare à tous coups?
Si vous estes mon coeur, si vous estes mon âme,
Comment puis-je estre en vie, et séparé de vous?

Beaux yeux, mon cher soucy, dont j'adore les charmes,
Si vous me vistes bien en partant de ce lieu,
Vous vistes bien mes yeux se couvrir de leurs larmes,
Pour ne point voir mon coeur qui leur disoit adieu.

Depuis si j'ay vescu, j'ay vescu par miracle,
Ou bien j'eus en naissant plus d'un coeur par le sort,
Non pour pouvoir jamais croire à plus d'un oracle,
Mais pour pouvoir vivant souffrir plus d'une mort.

Si mon oeil en pensant alléger mes supplices
S'est quelquefois tourné vers quelqu'autre beauté,
Ce que ce téméraire a choisi pour délices
Mon souvenir l'a pris pour une impiété.

Puis j'ay dict aussis tost, Si les flammes si belles
Du Soleil que je sers nous monstroient leur clarté,
Tous ces yeux ne seroient près d'eux que des chandelles,
Dont l'esclat ne se voit que par l'obscurité.

Mais quand je contemplois en ceste troupe mesme
Quelqu'un à sa moitié ses douleurs racontant,
Mon coeur triste et jaloux s'affligeant à l'extreme
Demandoit à mes yeux des larmes à l'instant.

Etienne Durand, "Where Are You Hidden"

Where are you hidden, eyes which feed my fire,
While lost and blinded I endure my smart?
If you are my heart and soul entire,
How can I live at all when we're apart?

Fair eyes, dear pain, whose charms I must adore,
If parting hence you did me well espy,
You saw my eyes with teardrops welling o'er,
That they might not my heart's farewell descry.

Since then if I have liv'd 'thas been by miracle,
Or I have had since birth more than one heart;
Not that I can believe more than one oracle,
But that I may more deaths than one support.

If, trying to assuage my constant pain,
My eye has ever mark'd another fair,
That which its boldness did as joy obtain
My memory did sacrilege declare.

At once I've said, "If those fair lights were here,
Of the glorious sun I serve, and here should shine,
These eyes of others were as candles mere,
Which one can only in the dark divine."

Whenever in a group I overheard
A lover to his love his woes lament,
At once my jealous heart itself bestir'd,
And my disappointed eyes their tears did vent.

J'ay passé maintes nuicts à me plaire en ces larmes,
Ne trouvant rien plus doux ny plus délicieux,
Pendant qu'Amour faisoit la garde avec ses armes,
De peur que le sommeil ne coulast en mes yeux.

Mais si par fois ce Dieu pour t'aller voir (ma Belle),
Cessoit de me garder, pendant qu'il me quittoit
Il mettoit près de moy le Songe en sentinelle,
Qui m'offroit tes beautez, et puis me les ostoit.

O Songe, luy disois-je, ô Songe que j'adore,
Arreste pour un peu, pourquoy t'envole-tu?
Puis je fermois les yeux pour resonger encore:
Mais estant sans sommeil ils estoient sans vertu.

Voilà comme j'ay peu profité de mes songes,
Et comme mes plaisirs se sont veuz emportez:
Mais las! si mes plaisirs ont esté des mensonges,
Mes tourments ont tousjours esté des véritez.

Mauvaise, c'est pour toy que ces peines j'endure,
Tu forme le dédale où je me vay perdant:
Mais si le Ciel m'a faict malheureux par nature,
Tu peux encor me rendre heureux par accident.

Toute seule tu peux à mon mal estre utile,
Tu peux guarir les maux que tu m'as faict souffrir:
Car tes blessures sont des blessures d'Achille,
Que l'autheur seulement a pouvoir de guarir.

Many a night I revel'd in these tears,
Finding no joy so delicate or sweet,
While Love stood guard as one who weapons bears,
Lest Sleep should in my eyes take up his seat.

But if perchance, my love, this god did go
To see you, and without his watch I lay,
Beside me he did still a dream bestow
Who your beauty offer'd, then straight took away.

"O dream," I said, "O dream which I adore,
But stay a while; O why then do you flee?"
And I clos'd my eyes to dream a little more,
But sleepless they could no more visions see.

Behold how little I have gain'd from dreaming,
And how my pleasures do depart from me;
Alas! If pleasures have been nought but seeming,
My pains have always been reality.

These torments, wicked one, for you I know;
You are the maze wherein myself I lose;
If Heaven did curse me with essential woe,
You can an accidental joy infuse.

Alone you can my pain alleviate,
The tortures which for you I do endure:
My wounds, like those struck by Achilles great,
The author only hath the power to cure.

Etienne Durand, "Stances a l'Inconstance"

Esprit des beaux esprits vagabonde inconstance
Qu'Æole Roy des vens avec l'onde conceut,
Pour estre de ce monde une seconde essence,
Recoy ces vers sacrez à ta seule puissance
Aussi bien que mon âme autrefois te receut.

Déesse qui par tout et nulle part demeure,
Qui préside à nos jours, et nous porte au tombeau,
Qui fait que le desir d'un instant naisse et meure,
Et qui fais que les Cieux se tournent à toute heure,
Encor qu'il ne soit rien ny si grand, ny si beau.

Si la terre pesante en sa base est contrainte,
C'est par le mouvement des atosmes divers,
Sur le dos de Neptun ta puissance est dépeinte,
Et les saisons font voir que ta Majesté saincte
Est l'âme qui soustient le corps de l'Univers.

Nostre esprit n'est que vent, et comme un vent volage,
Ce qu'il nomme constance est un branle retif:
Ce qu'il pense aujourd'huy demain n'est qu'un ombrage,
Le passé n'est plus rien, le futur un nuage,
Et ce qu'il tient présent il le sent fugitif.

Je peindrois volontiers mes légères pensées,
Mais desjà le pensant mon penser est changé,
Ce que je tiens m'eschappe, et les choses passées,
Tousjours par le présent se tiennent effacées,
Tant à ce changement mon esprit est rangé.

Etienne Durand, "To Inconstancy"

Vagrant Inconstancy, spirit of all mirth,
Born of King Aeolus and the heaving sea
To be the second essence of the earth,
Receive these verses sacred to thy worth
As in the past my soul receivèd thee.

Goddess who nowhere, everywhere doth dwell,
Who rules our days and guides us to the grave,
Who gives desire its birth and death as well,
And makes the skies perpetually swirl
Although there is no thing so great or brave.

If the massy earth is fastened to its base,
'Tis by the flux of atomies diverse,
On Neptune's back thy power shows its face,
And the seasons blazon thy majestic grace,
Thou soul which dost sustain the universe.

Our soul is nought but wind and so is made,
Its constancy a vain and stubborn dreaming:
What is today tomorrow is a shade,
The future a cloud, and every past unmade,
What it holds for real it knows an idle seeming.

Gladly I'd paint my thoughts that come and go,
But thinking them my thought itself is changed,
That which I seize escapes, the things I know,
In the present moment fly away and blow,
So is my spirit with this movement ranged.

Aussi depuis qu'à moy ta grandeur est unie
Des plus cruels desdains j'ay sceu me garantir,
J'ay gaussé les esprits, dont la fole manie
Esclave leur repos sous une tyrannie,
Et meurent à leur bien pour vivre au repentir.

Entre mille glaçons je sçay feindre une flame,
Entre mille plaisirs je fais le soucieux,
J'en porte une à la bouche, une autre dedans l'âme,
Et tiendrois à péché, si la plus belle Dame
Me retenoit le coeur plus longtemps que les yeux.

Doncques fille de l'air de cent plumes couverte,
Qui de serf que j'estois m'a mise en liberté,
Je te fais un présent des restes de ma perte,
De mon amour changé, de sa flame déserte,
Et du folastre object qui m'avoit arresté.

Je te fais un présent d'un tableau fantastique,
Où l'amour et le jeu par la main se tiendront,
L'oubliance, l'espoir, le desir frénétique,
Les sermens parjurez, l'humeur mélancolique,
Les femmes et les vents ensemble s'y verront.

Les sables de la mer, les orages, les nuës,
Les feux qui font en l'air les tonnantes chaleurs,
Les flammes des esclairs plustost mortes que veuës,
Les peintures du Ciel à nos yeux incogneuës,
A ce divin tableau serviront de couleurs.

Pour un temple sacré je te donne, ma Belle,
Je te donne son coeur pour en faire un autel,
Pour faire ton séjour tu prendras sa cervelle,
Et moy je te seray comme un prestre fidelle,
Qui passera ses jours en un change immortel.

Since to thy sovereign mightiness united,
I know no more the stings of cruel disdain;
I mock all those who madly are benighted
And thrall'd by tyrant passion unrequited,
Who, dead to joy, on earth to moan remain.

Among its thousand shapes I paint the flame,
Among a thousand pleasures I am wise;
For soul, for palate, I achieve my aim,
And I might sin but that the fairest frame
Retains my heart no longer than my eyes.

Daughter of air, goddess with plumes unfurl'd,
Who hast restor'd this slave to liberty,
I present thee with the fragments of my world,
My former love, my passion long since heal'd,
And with the object that enraptur'd me;

I present thee with a picture strange and dire,
With love and chance together hand in hand,
Forgetfulness and hope and wild desire,
And broken vows and melancholy fire,
And women and winds together in a band;

The sands of the sea and storms and clouds and air,
And cosmic fires, the brooding thunder's din,
And lightning, dead as soon as it is there,
Heaven's painting to our eyes all unaware,
Shall be the colours of this scene divine.

For a temple I present thee with my love,
For altar give thee her uncertain heart,
In her brain thou shalt ever dwell, a lodging brave;
And I shall be the priest who there will have
In ceaseless change his small immortal part.

Théophile de Viau, "Au moins ay-je songé"

Au moins ay-je songé que je vous ay baisee,
Et bien que tout l'Amour ne s'en soit pas allé,
Ce feu qui dans mes sens a doucement coullé,
Rend en quelque façon ma flamme rapaisee.

Apres ce doux effort mon ame reposee
Peut rire du plaisir qu'elle vous a volé,
Et de tant de refus a demy consolé,
Je trouve desormais ma guerison aisee.

Mes sens des-ja remis commencent à dormir,
Le sommeil qui deux nuicts m'avoit laissé gemir,
En fin dedans mes yeux vous fait quiter la place
Et quoy qu'il soit si froid au jugement de tous,
Il a rompu pour moy son naturel de glace,
Et s'est monstré plus chaud et plus humain que vous.

Théophile de Viau, "The Dream"

At least I've had a dream of kissing you,
And though my passion's not completely done,
The fire that through my veins has sweetly run
Has partially appeased the flame I knew.

After this gesture my relievèd soul
Can laugh a little at its stolen pleasure,
For past rebuffs some comfort I may treasure,
And I shall find a cure to make me whole.

My restorèd senses now begin to sleep,
And, having left me two long days to weep,
Within my eyes at length sleep takes your place;
And though it seems so cold to every view,
Revokes for me its quality of ice
And shows itself more warm and kind than you.

Théophile de Viau, "Elégie à Cloris"

Cloris lors que je songe en te voyant si belle
Que ta vie est subjette à la loy naturelle,
Et qu'à la fin les traicts d'un visage si beau
Avec tout leur esclat iront dans le tombeau,
Sans espoir que la mort nous laisse en la pensee
Aucun resentiment de l'amitié passee,
Je suis tout rebuté de l'aise et du soucy
Que nous fait le destin qui nous gouverne icy,
Et tombant tout à coup dans la mélancholie,
Je commence à blasmer un peu nostre folie
Et fay voeu de bon coeur de m'arracher un jour
La chere resverie où m'occupe l'amour.
Aussi bien faudra-t-il qu'une vieillesse infame
Nous gele dans le sang les mouvemens de l'ame,
Et que l'âge ensuivant ses revolutions
Nous oste la lumiere avec les passions.
Ainsi je me resous de songer à ma vie
Tandis que la raison m'en fait venir l'envie.
Je veux prendre un object où mon libre desir
Discerne la douleur d'avecques le plaisir,
Où mes sens tous entiers sans fraude et sans contrainte,
Ne s'embarrassent plus ny d'espoir ny de crainte,
Et de sa vaine erreur mon coeur desabusant,
Je gousteray le bien que je verray present,
Je prendray les douceurs à quoy je suis sensible
Le plus abondamment qu'il me sera possible.
Dieu nous a tant donné de divertissemens,
Nos sens trouvent en eux tant de ravissemens

142

Théophile de Viau, "Elegy to Cloris"

Cloris, when I think, seeing your beauty,
That your existence will be Nature's booty,
That finally those features proud and brave
Shall go in all their splendour to the grave,
That death will every mortal hope remove,
And leave no shadow of our former love,
I sicken at the pleasures to our state
Yet granted by all-dominating fate,
And fall at once into my melancholy
And start to puzzle at our pleasant folly,
And swear that one day I shall wrench away
This dear distraction which absorbs my day.
So must insensate age consume us whole
And freeze in our blood the motions of our soul,
And the revolutions of the passing age
Take from us light as well as passion's rage.
Thus I resolve to think on my own life
While yet my reason can enforce belief;
I shall think of all that my desire treasures
And see the pains unblinded by the pleasures;
My thoughts, of all deceit and striving bare,
Shall rid themselves of hope as well as fear;
My heart of all its former errors free,
I shall enjoy what present good I see:
I'll taste the sweetnesses my senses choose
As fully as abundant earth allows.
From God we have so much that may divert,
And our tastes themselves such rare delight impart,

Que c'est une fureur de chercher qu'en nous mesme,
Quelqu'un que nous aymions et quelqu'un qui nous ayme.
Le coeur le mieux donné tient tousjours à demy,
Chacun s'ayme un peu mieux tousjours que son amy,
On les suit rarement dedans la sepulture,
Le droit de l'amitié cede aux Loix de nature.
Pour moy si je voyois en l'humeur où je suis,
Ton ame s'envoler aux eternelles nuicts,
Quoy que puisse envers moy l'usage de tes charmes,
Je m'en consolerois avec un peu de larmes.
N'attends pas que l'Amour, aveugle, aille suivant
Dans l'horreur de la nuict des ombres et du vent.
Ceux qui jurent d'avoir l'ame encore assez forte
Pour vivre dans les yeux d'une Maistresse morte,
N'ont pas prix le loisir de voir tous les efforts
Que fait la mort hideuse à consumer un corps,
Quand les sens pervertis sortent de leur usage,
Qu'une laideur visible efface le visage,
Que l'esprit deffaillant et les membres perclus
En se disant adieu ne se cognoissent plus,
Que dedans un moment apres la vie esteinte,
La face sur son cuir n'est pas seulement peinte,
Et que l'infirmité de la puante chair
Nous fait ouvrir la terre afin de la cacher.
Il faut estre animé d'une fureur bien vive,
Ayant consideré comme la mort arrive
Et comme tout l'object de nostre amour perit,
Si par un tel remede une ame ne guerit.
Cloris tu vois qu'un jour il faudra qu'il advienne
Que le destin ravisse et ta vie et la mienne,
Mais sans te voir le corps ny l'esprit depery,

That he is mad who seeks life to improve
By loving, or by finding one to love.
The most giving heart the half alone doth give,
Each lover loves himself more than his love;
'Tis seldom that the tomb does not give pause,
And the laws of passion yield to Nature's laws.
I think, were I to see your spirit bright
Departing, fleeing to eternal night,
A few tears shed for your departed charms
Would console me for the solace of your arms.
O do not think that my blind love would follow
In horrid night, and wind, and shadows hollow.
Those who swear their love is strong enough
To court in death the favours of their love
Have not at leisure witnessed the resource
With which repulsive death consumes a corse,
The senses twisted from their former use,
By vivid ugliness defaced the face;
The spirit gone, and the useless limbs now made
Strangers before the corpse is even laid;
Within a moment, when the life has died,
The face not even painted on the hide,
And such the weakness of the stinking flesh
That to hide it deep in earth is our first wish—
It were indeed a most impetuous passion
That could consider death and this its fashion,
And how all objects of our love depart,
And find no cure for the distempered heart.
Cloris, you understand the day must dawn
When destiny will seize your life and mine;
But now, with soul and body unimpaired,

Le Ciel en soit loüé Cloris je suis guery:
Mon ame en me dictant les vers que je t'envoye,
Me vient de plus en plus ressusciter la joye,
Je sens que mon esprit reprend sa liberté,
Que mes yeux desvoilez cognoissent la clarté,
Que l'object d'un beau jour, d'un pré, d'une fontaine,
De voir comme Garonne en l'Ocean se traine,
De prendre dans mon Isle en ses longs promenoirs
La paisible fraischeur de ses ombrages noirs,
Me plaist mieux aujourd'huy que le charme inutile
Des attraicts dont Amour te fait voir si fertile.
Languir incessament apres une beauté
Et ne se rebuter d'aucune cruauté,
Gaigner au pris du sang une foible esperance
D'un plaisir passager qui n'est qu'en apparence,
Se rendre l'esprit mol, le courage abatu,
Ne mettre en aucun prix l'honneur ny la vertu,
Pour conserver son mal mettre tout en usage,
Se peindre incessament et l'ame et le visage,
Cela tient d'un esprit où le Ciel n'a point mis
Ce que son influence inspire à ses amis.
Pour moy que la raison esclaire en quelque sorte,
Je ne scaurois porter une fureur si forte,
Et des-ja tu peux voir au train de cest escrit,
Comme en la guarison s'avance mon esprit:
Car insensiblement ma Muse un peu legere
A passé dessus toy sa plume passagere,
Et destournant mon coeur de son premier object,
Dés le commencement j'ay changé de subject,
Emporté du plaisir de voir ma vene aisée
Seurement aborder ma flame r'apaisée
146

Praise Heaven, Cloris, I'm already cured.
My soul dictates the verses I essay
And revives in me the principle of joy;
I feel my spirit take its liberty,
And my eyes at last unveil'd most clearly see
The beauty of the day, the field, the spring,
And Garonne to the ocean wandering;
Upon my isle, where fair walks are display'd,
The quiet freshness of the leafy shade
More pleasure gives than all the futile charms
Which generous love would grant me in your arms.
To languish ever in a beauty's train
And be undaunted by her cruel disdain,
To win with heart's blood but the feeble hope
Of passing pleasure, vain illusion's shape,
To soften the spirit, render courage mute,
And value honour, virtue, not a whit,
To stoop to all to hold a dear disgrace,
To paint incessantly the soul and face—
These are the features of a craven spirit
Which Heaven grants not even common merit.
For me, whom Reason now has given sight,
I cannot contemplate such rude delight;
Already, as you see, this script announces
How rapidly my spirit's cure advances.
Insensibly my muse with casual aim
Has passed o'er you her light and wandering plume,
And my heart from former fancy turn'd away
From the first has changed the subject I portray,
Transported by the pleasure of my art
As it confronts my convalescent heart

Et joüer à son gré sur les propos d'aimer,
Sans avoir aujourd'huy pour but que de rimer,
Et sans te demander que ton bel oeil esclaire
Ces vers où je n'ay pris aucun soin de te plaire.

And plays at will on love's entangled theme
With no aim at the moment but to rhyme,
Nor asking if your fair eye will peruse
These lines that have not even tried to please.

Marc-Antoine de Saint-Amant,
"Je viens de recevoir une belle missive"

Je viens de recevoir une belle missive
De la Nymphe qui prit mon ame au trebuchet,
Et qui scellant mon coeur de son divin cachet
Y voulut imprimer son image lascive.

Il me fasche deja que cette heure n'arrive
Où je dois embrasser sa taille de brochet,
Et jamais verollé tapy dessous l'archet,
En suant ne trouva l'Orloge si tardive.

Phoebus, va t'en souler tes paillards appetis
Dans les bras amoureux de la belle Thetis;
Elle se plaint qu'au Ciel trop long temps tu demeures:
Nuit, couvre l'Univers de ton noir balandran:
Et puis que j'ay le mot justement à six heures,
Amour, conduy l'aiguille au milieu du Cadran.

Marc-Antoine de St.-Amant,
"I've Just Received A Very Pretty Letter"

I've just received a very pretty letter
From the nymph who has in wile ensnar'd my soul,
And stamped upon my heart her holy seal
That I may bear her wanton image better.

It maddens me the hours pass so dully
Until I hold her slim delicious form;
No pox'd one ever, sweating out his harm,
Could know the wretched clock to move more slowly.

Phoebus, go drown thy lecherous appetite
In the amorous arms of lovely Thetis white:
She protests thou'rt in the skies too long a while.
Night, shroud the universe in mantle black,
And since my appointment is at six o'clock,
Love, guide the needle to the middle of the dial.

Marc-Antoine de Saint-Amant, "Me voyant plus frisé"

Me voyant plus frisé qu'un gros Comte Allemant,
Le teint frais, les yeux doux, et la bouche vermeille,
Tu m'appelles ton coeur, ton ame, ta merveille,
Et me veux recevoir pour ton plus cher Amant:

Tu trouves mon maintien si grave et si charmant,
Tu sens à mes discours un tel goust en l'oreille,
Que tu me veux aimer d'une ardeur nompareille,
Où desormais ta foy sera de diamant.

Pour me donner un nom qui me soit convenable,
Cloris, ton jugement est plus que raisonnable,
Quand tu viens m'appeler un miroir à Putains,
Je n'en refuse point le titre, ny l'usage:
Il est vray, je le suis, tes propos sont certains,
Car tu t'es bien souvent mirée en mon visage.

Marc-Antoine de St.-Amant,
"Seeing Me Spruce As Some Fat German Count"

Seeing me spurce as some fat German count,
My skin fresh, eyes soft, mouth red and full,
You address me as your wonder, heart and soul,
And want me as your lover paramount.

You find my air so charming and profound
And you find my words so pleasing to your ear,
That you swear your love eternal will appear,
That your faith will be as firm as diamond.

Cloris, in finding for me a proper title,
Your judgment proves itself not vain or idle,
With this thoughtful designation "Mirror of whores."
I do not disavow my name or race:
'Tis true, I am, your wit is free from flaws—
You've often in my eyes seen your own face.

Marc-Antoine de Saint-Amant, "Entrer dans le bordel"

Entrer dans le bordel d'une démarche grave,
Comme un Coq qui s'appreste à jouër de l'ergot,
Demander Janneton, faire chercher Margot,
Ou la jeune Bourgeoise, à cause qu'elle est brave;

Fureter tous les troux, jusqu'au fonds de la Cave,
Y rencontrer Perrette, et daubant du gigot
Dancer le bransle double au son du larigot,
Pour y faire festin d'une botte de rave:

N'y voir pour tout tableaux que quelque vieux rebus,
Ou bien quelque Almanach qui sema ses abus
L'an que Pantagruel déconfit les Andoüilles;
Et du haut jusqu'au bas pour tous meubles de pris,
Qu'une vieille paillasse, un pot et des quenoüilles;
Voilà le passe-temps du Soudart de Cypris.

Marc-Antoine de St.-Amant, "Go in the Whorehouse"

Go in the whorehouse with a solemn pace
Like a cock preparing to display his spur;
Call Jenny, Margaret, or some other her,
Or the new city girl with the pretty face.

Explore each hole to the bottom of the cave,
Meet there Perrette and stew a haunch of pig,
And to the flute's sound dance the double jig,
Make on a turnip-bunch a banquet brave;

A rebus find in any picture's stead,
Or an almanac which its abuses spread
When Pantagruel destroyed the sausage-men;
For furniture, a mattress old, then spot
A pile of spindles and a chamber-pot
—Behold the sports of Venus' veteran!

Laurent Drelincourt, "Sur les Pierres précieuses"

Quoi! sort-il tant de feux, de rayons, de lumieres,
D'un si froid, si grossier, & si noir Elément?
Et tant d'Astres, naissans dans ces sombres Carrieres,
Font-ils donc de la Terre un second Firmament?

Minéraux éclatans, terrestres Luminaires,
Dont la tête de Rois brille superbement,
Je ne puis vous compter que pour des biens vulgaires,
Et pour moi votre éclat n'est qu'un foible ornement.

Invisible Soleil, qui donnas l'être au Monde,
Vien former dans mon coeur, par ta vertu féconde,
Pour célestes joyaux, l'Espérance & la Foi.
Mais que, cessant un jour d'espérer & de croire,
J'obtienne dans ton Ciel, & possede avec toi,
La Couronne sans prix des rayons de ta Gloire.

Laurent Drelincourt, "On Precious Stones"

What? So many fires, such rays of light,
From such a cold and darksome element?
Such stars born in the somber quarry's night
To make of Earth a second Firmament?

Outbursting minerals, terrestrial stars,
Which serve to shine upon the heads of kings,
I can account you nought but vulgar lures,
And flashy baubles what your beauty brings.

Invisible Sun which did the world create,
Descend into my heart, there generate
The precious jewels of Faith and Hope alone.
But may I cease to hope and to believe
One day, and in thy Heaven from thee receive
Thy beams of Glory as a priceless Crown.

Laurent Drelincourt, "Sur la Naissance de Notre Seigneur"

O Mystere fertile en merveilles étranges!
Ouvrez ici, Mortels, & vos coeurs & vos yeux;
Et vous, purs Séraphins, sainte Troupe des Anges,
Venez, d'un vol ardent, en ces terrestres lieux.

Celui, dont jour & nuit vous chantez les louanges,
A quitté, pour un tems, la demeure des Cieux:
Son habit de lumiere est caché sous des langes,
Il change en un toit vil son Palais glorieux.

Le Fort, l'Ancien des Jours, est foible & dans l'enfance:
L'Invisible se voit: Dieu même prend naissance:
L'Immortel est mortel, & l'Immense est borné.
Enfin, je l'apperçois couché dans une étable;
Et ravi, je m'écrie: Eternel nouveau-né,
Qu'en ton abaissement tu parois adorable!

Laurent Drelincourt, "On the Birth of our Saviour"

O mystery, of wonders fertile source!
Ye mortals, open here both hearts and eyes,
Ye Seraphim, divert your burning course
And come to earth, blest Legions of the Skies.

He whose praises night and day ye sing
Has left his dwelling in the Heavens a while;
Has hid his Light 'neath infant's covering,
His glorious Palace chang'd for lodging vile.

The mighty Ancient of Days a feeble child:
The unseen seen, and God in man reveal'd,
The immortal mortal, Infinity confin'd.
At last I see thee shelter'd in the hay;
Transfix'd I cry, "Eternal! Born this day!
In thine abasement how thou art enshrin'd."

GERMAN POEMS

Friedrich von Spee,
"Die gespons Jesu klaget ihren hertzen brand"

Gleich früh wan sich entzündet
  Der silber weisse tag;
Und uns die Sonn verkündet
  Wass nachts verborgen lag:
Die lieb in meinem hertzen
  Ein flämlein stecket an;
Dass brint gleich einer kertzen,
  So neimand leschen kan.

Wan schon Ichs schlag in Winde,
  Gen Ost-und-Norden brauss;
Doch ruh, noch rast ich finde,
  Last nie sich blasen auss.
O wee der qual und peine!
  Wo soll mich wenden hin?
Den gantzen tag ich weine,
  Weil stäts in schmertzen bin.

Wan wider dan entflogen
  Der Tag zu Nacht hinein,
Und sich gar tieff gebogen
  Die Sonn, und Sonnenschein;
Das Flämlein so mich queelet
  Noch bleibt in voller glut;
All stundt, so viel man zehlet,
  Michs je noch brennen thut.

Friedrich von Spee,
"The Spouse of Jesus Bewails her Passion"

Betimes when morning brightens
　　The day in silver-white,
And to us the sun enlightens
　　What hidden lay in night;
Then love within me yearning
　　Doth light a flame devout,
Like a candle fiercely burning,
　　Which no one can put out.

Though east and north winds freeze it,
　　They make it not expire,
Nor rest nor peace may ease it,
　　The flame of my desire.
Alas, the woe and anguish,
　　O wither shall I turn?
All the day I languish,
　　In pain so do I burn.

When once more has departed
　　The day unto the night,
And the sun again has started
　　To court'sy with its light;
The flame which me devours
　　Remains in fullest glow;
Through all the countless hours
　　Inflames me with its woe.

Das Flämlein dass ich meine,
  Ist JESU süsser Nam;
Es zehret Marck und Beine,
  Frist ein gar wundersam.
O Süssigkeit in schmertzen!
  O schmertz in süssigkeit!
Ach bleibe doch im Hertzen,
  Bleib doch in Ewigkeit.

O schon in pein, und qualen
  Mein Leben schwindet hinn,
Wan Jesu Pfeil und Stralen
  Durchstreichet Muth und Sinn;
Doch nie so gar mich zehret
  Die Liebe JESU mein,
Als gleich sie wider nehret,
  Und schenckt auch Frewden ein.

O Flämlein süss ohn massen!
  O bitter auch ohn ziel!
Du machest mich verlassen
  All ander Frewd, und Spiel;
Du zündest mein gemüthe,
  Bringst mir gross Hertzen leidt,
Du kühlest mein Geblüthe,
  Bringst auch ergetzligkeit.

Ade zu tausent Jahren,
  O Welt zu guter nacht:
Ade lass mich nun fahren,
  Ich längst hab dich veracht.
In JESU lieb Ich lebe,
  Sag dir von Hertzen grund;
In lauter Frewd Ich schwebe,
  Wie sehr ich bin verwund.

The flame which doth me harrow
   Is Jesus' sweetest name;
It eats up bone and marrow,
   And fiercely doth consume.
O agony in sweetness!
   O sweets in agony!
In my heart stay thou as witness,
   Stay to eternity!

Amid these pains and sorrows
   My life doth hence depart,
When Jesus' shining arrows
   Transfix my soul and heart;
But though in it I perish,
   The love of Jesus mine,
It ever doth me nourish,
   And pours out joy like wine.

O sweetest flame unmeasur'd!
   O bitter without end!
I leave all I have treasur'd,
   All joy or play could lend;
Thou set'st my soul on fire,
   Bring'st to my heart distress,
Thou coolest my blood's desire,
   And bring'st delightfulness.

Farewell for time unending,
   Good Night, O World, to thee;
My voyage is impending,
   My scorn I let thee see.
In the heart where it is founded
   I live in Jesus' love;
However I am wounded,
   I soar in bliss above.

Martin Opitz, "Ach Liebste, lass uns eilen"

Ach Liebste, lass uns eilen,
  Wir haben Zeit:
Es schadet das verweilen
  Uns beyderseit.

Der edlen Schönheit Gaben
  Fliehen fuss für fuss:
Das alles was wir haben
  Verschwinden muss.

Der Wangen Ziehr verbleichet,
  Das Haar wird greiss,
Der Augen Fewer weichet,
  Die Brunst wird Eiss.

Das Mündlein von Corallen
  Wird ungestalt,
Die Händ' als Schnee verfallen,
  Und du wirst alt.

Drumb lass uns jetzt geniessen
  Der Jugend Frucht,
Eh' als wir folgen müssen
  Der Jahre Flucht.

Wo du dich selber liebest,
  So liebe mich,
Gieb mir, das, wann du giebest,
  Verlier auch ich.

Martin Opitz, "Ah, Dearest, Let Us Haste Us"

Ah Dearest, let us haste us,
   While we have time;
Delaying doth but waste us
   And lose our prime.

The gifts that beauty nourish
   Fly with the year,
And everything we cherish
   Must disappear.

The cheeks so fair turn pallid,
   And grey the hair,
The flashing eyes turn gelid,
   And ice, desire.

From coral lips must flee then
   The outline bold;
The snowy hands decay then,
   And thou art old.

So therefore let us swallow
   Youth's precious fruit,
E'er we are forc'd to follow
   The years in flight.

As thou thyself then lovest,
   Love also me;
Give me, that when thou givest
   I lose to thee.

Martin Opitz, "Kompt, lasst uns ausspatzieren"

Kompt, lasst uns ausspatzieren,
Zu hören durch den Waldt
Die Vögel musiciren,
Das Berg und Thal erschallt.

Wol dem der frey kan singen,
Wie ihr, ihr Volck der Lufft;
Mag seine Stimme schwingen
Zu der auff die er hofft.

Ich werde nicht erhöret,
Schrey ich gleich ohne Rhu;
Die so mich singen lehret
Stopfft selbst die Ohren zu.

Mehr wol dem, der frey lebet,
Wie du, du leichte Schar,
In Trost und Angst nicht schwebet,
Ist ausser der Gefahr.

Ihr werdet zwar umbgangen,
Doch helt man euch in werth;
Ich bin von der gefangen
Die meiner nicht begehrt.

Ihr könnt noch Mittel finden,
Entfliehen aus der Pein;
Sie muss noch mehr mich binden,
Soll ich erlöset seyn.

Martin Opitz, "Come, let us go a-strolling"

Come, let us go a-strolling,
To hear, the woods around,
The birds their songs unrolling,
Till hill and dale resound.

Lucky is he who singing
Like you, ye folk of air,
His cheerful voice is bringing
Unto his hoped-for fair!

Fortune doth never reach me,
Though I sing without a pause;
She who did singing teach me
Herself doth stop her ears.

Lucky is he who living
Like you, ye airy band,
Knows hope's nor fear's misgiving,
Nor the touch of danger's hand.

Ye birds, indeed, are slighted,
But still of worth are thought;
But I am captivated
By one who wants me not.

Ye can escape, I mind me,
And from your anguish flee:
But she must yet more bind me
Before I can be free.

Paul Fleming, "Über seinen Traum"

Ists müglich, dass sie mich auch kan im Schlafe höhnen?
Wars noch nicht gnung, dass ich mich wachend nach ihr
    sehnen
und so bekümmern muss, im fall sie nicht ist hier?
Doch, sie ist ausser Schuld. Du, Morpheu, machtest dir,
aus mir ein leichtes Spiel. Der alte Schalck der lieffe,
In dem ich, gleich wie sie, frey aller Sorgen schlieffe.
Er drückt' ihr schönes Bild in einen Schatten ab.
Und bracht' es mir so vor. Die liebe Schönheit gab
der Seelen ihren Geist. Sie fingen sich zu lieben,
zu sehn, zu küssen an. Die süssen Freunde trieben
Ihr schönes Tuhn mit sich, so hertzlich und so viel,
biss dass, in dem der Geist noch hat sein Liebes-spiel,
und in dem Schatten schertzt, mein matter Leib erwachet.
Das Bild, in dem er sich noch so ergetzlich machet,
fleugt gantz mit ihm darvon, und kehrt an seinen Ort.
Was thu ich armer nun? die Seele die ist fort.
Mein Leib lebt auff den Schein. Wie wird mirs doch noch
    gehen?
Sag' ichs ihr, oder nicht? Sie wirds doch nicht gestehen.
Wer! O! wer wird mich denn entnehmen dieser Last?
Ach, Schwester, fühlst du nicht, dass du zwo Seelen hast?

Paul Fleming, "On his Dream"

And can she even in my sleep so scorn me?
Is not enough the longing which doth burn me
In waking hours, and pain when she's not here?
Yet is she blameless. Morpheus, 'tis clear
You make a mock of me. The idle knave
Came while we slept and not a care did have;
In a shadow he did print her image fair
And show'd it to me. Then my beauty rare
Did give her spirit to my soul. To love,
To see, to kiss, the pair began, so strove
In love's sweet ways with such enraptur'd zeal
That while my spirit love's allures did feel
And sported with its shade, my body woke.
The picture whence I such delight partook
Fled with my soul away, left me alone.
Alas, what shall I do? My soul is gone.
My body seems to live. Should I express it?
Tell her my dream or not? She'll not confess it.
O who will relieve me thus by cares oppress'd?
Don't you feel, Sister, two souls in your breast?

Paul Fleming, "Auff ihr Abwesen"

Ich irrte hin und her, und suchte mich in mir,
und wuste dieses nicht, dass ich gantz war in dir.
Ach! thu dich mir doch auff, du Wohnhauss meiner Seelen!
Komm, Schöne, gieb mich mir. Benim mir dieses quälen.
Schau, wie er sich betrübt, mein Geist, der in dir lebt?
Tödtst du den, der dich liebt? itzt hat er ausgelebt.
Doch, gieb mich nicht aus dir. Ich mag nicht in mich
    kehren.
Kein Todt hat macht an mir. Du kanst mich leben lehren.
Ich sey auch, wo ich sey, bin ich, Schatz, nicht bey dir,
So bin ich nimmermehr selbest in und bey mir.

Paul Fleming, "In her Absence"

Where'er I went I sought myself in me,
And knew not that I always was in thee.
Come set me free, dear dwelling of my soul,
Restore me to myself entire and whole.
Would'st kill the spirit prison'd in thy heart,
The soul that loves and tears itself apart?
Nay, hold me still, to me I'll not return;
Not death from thee but rather life I learn.
Absent from thee, wherever I may roam,
My exil'd self can never find its home.

Paul Fleming, "An Basilenen"

Ist mein Glücke gleich gesonnen,
mich zu führen weit von dir,
O du Sonne meiner Wonnen,
So verbleibst du doch in mir.
Du in mir, und ich in dir,
sind beysammen für und für.

Künftig werd' ich gantz nicht scheuen,
Kaspis, deine fremde Fluht,
und die öden Wüsteneyen,
da man nichts als fürchten thut.
Auch das wilde macht mir zahm,
Liebste, dein gelobter Nahm'

Überstehe diese Stunden,
Schwester, und sey unverwand.
Ich verbleibe dir verbunden,
und du bist mein festes Band.
Meines Hertzens Trost bist du,
und mein Hertze selbst darzu.

Ihr, ihr Träume, sollt indessen
unter uns das Beste thun.
Kein Schlaff der soll ihr vergessen.
Ohne mich soll Sie nicht ruhn.
Dass die süsse Nacht ersetzt,
was der trübe Tag verletzt.

Paul Fleming, "To Basilene"

If determinèd is Fate
To lead me far away from thee,
O thou sun of my delight,
Thou remainest yet in me.
Thou in me and I in thee,
Together for all time to be.

I shall never fear the vastness
Of the distant Caspian flood,
Or the lonely desert wasteness,
Where only fear invades the blood.
The very wilderness is tame,
Dearest, in thy lovèd name.

My love, my sister, do not change;
Live to survive this somber hour.
To thee my love shall not grow strange,
But bound shall be within thy power.
Ease to my heart thou truly art,
Nay, thou art my very heart.

Meanwhile dreams will serve to join us
And best remembrance still shall keep;
Heart, my sleep will not untwine us,
And without me thou shalt not sleep;
So sweet night again supplies
What the dismal day denies.

Lebe meines Lebens Leben,
stirb nicht meines Todes Todt,
dass wir uns uns wiedergeben,
abgethan von aller Noth.
Sey gegrüsst, bald Trost, itzt Quahl
tausent, tausent, tausent mahl.

Live, thou life of my own life,
Do not die, death of my death.
One day free from pain and strife
We'll share again our mutual breath.
Farewell my comfort, present pain,
Ten thousand farewells, and yet again.

Paul Fleming, "Zur Zeit seiner Verstossung"

Ein Kauffmann, der sein Gut nur einen Schiffe traut,
ist hochgefährlich dran, in dem es bald kan kommen,
dass ihm auff einen Stoss sein gantzes wird genommen.
Der fehlt, der allzuviel auff ein Gelücke traut.

Gedenck' ich nun an mich, so schauret mir die Haut.
Mein Schiff das ist entzwey. Mein Gut ist weggeschwom-
    men.
Nichts mehr das ist mein Rest; das machet kurtze Summen.
Ich habe Müh' und Angst, ein ander meine Braut.

Ich unglückseeliger! mein Hertze wird zerrissen,
mein Sinn ist ohne sich. Mein Geist zeucht von mir aus.
Mein alles wird nun nichts. Was wird doch endlich drauss?
Wer eins doch übrig noch, so wolt' ich alles missen.
Mein theuerster Verlust der bin selb-selbsten ich.
Nun bin ich ohne Sie, nun bin ich ohne mich.

Paul Fleming, "In Time of Rejection"

A merchant who entrusts his whole estate
Unto one ship is foolish; all too soon
A single stroke may all his riches drown;
He errs who from one cast all doth await.

If on myself I think, I desperate grow.
My ship is sunk; my riches float away;
Nothing remains; there is no more to say:
Another has my bride, I have my woe.

Unhappy me! My heart is torn apart,
My wits are fled, my spirit given o'er;
My everything is nought. What's now in store?
Had I one thing alone, I'd feel no smart:
Myself my dearest loss I must proclaim,
Now without her, without myself I am.

Paul Fleming, "An meinen Erlöser"

Erhöre meine Noth, du aller Noth Erhörer,
Hilff Helffer aller Welt, hilff mir auch, der ich mir
selb-selbst nicht helffen kan; ich suche Trost bey dir.
Herr, du hast Rath und That. Dich preisen deine Lehrer,

wie du es denn auch bist, für einen Glaubens-mehrer.
Ich bin desselben Lehr. Hier steh' ich, Ich steh' hier.
Erfülle mich mit dir und deines Geistes Zir.
Er ist es, Er dein Geist, der rechte Glaubens-mehrer.

Artzt, Ich bin kranck nach dir. Du Brunnen Israel,
dein kräfftigs Wasser löscht den Durst der matten Seel'
Auch dein Blut, Oster-Lam, hat meine Thür erröhtet,
die zu dem Hertzen geht. Ich steiffe mich auff dich
du mein Hort, du mein Felss. Belebe, Leben, mich.
Dein Todt hat meinen Todt, Du Todes Todt, getödtet.

Paul Fleming, "To my Redeemer"

Hear my cry, thou hearer of all cries,
Help, help of all the world, help also me;
I cannot help myself; only in thee
I comfort find and counsel. Worthy prize

Of all thy teachers, only faith-restorer
Empty of faith I am. O fill me here
With thee and with belief, with spirit's cheer;
Only thy spirit frees from doubt and error.

Sick for thee, Doctor, Fount of Israel,
Whose water slakes the thirsty tired soul,
Thy blood, Lamb of Easter, marks my door with red;
Supporter of hearts, I rest myself on thee,
My fortress, rock. My life, live thou in me.
Thy death, death's death, hath struck my own death dead.

Paul Fleming, "Andacht"

Ich lebe. Doch nicht ich. Derselbe lebt in mir,
Der mir durch seinen Todt das Leben bringt herfür.
Mein Leben war sein Todt, sein Todt war mir mein Leben,
Nur geb' ich wieder Ihm, was Er mir hat gegeben.
Er lebt durch meinen Todt. Mir sterb' ich täglich ab.
Der Leib, mein Irdnes Theil, der ist der Seelen Grab.
Er lebt nur auff den schein. Wer ewig nicht wil sterben.
Der muss hier in der Zeit verwesen und verderben,
Weil er noch sterben kan. Der Todt, der Geistlich heisst,
Der ist als denn zu spät, wann uns sein Freund hinreisst,
Der unsern Leib bringt um. HERR, gieb mir die Genade,
Dass dieses Leibes-Brauch nicht meiner Seelen schade.
Mein Alles und mein Nichts, mein Leben, meinen Todt,
Das hab' ich bey mir selbst. Hilffst du, so hats nicht noth.
Ich wil, ich mag, ich sol, ich kan mir selbst nicht rahten,
Dich wil ichs lassen thun; du hast bey dir die Thaten.
Die Wünsche thu ich nur. Ich lasse mich gantz dir.
Ich wil nicht meine seyn. Nim mich nur, gieb dich mir.

Paul Fleming, "Devotion"

I live; yet 'tis not I. He lives in me,
Who through his death my life did fast decree.
My life to him was death, his death my life,
Now give I him again what once he gave.
Through the death of me he lives. I die each day,
The grave of my body shuts my soul away;
It only seems to live. Who will not die
Must here in time decay and waste and sigh,
While yet he can, die. The spirit's death
Comes then too late, when his friend has robb'd our breath
And laid our body low. Lord, give me grace,
That my body's use may not my soul disgrace.
My Everything, my Nought, my Death, my Life
I have in me. If thou help'st I am safe.
Nor will, nor may, nor can I judge my needs;
That leave I thee, for thou alone hast deeds;
But wishes I. To thee then give I me.
I will not be mine. Only take me; give me thee.

Andreas Gryphius, "Über die Geburt Jesu"

Nacht, mehr denn lichte Nacht! Nacht, lichter als der Tag,
Nacht, heller als die Sonn', in der das Licht geboren,
Das Gott, der Licht, in Licht wohnhafftig, ihm erkohren:
O Nacht, die alle Nacht' und Tage trotzen mag!

O freudenreiche Nacht, in welcher Ach und Klag,
Und Finsternüss, und was sich auff die Welt verschworen
Und Furcht und Höllen-Angst und Schrecken ward ver-
lohren.
Der Himmel bricht! doch fällt numehr kein Donnerschlag.

Der Zeit und Nächte Schuff, ist diese Nacht ankommen!
Und hat das Recht der Zeit, und Fleisch an sich genommen!
Und unser Fleisch und Zeit der Ewigkeit vermacht.
Der Jammer trübe Nacht, die schwarze Nacht der Sünden
Dess Grabes Dunckelheit, muss durch die Nacht verschwin-
den.
Nacht lichter als der Tag; Nacht mehr denn lichte Nacht!

Andreas Gryphius, "On the Birth of Jesus"

Night more than any light! Night more than day!
Night brighter than the sun where light is born;
Which God, who dwells in light, chose as his own!
O Night which days and nights all comfort may!

O Night of joy where all lament and pain
And darkness grim and all to earth betray'd
And fear of Hell and horror are allay'd!
Though Heaven opes, no thunder falls amain.

Who made all days and nights this night is come,
And taken weights of time and flesh to him,
And render'd flesh and time forever bright.
The wretched night, the dark night of our sins,
The darkness of the grave, to nought returns.
Night more than day! Night more than any light!

Andreas Gryphius, "An sich selbst"

Mir grauet vor mir selbst, mir zittern alle Glieder
Wenn ich die Lipp' und Nass' und beyder Augen Klufft,
Die blind vom wachen sind, dess Athems schwere Luft
Betracht', und die nun schon erstorbnen Augen-Lieder.

Die Zunge, schwartz vom Brand fällt mit den Worten
    nieder,
Und lalt ich weiss nicht was; die müde Seele rufft
Dem grossen Tröster zu, das Fleisch reucht nach der Grufft,
Die Aertzte lassen mich, die Schmertzen kommen wieder.

Mein Cörper ist nicht mehr als Adern, Fell', und Bein.
Das sitzen ist mein Tod, das liegen meine Pein.
Die Schenckel haben selbst nun Träger wol von nöthen!
Was ist der hohe Ruhm, und Jugend, Ehr und Kunst?
Wenn diese Stunde kompt: wird alles Rauch und Dunst.
Und eine Noth muss uns mit allem Vorsatz tödten.

Andreas Gryphius, "To Himself"

I shudder at myself, my limbs do quake,
When lip and nose and caverns of the eyes
With watching blind I see, when heavy sighs
Of wind I breathe, and dying eyelids shake.

The blacken'd tongue lolls out nor words doth have,
But stammers God knows what, the tired soul
Cries to the Comforter; the pains appal,
The doctors leave; my flesh smells of the grave.

My body's nought but skin and bone and vein,
To sit up is my death, to lie my pain,
And my legs have need of carriers to be carried.
Where are youth, glory, honour, art and power?
All turns to smoke and mist when comes this hour;
By a common misery we're killed and buried.

Christian Hofmann von Hofmannswaldau, "Vergänglichkeit der Schönheit"

Es wird der bleiche tod mit seiner kalten hand
Dir endlich mit der zeit um deine brüste streichen,
Der liebliche corall der lippen wird verbleichen;
Der schultern warmer schnee wird werden kalter sand,

Der augen süsser blitz, die kräffte deiner hand
Für welchen solches fällt, die werden zeitlich weichen,
Das haar, das itzund kan des goldes glantz erreichen,
Tilgt endlich tag und jahr als ein gemeines band.

Der wohlgesetzte fuss, die liebliche gebärden,
Die werden theils zu staub, theils nichts und nichtig werden,
Denn opfert keiner mehr der gottheit deiner pracht.
Diss und noch mehr als diss muss endlich untergehen,
Dein hertze kan allein zu aller zeit bestehen,
Dieweil es die natur aus diamant gemacht.

Christian Hofmann von Hofmannswaldau, "The Transience of Beauty"

One day pale death shall come with icy hand
And stroke at last, my dearest one, your breasts,
The coral of your lips fade at his tests,
The warm snow of your shoulders turn cold sand.

Your eyes' sweet lightning and your fingers' force,
On which it falls, shall fall into decay;
Your hair which rivals gold with shining ray
The days and years shall quench without remorse.

Your shapely foot, your gracious movements sweet,
One fall to dust, the others turn to nought;
Then none shall worship more your Godhead's pride.
These beauties, yes, and more shall perish'd be,
Only your heart will last eternally:
Of diamond made, it ever must abide.

Johann Scheffler ("Angelus Silesius"), from
Der Cherubinische Wandersmann

Ich weiss nicht/ was ich bin/ ich bin nicht/ was ich weiss:
Ein Ding und nicht ein Ding/ ein Stüpfchen und ein Kreis.

Ich bin so gross als Gott/ er ist als ich so klein:
Er kann nich über mich/ ich unter ihm nicht sein.

Wer nichts begehrt/ nichts hat/ nichts weiss/ nichts liebt/
    nichts will/
Der hat/ der weiss/ begehrt und liebt noch immer viel.

Wer unbeweglich bleibt in Freud'/ in Leid/ in Pein/
Der kann nunmehr nich weit von Gottes Gleichheit sein.

Ich selbst muss Sonne sein/ ich muss mit meinen Strahlen
Das farbenlose Meer der ganzen Gottheit malen.

Gott hat nicht Unterscheid/ es ist ihm alles ein:
Er machet sich so viel der Flieg' als dir gemein.

Dass dir im Sonnesehn vergehet das Gesicht/
Sind deine Augen schuld und nicht das grosse Licht.

Ich bin Gott's ander Er/ in mir find't er allein/
Was ihm in Ewigkeit wird gleich und ähnlich sein.

Wir beten: es gescheh/ mein Herr und Gott/ dein Wille;
Und sieh/ er hat nich Will'/ er ist ein ew'ge Stille.

Was ist Gotts Eigenschaft? Sich ins Geschöpf ergiessen/
Allzeit derselbe sein/ nichts haben/ wollen/ wissen.

Wem nichts wie alles ist und alles wie ein nichts/
Der wird gewürdiget des Liebsten Angesichts.

Johann Scheffler ("Angelus Silesius"), from
The Cherubic Wanderer

I know not what I am, and what I know am not:
A thing and not a thing, a circle and a dot.

I am as large as God, and He as small as I;
I cannot lower be; He cannot be more high.

He who nought desires, or has, knows, loves or wills,
Has, knows, desires and loves, and God's abundance fills.

He who remains unmov'd in joy and trial and pain
Can never be too far from God's own image plain.

Myself must be the sun, and paint with my own rays
The Godhead in the reach of its uncolor'd seas.

For God 'tis all the same, distinctions cannot be;
He enters in the fly as fully as in thee.

That when thou see'st the sun straightway thou hid'st thy
    face,
'Tis not the heaven's great light but thy eyes bear disgrace.

I am God's other self, in me He finds alone
What else eternally unrealiz'd must remain.

We pray: Eternal Lord and God, Thy will be done!
But see, He has no will, the still eternal One!

What is God's quality? In the creature still to flow,
And ever be the same, nought have nor will nor know.

He to whom nought is all, to whom all is as nought
Is granted the vision fair by every being sought.

Warum pflegt doch der Herr mit Sündern umzugehn?
Warum ein treuer Artzt den Kranken beizustehn?

Das Tröpflein wird das Meer/ wenn es ins Meer gekom-
    men/
Die Seele Gott/ wenn sie in Gott ist aufgenommen.

Gott ist ein Geist/ ein Feu'r/ ein Wesen und ein Licht
Und ist doch wiederum auch dieses alles nicht.

Mensch/ was du liebst/ in das wirst du verwandelt werden/
Gott wirst du/ liebst du Gott/ und Erde/ liebst du Erden.

Die Lieb' ist Flut und Glut: kann sie dein Herz empfinden/
So löscht sie Gottes Zorn und brennt hinweg die Sünden.

Mensch/ wirst du nicht ein Kind/ so gehst du nimmer ein/
Wo Gottes Kinder sind: die Tür ist gar zu klein.

Christ mein/ wo läufst du hin? Der Himmel ist in dir/
Was suchst du ihn dann erst bei eines andern Tür?

Was ist nicht sündigen? Du darfst nich lange fragen:
Geh hin/ es werden's dir die stummen Blumen sagen.

Freund/ es ist auch genug. Im Fall du mehr willst lesen/
So geh und werde selbst die Schrift und selbst das Wesen.

Why is so much the Lord with sinners to be seen?
Why does a doctor then with sick men still remain?

The droplet becomes the sea when into the sea it flows;
The soul becomes God, when into God it goes.

God is a spirit, a fire, an essence and a light,
Yet is He none of these, no figure shows Him right.

O Man, that which thou lov'st, to that wilt thou be chang'd.
To God, if God thou lov'st, if earth, with earth be rang'd.

Love is a flood and fire, if thy heart can Love assay,
'Twil put God's anger out and burn thy sins away.

If thou canst not be child thou surely shalt not go
To where God's children are: the door is far too low.

Halt, where runnest thou? Heaven is in thee;
Seek'st thou God elsewhere thou shalt Him never see.

What is it not to sin? No more the question, pray:
Go out; the tongueless flowers at once the answer say.

Friend, enough is said. In case thou more would'st read,
Go out, thyself become the writing and the seed.

David Schirmer, "Sie Quället Ihn"

Liebste Seele meiner Seelen,
Soll ich mich denn gantz und gar,
Über dich zu tode quälen?
Gieb mich doch nicht der Gefahr.
Tödte lieber deinen Feind,
Der es nie, wie ich, gemeint.

Lass mich docht nicht ohne Leben
Hier mein Leben bringen zu.
Du kanst Kraft und Seele geben,
Du geliebte Schönheit du,
Dass ich, ausser Noth und Pein,
Könne voller Freuden seyn.

Unsrer Wälder grünen Füsse
Bleiben deiner Tugend hold.
Und die reinen Silber-Flüsse
Führen deinet wegen Gold.
Alles wartet nur auf dich.
Ach, wenn wirstu trösten mich?

Komm, du kühler Tag gegangen,
Komm du Rosen volle Nacht!
Und lass dieses mich empfangen
Was mich so betrübet macht.
Komm Labelle meine Zier!
Tod und Leben steht bey dir.

David Schirmer, "To my Tormentor"

Soul of my soul, why must I languish,
Meet my death through your disdain?
From this danger, from this anguish,
Let me know relief again!
Rather kill some worthy foe
Than me, whose crime is love to show.

Do not let me lifeless lie
Until my wretched life is through!
You can my lost strength supply,
You, beloved beauty, you,
That I, free from all loss and pain,
Shall know the fullest joy again.

The green feet of the fragrant woods
Your fair reflected virtue hold,
The purest river's silver floods
Run for your sake only gold.
All nature waits your form to see,
Alas, when will you comfort me?

Come and go, cool lovely day,
Come, night when all the roses blow;
O that my arms might have a way
To hold the cause of all my woe!
Come, La Bella, jewel so rare,
With you life and death you bear.

David Schirmer, "Als sie gestorben"

O Brief! O Donner-Wort! mein schönes Lieb ist hin.
Was mach ich nun mit mir? mit mir, ach! mit mir Armen?
Wer wird sich über mich hinfort, wie vor erbarmen?
Ich sterb, ich sterbe mit, dass ich stets bei ihr bin.

Hier hastu, Marnia, hier hastu meinen Sinn.
Hier hastu meinen Geist, den lieben, den noch warmen.
Hier hastu meinen Muth. Hier hastu Pein und Harmen.
Hier hastu mich, dein Gantz, du Himmels Bürgerin.

Rauss Hertze, rauss, ihr nach! Rauss! folge deiner Schönen.
Rauss, Seele, rauss, empor! Such ihre Liebligkeit.
Fahr in Elysien, und kürtz ihr ihre Zeit.
Diss eintzig ist mein Trost, diss eintzig ist mein Sehnen:

Lebstu nicht, Marnia, so lebstu doch in mir.
Und sterb ich nicht alsbald so sterb ich doch in dir.

David Schirmer, "On her Death"

O letter! Thund'rous word! My love is gone!
What shall I do, alone and comfortless?
Who now will pity show to my distress?
I die that I may be with her, my own.

Here hast thou, Marnia, my entire brain,
Here hast thou my yet warm and living soul,
And here my heart with pains and sorrows full,
Here hast thou me, thou Heaven's citizen.

Away, my heart, and follow thy fair love.
Away, my soul, and seek her charms on high,
To Elysium go and help her time pass by,
Now all my comfort shall I seek above.

My Marnia, though dead, thou liv'st in me,
And though I live, yet do I die in thee.

David Schirmer, "Über seinen Eyd"

Dir, meine Marnia, dir schwur ich einen Eyd
auf deiner Asche dort und dort auf deinen Beinen,
ich wolte keine mehr, als dich alleine meynen.
Ietzt soll ich treuloss seyn, ietzt findet sich der Streit.

Hier ist dein Ebenbild. Hier geht mein neues Leid,
der Mund, das braune Haar, die sehen gleich den deinen,
kein Rose-Blat kan sich so mit einander einen,
als ihre schöne Zucht und deine Trefflichkeit.

Was fang ich endlich an mit ihr, mit mir, und dir?
Ich bin aufs neue wund. Sie gönnt mir ihre Blicke.
dich nur, nur einzig dich, dich halt ich nicht zurücke.
Diss ist die neue Pein, die mich selbst raubet mir.

Sey ruhig, Marnia, lass sich den Eyfer stillen.
Ich liebe sie, und diss, vorwar, umb deinet willen.

David Schirmer, "On his Oath"

My Marnia, I swore an oath to thee,
There upon thine ash and on thy bone,
That no one should I love save thee alone.
Now am I faithless; the conflict now I see.

Here is thy double. My pain begins anew;
Her mouth, her chestnut hair, are like to thine;
No more alike could be rose-petals twain
Than her modest charm and thy beauty rare and true.

What shall I do with her, with me, with thee?
Again I feel love's wound. She grants her look.
Thou only, thou alone, dost hold me back.
My new pain steals myself away from me.

Be peaceful, love, thy jealousy forsake;
I love her, true, but only for thy sake.

David Schirmer, "An seine neue Buhlschafft"

Sie, meine Marnia, kam an das todte Meer,
der Charon, solte sie mit andern überführen,
du, Schöne, wer du bist, rief er, hier gilt kein zieren.
Leg deine Schönheit ab, und denn kom wieder her.

Sie that, was er befahl. Was ich nicht mehr begehr,
sprach sie, das nim nur hin. Hier liegt des Hertzens rühren,
hier liegt der Wangen Blut, hier liegt der Pracht duplieren,
hier liegt mein gantzer Leib, ja hier, hier lieget er.

Mercur der sah ihr zu, und sprach: soll denn dein lachen,
Der Mund, der Hals, diss Haar so gar verdorben seyn?
nein, Edle Marnia, nein, Edle Nymphe, nein,
sie sollen deinen Schatz noch oftermals anlachen.

Drauf hub er alles auf, und bracht es, Nymphe, dir.
Nun lieb ich dupelt dich von wege dein und ihr.

David Schirmer, "To his New Love"

My Marnia came unto Death's grim flood,
Where Charon waited; "Fair One," straight cried he,
"Who'er thou art, thy beauty lay away,
For here all ornaments do we exclude."

She did as order'd: "What I need no more
I freely cast aside. Here lies my heart,
My rosy cheeks, my mouth's divided art,
Here lies my body and all my beauty's store."

Mercury saw and spoke: "And shall thy laugh,
Thy mouth, thy throat, this hair, be lost forever?
No, noble Marnia, fair nymph, thou shalt thy lover
Yet oft again delight with smiles enough;"

Then gathering all, to thee did all assign.
Now love I doubly, for her sake and for thine.

David Schirmer, "Er hat Vergünstigung"

Sie war und war es nicht. Noch denn kam sie mir für,
die todte Marnia, mit frölichen Geberden.
Ach, sprach sie, mein Poet, du magst verliebet werden.
Geh, mein gewesner Schatz, geh, ich vergönn es dir.

Sie, die dir wohlgefällt, ist ähnlich meiner Zier,
so sich ietzund durch dich noch zeigt der kalten Erden.
Geh, nim mein Bildnüs an, wo mein und deine Heerden
Im Grünen dort sich sat geweidet neben mir.

Wir beyde geben dir den Krantz der Ewigkeiten,
ich an dem Elbenstrom, sie ümb den Elsterstrand.
Fang an, und stim auf sie die übergöldten Saiten.
Ich bleibe nun durch dich, wie sie durch mich, bekant.

Wol uns! Wir sterben nicht. Das Reichtum der Poeten
kan unsern letzten Todt auch in dem Tode tödten.

David Schirmer, "The Permission"

'Twas she and 'twas she not; yet she appeared,
Dead Marnia, with gesture light and gay.
She spoke: "Ah poet, love again you may.
Take her, my dear that was, the past is cleared.

She whom you love again my likeness has,
Which the cold and silent earth to you unlocks.
Go, take my picture to you, where our flocks
In former times beside us used to graze.

We both bestow eternity's rewards,
I beside Elbe, she on Elster's shore.
Go to her, strike again the golden cords.
I live through you, as she through me, e'ermore.

We fortunate die not. The poet's breath
Can kill our death itself even in death."

Catharina Regina von Greiffenberg,
"Von der hohen Erschaffungs Gnade"

Herr, deine Heiligkeit, sich selber zu besehen
hatt' eine Gottes-Lust. die Allheit fund' in ihr
ein reichs Ergötzungs-Feld, betrachtend ihre Zier.
Sie konte, Süssheit satt, auf Wollust Weiden gehen.

Verstand, hatt tiefen Sinn', sich selber zu verstehen.
Ihr' Allvergnügung fand' in dir auch, die Begier.
der Wille hat geschöpfft sein wollen nur aus dir.
dass du uns schuffst, geschah allein uns zuerhöhen.

Ach Abgrund-guter Gott! Ach wesentliche Gnad',
unausgesprochne Lieb, wie soll ich dich nur loben,
Dich Güt im äusersten ja nie erreichten Grad?
Wir und das ganze Seyn, seyn deine Wunder-Proben.
wann deine Gnad nicht wär, wir wären alle nicht.
gib, dass, als Strahlen, wir gehn lobend' in ihr Liecht!

Catharina Regina von Greiffenberg, "On the Supreme Grace of Creation"

Lord, thy Holiness hath godly lust
To see itself; Totality hath found
Fields of delight within its beauty bound,
Through joyous meadows, fill'd with sweets, hath pass'd.

And Understanding, itself to understand,
Desire, to be fulfill'd, themselves do see;
And Will hath forg'd its willing but from thee:
Thou hast made us only so that we may stand.

O God, unfathom'd good, essential Grace,
How can I praise thee, inexpressible Love,
Ultimate Good, unreach'd, beyond all space?
We and all Being do thy wonders prove.
Without thy grace we would not be. O may
We go, as beams, rejoicing to thy day!

Catharina Regina von Greiffenberg,
"Über Gottes gnädige Vorsorge"

Ach hoher Gott, vor dem die Sternen gleich dem Staube,
die Sonn' ein Senffkorn ist, der Mond ein Körnlein Sand,
der ganze Erden Ball ein Pflaumen auf der Hand.
verwunderns voll hierob, ich mich schier ganz betaube.

Wann deine Hauptobacht', auf mich ein nichts, ich glaube,
ja! reich erfahrner spür', im Tausendschickungs-Stand:
So scheints, auf mich allein sey all dein Fleiss gewandt.
nur dieses Wunders Art zu preissen mir erlaube.

Ich bin ein nichts, aus nichts: durch deine Gnad so viel,
dass deiner Güter Mäng' ich ein eintreffends Ziel.
der Menschen bösser Sinn möcht diss vor Hoffart achten.
Doch ists der Demutgrund, Gott, deine Werk betrachten.
Ich bin, wie ich gesagt, ein Nichts: mein Alles du.
hat (Wunder!) Allheit dann in Nichtes ihre Ruh?

Catharina Regina von Greiffenberg, "On God's Gracious Providence"

O highest God, to whom the stars are dust,
The sun a seed, the moon a grain of sand,
This ball of earth a speck upon the hand:
In wonder and amazement I am thrust.

When I, a nothing, see thy Providence,
Yea, feel it on me ever thousand-fold,
It seems that me alone thy strength doth mould;
Let me but praise these marvels so immense.

I am a nought, of nought, yet through thy grace
So much am that thy gifts I all embrace;
Let evil man this thought for pride eschew.
'Tis much humility thy works to view;
A nothing I, thou art my all and best;
Doth Omnipotence in Nothing take its rest?

Quirinus Kuhlmann, "Der XXIII. Liebeskuss: die Geburtsnacht des Herrn"

O Nacht! du grosse Nacht! die heller als der Tag!
O Nacht! ja Licht! und Licht, das Sonnen übersteiget!
O Nacht! dergleichen nie der Kreis zu sehen pflag!
O Nacht! darinnen sich das grösste Wunder zeiget!

O Nacht! die schon dort pries der Patriarchen Sag!
O Nacht! da alles spricht! da Berg und Fels nicht schweiget!
O Nacht! die den umschloss, den nichts umschlüssen mag!
O Nacht! vor dessen Kind die Welt sich zitternd neiget!

O Nacht! der Himmel bebt ob dem ganz neuen Lauf!
O Nacht! dass der sein Mond, der Mond und Sonne blümet!
O Nacht! dass der dir scheint, den Mond und Sonne
    rühmet!
O Nacht! die ganz durchsternt der Cherubinenhauf!
Hier will ich Tycho sein und dies Gestirn erlernen,
Bis sich mein Geist gesellt zu solchen Himmelssternen!

Quirinus Kuhlmann, "The Nativity of the Lord"

O Night! Great Night! Thou brighter than the day!
O Night! Aye light! And light which dims the sun!
O Night the cosmos never did survey!
O Night! In which all wonders are outdone!

O Night! Whose praise the Patriarchs' mouths did sound!
O Night! When cliff and mountain are not dumb!
O Night! Surrounding Him nought can surround!
O Night! To whose child the world kneels and is numb!

O Night! The Heavens shake at this career!
O Night! Whose moon the moon and sun did raise!
O Night! Where shines Whom moon and sun do praise!
O Night! Which shineth through Cherubic choir!
I will be Tycho, this constellation view,
Until my soul doth join that starry crew!

DUTCH POEMS

Jacob Revius, "Scheppinge"

God heeft de werelt door onsichtbare clavieren
Betrocken als een luyt met al sijn toebehoor.
Den hemel is de bocht vol reyen door en door,
Het roosken, zon en maen die om ons hene swieren.

Twee grove bassen die staech bulderen en tieren
Sijn d'aerd' en d'oceaan: de quinte die het oor
Verheuget, is de locht: de reste die den choor
Volmaket, is t'geboomt en allerhande dieren.

Dees luyte sloech de Heer met sijn geleerde vingers,
De engels stemden in als treffelicke singers,
De bergen hoorden toe, de vloeden stonden stil:
De mensch alleen en hoort noch sangeren noch snaren,
Behalven dien 't de Heer belieft te openbaren
Na sijn bescheyden raet en Goddelijcken wil.

Jacob Revius, "Creation"

With strings invisible God made the world,
A lute with all its separate parts array'd:
Heaven the soundboard wherein are inlaid
As sound-holes sun and moon around us hurl'd.

The earth and ocean make the rumbling bass,
Raging and roaring, while as treble sweet
The air delights the ear; the choir complete
With trees and animals, each in its place.

The Lord did play this lute with learnèd fingers.
The angels join'd the song as mighty singers,
The hills gave ear, the rivers all stood still.
'Tis Man alone hears neither string nor voice,
Except for those whom God takes as his choice
According to his wisdom and his will.

De mensch een penninck is van Godes hant geslagen
Om zijn gelijckenis in heylicheyt te dragen:
De duyvel, die hem sulck een ere niet en gunt,
Gods beelt heeft wtgewist, en t'sijn daer op gemunt.
Hoe sal den sondaer wt dit ongeval geraken?
Den stempel die hem sloech, can hem alleen hermaken.
De Heere, die ons schiep rechtveerdich, wijs, en goet,
Met zijnen grooten Geest ons weer herscheppen moet.

Jacob Revius, "Renewal"

Man is a penny minted by God's hand,
On which the holy likeness clear doth stand:
The devil, grudging man such honour fair,
Recasts and stamps his own grim image there.
How can the sinner rise from this disgrace?
The seal that form'd him can reform his face.
The Lord who made us wise and just and true
Can with his spirit mould the coin anew.

Jacob Revius, "Gods Besluyt"

Gelijck als in een colck een steentgen valt te gronde
Het water werpt terstont een ringsken in het ronde,
En van het eene comt een ander schieten uyt,
Waervan een ander strax, en weer en ander spruyt,
Soo dat in corten tijdt de oogen daer op dwalen,
De grootte noch 't getal niet connend' achterhalen:
Soo gaetet oock met my, o groote God en Heer,
Van doe mijn tong began te stamelen u eer,
Het eene denck ik na, het ander valt my inne,
U wijsheyt, u gericht, u waerheyt, uwe minne
Omringen my te saem in eenen oogenslach:
En, wil ick van het een of 't ander doen gewach,
U raet en u besluyt my so geheel verslinden
Dat ick daer in noch gront noch oever weet te vinden.

Jacob Revius, "God's Virtues"

Just as when in a pool a pebble falls
And the water at once in ripples wide unrolls,
And after one, another circle forms,
Then quickly another and yet another comes,
That the eyes are in an instant dazzl'd quite
And the number and size no longer estimate:
Just so with me, O God and sovereign Lord,
Since first my stammering tongue thy praise did spread;
Thy attributes I count, due praise to give;
Thy wisdom, justice, truthfulness and love
Surround me in the twinkling of an eye,
And will I one or th'other just portray,
Thy counsel and thy providence so blind
That neither bank nor bottom can I find.

Jacob Revius, "Gods Kennisse"

Wanneer het spade licht begint hem wt te spreyen
Opt vlackste vande see, de vischkens haer vermeyen
En meynen; datter blinckt dat het al sterren zijn,
Hoewelse niet en sien als eenen wederschijn;
Maar die hier inde locht en boven 't water leven
Die sien des hemels heyr bescheydelijcken sweven:
Soo is het met den mensch: al wat hij hier aensiet
Van God en van zijn rijk en is het wesen niet,
Maer een geringen schijn, waer van de naeckte waerheyt
Aenschouwen die daer sien de goddelijcke claerheyt.

Jacob Revius, "The Knowledge of God"

When starlight shines on the surface of the sea,
The fishes underneath do all agree,
And think that there the stars of Heaven show,
Although reflection scant is all they know;
But we who here above the water live
Can see the bright hosts of the night arrive.
So Man: all that he sees on earth this while
Of God and of his glory is not real,
'Tis image mere; who naked truth can bear,
They only see God's shining visage clear.

Jacob Revius, "Gods Evenbeelt"

In een schoon waterken vertonet hem de sonne
Niet in een vuyle somp, of rustelose bronne:
Want is het water dick, of voeltet sonder endt
Dien claren wederschijn wert t'enemael geschent.
O siele, die Gods beelt in u behouden willet
d'onsuyverheyt vermijdt, en de beroerten stillet:
Want Gods gelijckenis vertoont sich aldermeest
In een gestadich hert en onbesmetten geest.

Jacob Revius, "God's Likeness'

A clear pool alone reflects the sun,
Not a dirty sump, or fountain which doth run:
For in water impure or water ever roil'd
The clear reflection instantly is spoil'd.
O Soul that will God's image hold within,
Shun undue motion and reject all sin;
For the likeness of God can show itself but there
Where the heart is still, the spirit clean and fair.

Jacob Revius, "T' Selve"

In een eng waterken niet wel en connen lichten
Twee beelden te gelijck of vele aengesichten,
    Maer t'eene nootelijck het ander houdet uyt.
O mensche, mercket wat dees reden u beduyt:
Wildy in Godes beelt u degelijck verblijen,
So keret uyt het hert des duyvels schilderyen
    Van gelt, van lust, van pracht. want t'liefelijck aenschijn
    Ws Heeren wilder niet, of T'wil alleene sijn.

Jacob Revius, "On the Same'

A narrow pool cannot in sense contain
Reflections more than one, or faces twain;
Of necessity one holds the other out.
Mark well, oh Man, the meaning free from doubt:
Wilt thou God's picture faithfully present,
Drive from thy heart those pictures devil-sent,
Of gold, of lust, of pride; the face divine
Only alone within thy heart will shine.

Joost van den Vondel,
"Uitvaert van Maria van den Vondel"

Wanneer dit tijtlijk leven endt,
Begint het endelooze leven,
By Godt en engelen bekent,
En zaligen alleen gegeven.

Daer zit de Godtheit op den troon,
In 't middenpunt van alle ronden,
Dat overal, en eenigh schoon,
Noit zijnen omvang heeft gevonden.

Dit trekt alle oogen naer zich toe,
Als d'eerste zon van alle zonnen,
De bron van 't licht, noit straelens moê,
Van geene schaduwen verwonnen.

Wat goet zich in 't geschapen spreit
By sprengkelen, is hier volkomen
In schoonheit, maght, en heerlijkheit,
Een zee, de springaêr aller stroomen.

Wat herquam van het enkel Een
Doolt, als in ballingschap verschoven,
Vint geene rustplaets hier beneên,
En zoekt het vaderlant daer boven.

Zoo waelt de lely van 't kompas,
Die met den zeilsteen wert bestreeken,
Rondom, en zoekt de starlichte as
Haer wit, waer van zy was versteeken.

Joost van den Vondel, "Maria's Journey"

When first this life of time is past,
Eternal life itself unrolls,
Known to God and angels blest
And given but to blessèd souls.

There sits God upon his throne
In the middle point of all the spheres,
Beauty eternal and alone,
Whose compass knows nor space nor years.

He draws to him all eyes and beams,
The sun of suns, untouch'd, unspotted,
The well of light, with untiring streams
By hint of shadow never blotted.

The good we in creation see
In droplets scant is there entire
In beauty, power, majesty,
A sea, the source of all desire.

What comes here from the eternal One
Wanders in banishment from its love,
And resting-place below finds none,
And seeks its native home above.

So shrinks the needle from her proper place
When the alien loadstone is applied,
Then quivers and seeks her starry base,
The goal which to her is denied.

Maria steegh met haer gemoedt,
Van werreltsche ydelheên gescheiden
En los, naer dit volkomen goet,
Waertoe d'elenden 't hart bereiden.

Twee vleugels, ootmoet en gedult,
Verhieven haer uit aertsche dampen,
Daer 't eeuwigh Een 't gebrek vervult,
En vleesch en geest niet langer kampen.

Haer leste stem en aêm was Godt,
De troost der aengevochte harten,
Het beste deel, en hooghste lot.
Zoo voerze heen uit alle smarten.

Wat kroontge, op dat uw liefde blijk',
Met parle, zilver, en gesteente,
En palm, en roosmarijn, het lijk?
O Speelnoots, dit's een dor gebeente.

Zy leefde tien paer jaeren lang,
Maer nu van 's werrelts last ontbonden,
Verwachtze om hoogh geen' ondergang.
Het hemelsche uurwerk telt geen stonden.

Een rey van englen kroon' de ziel
Met lauwerier in 's hemels hoven,
Nu 't kleet des lichaems haer ontviel.
Zy noode ons met gebeên daer boven.

Maria and her spirit flew,
From earthly vanity unpair'd
And free, to the realm of good and true,
Whither that longing heart prepar'd.

Humility, patience, two strong wings,
Rais'd her from the mists of earth,
The One to the spirit such help brings
That resists the body from its birth.

Her last word, her last breath, was God,
The comfort of the beleaguer'd heart,
The single, highest, best reward,
So flew home, free from every smart.

Why mantle for your love to see
With silver, gold and precious stones,
With palms and flowers and rosemary
This body? Comrades, 'tis but bones.

She liv'd in years an irksome score,
But now is from that weight unbound,
And knows on high no sorrow more:
Heaven's clockwork has no hours to sound.

A band of angels crown her soul
With laurels that in Heaven grow,
The body's dress away doth fall,
May her prayers raise us from below!

Constantijn Huygens, "Kommerlick Ontwaken"

Sonn, zijt ghij daer allree! Dagh, zijt ghij weer aen 't
    kriecken?
Nacht, zijt ghij soo voorbij, zoo vroegh, met sulcke
    wiecken,
Soo vochtigh en soo vlugg? O swarten oogenblick,
O Doodshalf, daer ick mij soo gaeren in verstick,
Hoe loopt ghij soo te loôr, en laet mijn' Ziel verleghen
Om ongevoelickheid, den aller dooden seghen,
En ruckt mij onvoorsiens uw' bruyne deken af,
Uw' sarck-steen van mijn bedd, mijn boven-aerdsche graf?
Ick was, en wist het niet; ick lagh, en hadd geen wesen
Van leggen noch van zijn; met d'ongenucht van 'tvreesen,
Met d'onrust vande hoôp en hadd ick niet gemeens,
Mijn hert, mijn' herssenen, mijn' sinnen waren eens.
Wat scheelt het nu, mijn hert, mijn' herssenen, mijn' sinnen,
Wat scheelt het nu van eens! hoe woelen wij van binnen,
Hoe vallen wij te hoop van d'ure dat ick waeck
En sluype 't mijnent in door 'tsplijten vanden vaeck!

Constantijn Huygens, "Troubled Awakening"

What, Sun, already here? Dost break, O Day?
And Night, so soon and swiftly flown away,
So hasty and abrupt? O moment black,
O welcome half of death, must I awake?
Why must thou then be gone and leave devoid
My soul of that unfeelingness it had,
That blessing of the dead; why roughly tear
The black drapes from my over-earthly bier?
I was, and knew it not, and lay without
The disease of hope, the bitterness of doubt.
No more had I to do with fears that run;
My heart and mind and senses were at one.
How struggle now my senses, mind and heart?
How struggle they at once? How sorrows start,
What conflict with myself in this my waking,
As I creep into myself through slumber's breaking!

Constantijn Huygens, "Van d'ure dat ick waeck"

Van d'ure dat ick waeck
En sluype 't mijnent in door 't splijten vanden vaeck,
Staet Sterre voor mijn' ooghen,
Mijn' ooghen trane-vocht, die dan maer eerst en drooghen,
Gelijck de dauw verdwijnt
Van dat de Morghen-sonn de droppelen beschijnt.
Sterr, segh ick, Morghen-Sterre,
Die verre van mij staet, en noch, en noch soo verre,
En noch soo verre laet,
Als daer het hooghste licht van all' in 't ronde gaet,
Hoe kont ghij Sterre wesen
En houden teghens mij soo staegh, soo fieren wezen,
En staen als een Comeet
Die, verr van tintelen, van wencken niet en weet?
Kan 't Sterren-licht bevriesen,
En gaen de Sterrheit quijt, en heel de daed verliesen
En houden heel den naem?
En, Sterre, staet ghij toe dat sich Nature schaem'
Der plaetse die s'u gonde
Van doe sij 'thelle holl der Hemelen berondde,
En van genoeghen loegh
Mits dats' u naerde Sonn de tweede plaets opdroegh?
All kont ghij mij vergeten,
Die heldere geboort en mooght ghij niet ontweten,
En onder uw geslacht
Soo minigh minder licht dat stadich staet en lacht.

Constantijn Huygens, "From the moment of my waking"

From the moment of my waking,
As I creep into myself through slumber's breaking,
Stands Star before my eyes,
These tear-drench'd eyes her favour only dries,
Like drops of morning-dew,
When the sun upon them brightly shines anew.
"Star," say I, "Morning-Star,
Which far above me stands, so far, so far,
And still so far doth glow,
Since Heaven's high light in circular path doth go,
How can'st thou Star be styl'd
And follow with me ways so proud and wild?
A comet thou must be,
Which neither twinkles at nor nods to me.
How can starlight freeze,
And its quality of Starness wholly lose,
And yet retain its name?
Dost admit, my Star, that Nature must feel shame
That she such place did grant thee,
What time mid Heaven's bright course she did implant thee,
And laugh'd in sheer delight,
And thee next to the sun did dedicate?
Though me thou dost forget,
Thy brighter birth thou can'st not disown yet;
Among thy sex remain
So many who still laugh and steady shine."

Constantijn Huygens, "Nieuwe Jaer"

'Tis uijt. de leste Sonn gingh gisteren in Zee,
Getuijghe van mijn jaer voll ongeregeltheden.
O dien daer dusend jaer zijn als de dagh van heden,
Voor wien ick desen dagh mijn vuijle ziel ontklee

Van 'tsmodderigh gewaed van veertigh jaer en twee,
En drij, en noch eens twee, die Ghij mij hebt geleden,
All vergh ick 't dijn geduld met sondighe Gebeden,
Gunt mij een schoonder pack dan ick 'er oyt aen dee.

In d'eerste niewicheid sal 'tVleesch en Bloed wat prengen,
En 'tpast haer moijelick: maer ick betrouw dijn' hand;
Die sal 't mij lichtelick wat ruijmen en wat lenghen.
Maeckt mij maer op de Reis naer 'teewigh Vaderland
In dese Wilderniss een' dijner Israelyten,
En laet dit niewe Kleed mijn leven niet verslijten.

Constantijn Huygens, "New Year's Day"

'Tis done. The sun sank yester in the sea,
The witness of my year's unruly run.
O thou to Whom a thousand years are one,
For whom this day my foul soul I do free

Of the muddy garb of forty years and more,
These years which thou hast granted me to wear;
Though I try thy patience with my sinful prayer,
Grant me a fairer gown than that I wore.

At first shall flesh and blood a little pinch,
And the fit be narrow, but I trust thy hand;
Thou shalt my gown let out or stretch an inch.
But let me seek the eternal Fatherland,
In this wilderness an Israelite devout,
And let my garment new never wear out.

Constantijn Huygens, "Goede Vrijdagh"

Wat lett de Middagh-sonn? hoe lust haer niet te blincken?
Is 't avond opden Noen? Ten minsten, Volle Maen,
En, Sterren, haer gevolgh, hoe haest ghij 'tondergaen?
Moet ghij ter halver loop van 't koele zee-natt drincken?

Neen, neen; ick sie 't u aen, ghij voelt den moed ontsincken
Voor 'tschandighe Schavott, daer Sions dochtren staen
En swijmen voorden schrick van 'theiligh, *'Tis voldaen*,
En op den drooghen Bergh in tranen gaen verdrincken.

O myn Volldoende God, vergeeft ghij mij een woord?
'Tvoldaen voldoet mij niet, ten zij ghij mij vermoort
En van mijn selven scheurt, en brieselt de gewrichten
Van mijn' verstockte Ziel, soo dats' haer weder-plichten
Gedwee en morruw doe: soo dat ick haev en huijs,
En lijf en lust en tyd leer' hangen aen dit Cruijs.

Constantijn Huygens, "Good Friday"

What ails the midday sun? Why shines it not?
Is night at noon then come? Tell me, thou moon,
With thy starry train, why sinkest thou so soon?
Must ye sea-water drink e'er half your route?

Nay, nay, now I perceive your strength abated
At the shameful Cross, where Zion's daughters stand
And drown in tears upon the barren land
At those awesome holy words, " 'Tis consummated." *

My consummating God, may I presume?
This consummation doth me not consume,
Unless thou dost me kill, and soften so
My harden'd soul it may its duty know
And humbly do, so that I hearth and house,
And body, will and time hang on this Cross.

* The full complexity of the original cannot be caught in translation. Actually, in place of the biblical " 'Tis volmaekt" ("It is consummated"), Huygens writes " 'Tis voldaen" ("It is paid for").
The verb "voldoen," however, may mean "to satisfy" as well as
"to pay for," and consequently line 10 may have the readings "This
payment does not satisfy me" and "This payment does not pay for
me" in addition to the implied meaning which I have chosen to
render.

Constantijn Huygens, "Paeschen"

Den Engel is voorbij: de grouwelicke nacht
Der eerstgeborenen is bloedeloos verstreken:
Ons' deuren zijn verschoond; soo warense bestreken
Met heiligh Paeschen-bloed, dat d'uytgelaten macht,

Die Pharâos kinderen en Pharâo t'onderbracht,
Doorgaens verschrickelick, verschrickt heeft voor het
    teeken.
Wij zijn door 'troode Meer de slavernij ontweken,
Aegypten buytens reicks. Is alle dingh volbracht?

Is 'tschip ter haven in? Oh, midden in de baren,
De baren van ons bloed, veel holler dan dat meer.
Den Engel komt weerom en 'tvlammige geweer
Dreight niewen ondergang. Heer, heet hem over varen.
Merckt onser herten deur, o Leeuw van Judas Stamm,
En leert ons tydelijk verschricken voor een Lam.

Constantijn Huygens, "Easter"

The Angel passes by; the horrid night
Of the first-born wanes, and touches not our brood—
Our doors are spared; so they with holy blood
Of Paschal lamb are mark'd that the uncheck'd might

Which Pharaoh's children and Pharaoh himself hath kill'd,
That fearful might itself hath fear'd the Sign—
We have fled our slavery through the Red Sea's plain,
Beyond Egyptian reach—Is all fulfill'd?

Is our ship in port? In billows still, alas,
Much fiercer than that sea, of our own blood!
The Angel comes again, the flaming sword
Theatens destruction new! Lord, bid him pass!
O Lion of Judah's race, the heart's door smear,
And teach us in our time a Lamb to fear!

Constantijn Huygens, "Sondagh"

Is 't Sabbath dagh, mijn ziel, of Sondagh? geen van tween.
De Sabbath is voorby met syne diesntbaerheden:
En de sonn die ick sie scheen gisteren als heden.
Maer die ick niet en sie en schijnt niet soo se scheen.

Son, die ick niet en sie als door mijn' sonden heen,
Soon Gods, die desen dagh het aerdrijck weer betreeden,
Fier als een Bruydegom ter loop-baen ingereden,
'Ksie Sondagh sonder end door dijne Wonden heen.

'Tzy dan oock Sondagh nu, men magh't Gods Soon-dagh
    noemen,
Ja, en Gods Soen-dagh toe. Maer laet ick ons verdoemen,
Waer ick van drijen gae ick vind ons inde Schuld.
God Son, God Soon, God Soen, hoe langh duert dijn ge-
    duld?

Hoe langhe lydt ghij, Heer, dijn' Soondagh, Soendagh,
    Sondagh
Ondanckbaerlick verspilt, verspeelt, verspelt in Sond-dagh?

Constantijn Huygens, "Sunday'

Is it Sabbath, my soul, or Sunday? Neither one.
The Sabbath of the old law is no more:
The sun I see today did shine before;
The sun I see not shines not as it shone.

Sun that I do not see but through my sin,
God's son who once again dost walk the earth,
Bright as a bridegroom in Thy shining worth,
Thy wounds I see Sunday undying in.

Sunday it is, but should be Son-day named,
God's Sum-day too, which shows we should be damned
In justice; each of three shows our disgrace.
God's Sun, God's Son, God's Sum, how great Thy grace?

How long allow'st Thou, Lord, Thy Sum-day, Son-day,
    Sunday,
Ungrateful man to spoil and spill and spell as Sin-day?

Heiman Dullaert, "Christus stervende"

Die alles troost en laaft, verzucht, bezwymt, ontverft!
Die alles ondersteunt, geraakt, o my! aan 't wyken.
Een doodsche donkerheit komt voor zijne oogen stryken
Die quynen, als een roos die dauw en warmte derft.

Ach werelt, die nu al van zyne volheid erft;
Gestarnten, Engelen met uwe Hemelryken;
Bewoonderen der Aarde, ey, toeft gij te bezwyken,
Nu Jezus vast bezwykt, nu uwe Koning sterft?

Daar hy het leven derft, wil ik het ook gaan derven:
Maar hoe hy meerder sterft, en ik meer wil gaan sterven,
Hoe my een voller stroom van leven overvloeit.
O hooge wonderen! wat geest is zoo bedreven,
Die vat hoe zoo veel sterkte uit zoo veel zwakheid groeit,
En hoe het leven sterft om dooden te doen leven?

Heiman Dullaert, "Christ Dying"

The comforter of all, expiring, wan,
The world's support, condemn'd to death and anguish;
A fatal darkness dims those eyes which languish
Like roses faint, depriv'd of dew and sun.

O world, O heir of this abundant prize,
O angels, starry powers in your spheres,
Inhabitants of earth, have ye no tears,
While Jesus sinks his head, while your king dies?

Since he departs from life, I long for death:
But even as I wish an end to breath,
A brimming stream of life o'erflows my soul.
O highest wonder! How can it be said
That strength can come from feebleness so whole,
That life can die to save from death the dead?

Heiman Dullaert, "De bekeerde moorder"

Die langs het aardryk zworf om op wat buit te passen,
Wiens flukse wakkerheid de reizenden verriedt,
Heeft hier, dus vast geknelt, de volheit zelf bespiedt,
En komt het Hemelryk tot roofgoet te verrassen.

Die diep in eenzaamheid de hand wiesch in de plassen
Van een verdoemend bloet, wort hier, daar 't yder ziet,
In 't zaligende bloet, dat Jezus vast vergiet,
Aan hand, aan lijf, aan ziel, van bloedschult afgewassen.

Hy, in zijn Moorderschap aan schaduwen verplicht,
Word in 't geloof bedaagt van een genadelicht,
Terwyl zijn quynend oog 't natuurlyk licht gaat derven,
De Kruisnacht, door het recht den Booswicht aangezeit,
Word den Boetwaerdigen een dag van zaligheit:
Die dood was toen hy leefde, ô! leeft hier in zyn sterven.

Heiman Dullaert, "The Good Thief"

He wander'd on the earth in search of pelf,
His craft despoil'd the traveler on his way;
But here, nail'd fast, he sees the All itself,
And seizes Heaven as a robber's prey.

In loneliness he dipp'd his hand in blood
Which call'd for vengeance; body, hand and soul
He now is wash'd in that redeeming flood
From Jesus' side, where it is seen by all.

As murderer then to shadows sworn and plight,
As faithful now bath'd in the gracious light,
To his fading eye the earth its rays denying.
Night of the cross, to the miscreant decreed,
To the penitent becomes the day of meed:
He died in life, he lives now in his dying.

Heiman Dullaert, "Aen myne uitbrandende kaerse"

O haast gebluschte vlam van mijne kaers! nu dat
Gy mijnen voortgang stut in 't naerstig onderzoeken
Van nutte wetenschap, in wysheidsvolle boeken
Voor een leergierig oog zo rykelyk bevat,

Verstrekt gy my een boek, waar uit te leeren staat
Het haast verloopen uur van mijn verganklyk leven;
Een grondles, die een wys en deuchdzaam hart kan geven;
Aan een aandachtig man, wien zy ter harte gaat.

Maar, levend zinnebeeld van 't leven dat verdwynt,
Gy smoort in duisternis ny gy uw licht gaat missen;
En ik ga door de dood uit myne duisternissen
Naar 't onuitbluschlyk licht, dat in den Hemel schynt.

Heiman Dullaert, "On my Candle Burning Out"

O rapidly extinguished candle flame,
Since thou dost fail me in my busy search
For useful knowledge hid in volumes rich
For the eye which lust of knowing still doth claim,

Supply me with a book wherein to learn
My life's too brief and quickly running hour:
A lesson which the virtuous heart may pour
Into the heart of him who can discern.

Emblem which doth our transient life define,
Thou chok'st in darkness as thy light doth die,
But I through death from out my darkness fly
To the unquench'd light which doth in Heaven shine.

Jan Luyken, "De Ziele betracht de nabijheid Gods"

Ich meende oock: de Godtheyt woonde verre,
In eenen troon, hoogh boven maen en sterre,
En heften menighmael mijn oogh,
Met diep versuchten naer om hoogh.

Maer toen ghy u beliefden topenbaren,
Toen sagh ick niets van boven nedervaren;
Maer in den grondt van myn gemoet,
Daer wierdt het lieflyck ende soet.

Daer quamt ghy uyt der diepten uytwaerts dringen,
En, als een bron, myn dorstigh hart bespringen,
Soo dat ick u, ô God, bevondt,
Te zyn den grondt van mynen grondt.

Dies ben ick bly, dat ghy, mijn hoogh beminden,
My nader zyt dan al myn naeste vrinden.
Was nu alle ongelyckheyt voort,
En 't herte reyn gelyck het hoort,

Geen hooghte, noch geen diepte sou ons scheyden,
Ick smolt in Godt, myn lief: wy wierden beyde
Een geest, een hemels vlees en bloedt,
De wesentheyt van Godts gemoedt,

Dat moet geschien. Och help getrouwe Heere,
Dat wy ons gantsch in uwen wille keeren!

Jan Luyken, "The Soul Considers its Nearness to God"

I thought that Godhead made its home afar,
Enthroned beyond the moon and every star,
And often lifted up my eyes
Thither with deep and heartfelt sighs;

But when it pleased thee to illuminate me,
I saw no heavenly light descend to greet me;
But at my spirit's deepest root
All was lovely, all was sweet.

For thou cam'st from the depths and outwards spread,
And like a well my thirsty heart was fed;
So was it, God, that thee I found
To be the ground beneath my ground.

Then I rejoiced that thou, my highest dearest,
Wert closer to me than my earthly nearest!
All disproportion fled from me,
My heart was pure, as it should be.

No heights, no depths shall separate us twain;
I melt in God, my Love; we shall remain
One soul, one heavenly flesh and blood,
The being and the mind of God.

It must occur; O help, eternal Lord,
To turn us to thy will and to thy word.

Jan Luyken, "De Ziel betracht den Schepper uit de Schepselen"

Ik zag de schoonheid en de zoetheid aller dingen
En sprak: "wat zijt gij schoon!" Toen hoorde mijn gemoed:
"Dat zijn wij ook, maar Hij, van wien wij 't al ontvingen,
Is duizendmaal zo schoon en duizendmaal zo zoet!"

En dat zijt gij, mijn Lief, zoud' ik u niet begeren?
Is hier een lelieblad op aard zo blank en fijn,
Wat moet, o eeuwig Goed, o aller dingen Here,
Wat moet de witheid van uw zuiverheid dan zijn!

Is 't purper ook zo schoon der rozen die hier bloeien
—Bedauwd met paarlen, als de morgenzon haar groet—,
Hoe moet het purper van uw Majesteit dan gloeien!
Ruikt hier een violet zo lieflijk en zo zoet,

Als 't westewindje door de hoven zacht gaat weiden,
—Zo ik het menigmaal bij koelen morgen vond—,
Wat moet zich dan een reuk door 't Paradijs verspreiden,
Zo lieflijk vloeinde uit uw vriendelijken mond!

Is hier de zon, gelijk een bruidegom gerezen,
Zo schoon en blinkende op het hoogste van den dag,
Wat moet uw aangezicht dan klaar en helder wezen!
O God, mijn schoonste Lief, dat ik u eenmaal zag!

Jan Luyken, "The Soul Contemplates the Creator in the Creation"

I saw the beauty and the sweetness of all things,
And said: "How fair you are!" Then heard an answer clear:
"Indeed we are, but he from whom our beauty springs
Is a thousand times more sweet, a thousand times more fair."

And that thou art, my Dearest, the goal of my desire!
If a lily here on earth is fair, and white, and clean,
What must, eternal Good, Lord of all things and higher,
What must the whiteness be of thy purity serene?

So lovely is the scarlet of the roses here below,
Glistening with pearls as the morning sun doth greet them,
How must the scarlet of thy majesty then glow!
If violets smell sweet each time we bend to meet them,

As the little western wind blows softly through the field
(I've marked it many times in the mornings fresh and cool),
What then the sweetness that thy kindly mouth must yield,
What blessed odours sweet through Paradise must roll.

If here the Sun appears, a bridegroom richly dressed,
So fairly shining down on the beauties of the day,
What must thy countenance be, so beautiful and blest!
O God, my dearest Love, I would see thee without stay!

Jan Luyken,
"De Ziele in aandacht over de nieuwe Creatuur"

Toen 't zaadje sturf in 's aardrijks schoot
En scheen vergeten en verloren,
Toen groenden 't bloempje door dien dood
En kwam gelijk een nieuwgeboren
Uit duistere aarde in 't schone licht
Om reuk en verwen voor te dragen,
Begroet van 's hemels aangezicht
Met dauw en zonneschijn in 't dagen.

Zo wast de nieuwe creatuur:
Als eigen wil gaat in 't verderven
In dood en graf, al smaakt het zuur,
Daar groent een leven door dat sterven,
Een bloem in 't Paradijs zo schoon,
Al zien 't geen werelds blindgeboren:
Hij staat voor God en zijnen Zoon
En ruikt door aller englen koren.

O Jezus-lief! O eeuwig Goed!
Hoe vurig lust het mij te worden
Een bloempje aan uw rozenhoed,
Daar nooit een lovertje verdorden!
O Here Jezus, voert mij aan
Om altijd in den dood te gaan!

Jan Luyken, "The Soul's Devotion at the Rebirth of Life"

When the seedlet died in the lap of earth,
And seemed forgotten and forlorn,
The flower came to green rebirth,
From death to life as newly born.
From gloomy earth to the lovely light,
To give its hue and scent to all,
With heaven's face to greet its sight,
While dew and sunshine on it fall.

So grows the new and lovely creature,
Then goes to death of its own will,
To death and the grave; the taste is bitter,
But its dying yields a green life still,
A flower in Paradise so fair,
Though unseen by a blinded race,
It exhales to God its fragrance rare,
In the host of angels takes its place.

O dearest Jesus! Eternal Good!
How ardently I long to be
A flower on your rose-deck't head,
Where never withering may be!
My Lord, my Jesus, make me strive
To long for death while yet alive.

SPANISH POEMS

San Juan de la Cruz, "Canciones del alma en la íntima
comunicación de unión de amor de Dios"

¡Oh llama de amor viva,
Que tiernamente hieres
De mi alma en el más profundo centro!
Pues ya no eres esquiva,
Acaba ya si quieres,
Rompe la tela deste dulce encuentro.

¡Oh cauterio suave!
¡Oh regalada llaga!
¡Oh mano blanda! Oh toque delicado,
Que a vida eterna sabe,
Y toda deuda paga!
Matando, muerte en vida la has trocado.

¡Oh lámparas de fuego,
En cuyos resplandores
Las profundas cavernas del sentido,
Que estaba obscuro y ciego,
Con extraños primores
Calor y luz dan junto a su querido!

¡Cuán manso y amoroso
Recuerdas en mi seno,
Donde secretamente solo moras:
Y en tu aspirar sabroso
De bien y gloria lleno
Cuán delicadamente me enamoras!

San Juan de la Cruz, "Song of the Soul in Union with God"

Oh living flame of love
Which tenderly doth wound
My soul within its secret deepest center!
Since not averse you prove,
Oh end what you do sound,
And tear the fabric of this sweet encounter.

Oh cautery so smooth!
Oh so desired pain!
Oh gentle hand! Oh touch most delicate,
Which eternal life endueth,
And doth all debts unchain!
In killing, you do life perpetuate.

Oh lamps of fire pure,
In whose resplendent blaze
The caverns of my senses most profound,
Just now blind and obscure,
Find strangely lovely rays,
And give their love the heat and light now found.

How amorous and mild
The thoughts you give my breast,
Where secretly in solitude you dwell:
By your sweet breath beguil'd,
In grace and glory best,
How delicately you do love compel!

Lope de Vega,
"¿Qué tengo yo, que mi amistad procuras?"

¿Qué tengo yo, que mi amistad procuras?
¿qué interes se te sigue, Jesus mio,
que a mi puerta cubierto de rozio
passas las noches del hibierno escuras?

¡O quanto fueron mis entrañas duras!
pues no te abrí, ¡que estraño desvario!
si de mi ingratitud el hielo frio
secó las llagas de tus plantas puras.

¿Quántas veces el Angel me decia:
Alma, asomate ahora a la ventana,
verás con quanto amor llamar porfia?
¿Y quántas, hermosura soberana,
mañana le abriremos, respondia,
para lo mismo responder mañana?

Lope de Vega,
"What Interest, my Jesus, Drives You Thus?"

What interest, my Jesus, drives you thus?
What have I that you for my friendship sue?
That at my door you wait, cover'd with dew,
That there dark winter's nights you aye do pass?

Of what untemper'd hardness is my heart
Which opens not to you! What madness bold
That my ingratitude with icy cold
The wounds of your pure feet doth chap apart!

How many times my angel good insists:
"Go to the window, Soul, look out and see
With how much love in knocking he persists!"
How many times, O Beauty sovereign,
Have I replied: "Tomorrow it shall be,"
Only tomorrow to say the same again!

Pastor, que con tus silvos amorosos
me despertaste del profundo sueño,
tú, que hiciste cayado de esse leño,
en que tiendes los brazos poderosos:

Vuelve los ojos a mi fé piadosos,
pues te confiesso por mi amor y dueño,
y la palabra de seguirte empeño
tus dulces silvos, y tus pies hermosos.

Oye, pastor, que por amores mueres,
no te espante el rigor de mis pecados,
pues tan amigo de rendidos eres.
Espera pues, y escucha mis cuidados,
¿pero cómo te digo que me esperes,
si estás para esperar los pies clavados?

Lope de Vega,
"Shepherd Who Did Me from the Depths of Sleep"

Shepherd who did me from the depths of sleep
Awaken with your lover's whistle, you
Who from this wood a shepherd's crook did hew
On which your mighty arms at rest you keep,

Oh turn your eyes in pity on my faith,
Since I confess you for my love and lord
And still to follow you do pledge my word,
To follow your fair feet and your sweet breath.

Listen, Shepherd, since you die for love,
Do not be frightened by my harshest sin,
Since to the weary still a friend you prove.
Wait, then, and listen to the cares I've wail'd.
But stop! To entreat you why do I begin?
I see to make you wait your feet are nail'd.

Francisco de Quevedo,
"Amor constante mas allá de la muerte"

Cerrar podrá mis ojos la postrera
Sombra, que me lleváre el blanco dia;
Y podrá desatar esta alma mia
Hora á su afan ansioso lisonjera;

Mas no de esotra parte en la ribera
Dexará la memoria, en donde ardia:
Nadar sabe mi llama la agua fria,
Y perder el respeto á ley severa.

Alma á quien todo un Dios prision ha sido:
Venas que humor á tanto fuego han dado;
Medulas que han gloriosamente ardido;
Su cuerpo dexarán, no su cuidado:
Serán ceniza, mas tendrá sentido:
Polvo serán, mas polvo enamorado.

Francisco de Quevedo,
"A Love Constant beyond Death"

The last shade that takes from me white day
May close my eyes and may release my soul
At once, and may with flattery fulfill
The spirit's eager urge to be away.

But my soul shall not the memory forsake
Of where it burn'd there on the other shore;
My passion swims in waters cold and, more,
The rigid law of nature still doth break.

A soul which has a god entire confin'd,
Veins which have given fuel to such a fire,
A marrow which so gloriously has burn'd,
Shall from their body, not their care, remove,
Shall turn to ash, but ash which knows desire,
Dust they shall be, but always dust in love.

Francisco de Quevedo, "Persevera en la exâgeracion de su afecto amoroso, y en el exceso de su padecer"

En los claustros de l'alma la herida
Yace callada; mas consume hambrienta
La vida, que en mis venas alimenta
Llama por las medulas estendida.

Bebe el ardor hydrópico mi vida,
Que ya ceniza amante y macilenta,
Cadaver del incendio hermoso, ostenta
Su luz en humo y noche fallecida.

La gente esquivo, y me es horror el dia:
Dilato en largas voces negro llanto,
Que á sordo mar mi ardiente pena envia.
A los supiros dí la voz del canto,
La confusion inunda l'alma mia,
Mi corazon es reyno del espanto.

Francisco de Quevedo, "The Excess of Amorous Suffering"

The wound within the cloisters of my soul
Lies silent; yet doth hungrily consume
My life, which in my veins doth feed the flame
Which through my pith and marrow doth unroll.

Hydroptic ardour still my life doth drink;
Its light is turn'd to amorous ashes pale,
The corpse of beauteous fire which doth fail
And unto smoke and dying night doth sink.

I flee all men, and horror to me is day;
I cry aloud my black lament of wrong,
Which sorrow sends to the sea's unlistening ear
Unto my sighs I give the voice of song,
Confusion floods my soul, sweeps it away,
My heart becomes an empire of fear.

Francisco de Quevedo,
Lágrimas de un Penitente: Psalmo IV

¿Dónde pondré, Señor, mis tristes ojos
que no vea tu poder divino y santo?
Si al cielo os levanto,
del Sol en los ardientes rayos rojos
te miro hacer asiento;
si al manto de la noche soñoliento
leyes te veo poner a las estrellas;
si los bajo a las tiernas plantas bellas,
te veo pintar las flores;
si los vuelvo a mirar los pecadores
que viven tan sin rienda como vivo,
con amor excesivo
allí hallo tus brazos ocupados,
más en sufrir que en perdonar pecados.

Francisco de Quevedo, *Tears of a Penitent*, Psalm IV

Where can I turn, O Lord, my sadden'd eyes
That I may not thy sacred might perceive?
If I them upward heave,
I mark thee in the sun's red burning rays,
And see thee take thy place;
If the mantle of the drowsy night I trace,
I see thee giving laws unto the stars;
If I lower them to tender lovely flowers,
I see thou hast them painted;
If I turn to gaze at those with sin acquainted,
Who live, like me, in license unrestrain'd,
Thy love extreme I find,
And thy arms more busy suffering I see
Than granting pardon of my sins to me.

Francisco de Quevedo,
Lágrimas de un Penitente: Psalmo x

¿Hasta cuándo, salud del mundo enfermo,
sordo estarás a los suspiros míos?
¿Cuando mis tristes ojos, vueltos ríos,
a tu mar llegarán desde este yermo?
¿Cuando amanecerá tu hermoso día
la escuridad que el alma me anochece?
Confieso que mi culpa siempre crece,
y que es la culpa de que crezca mía.
Su fuerza muestra el rayo en lo más fuerte
y en los reyes y príncipes la muerte;
resplandece el poder inaccesible
en dar facilidad a lo imposible;
y tu piedad inmensa
más se conoce en mi mayor ofensa.

Francisco de Quevedo, *Tears of a Penitent*, Psalm x

How long, health of this sickly world, how long,
Wilt thou be deaf unto my fervent sighs?
When will, to rivers turn'd, my sadden'd eyes
Rejoin thy sea from this wasteland of wrong?
When will thy lovely day consent to dawn
On the darkness which benights my wretched soul?
I must confess my guilt doth still unroll,
And that this growing guilt is all my own.
Lightning displays its strength on strongest things,
And death its power shows on princes and kings;
The highest might most clearly we do see,
When it performs impossibility;
Thy pity so immense
Best knows itself in my most grave offense.

Francisco de Quevedo, "Reconocimiento propio, y ruego piadoso antes de comulgar"

Pues hoy pretendo ser tu monumento,
Porque me resucites del pecado,
Habítame de gracia renovado
El hombre antiguo en ciego perdimiento.

Sino retratarás tu nacimiento
En la nieve de un ánimo obstinado,
Y en corazon pesebre acompañado
De brutos apetitos, que en mi siento.

Hoy te entierras en mí, siervo villano,
Sepulcro á tanto huesped vil y estrecho,
Indigno de tu Cuerpo soberano.
Tierra te cubre en mí de tierra hecho:
La conciencia me sirve de gusano:
Marmol para cubrirte dá mi pecho.

Francisco de Quevedo, "Prayer before Communion"

Since I would be today thy monument
So that from sin thou may'st my soul revive,
Inhabit me, I beg, and make alive
My former self, from blind imprisonment.

If not, thou'lt trace again thy birth so low
In the cold snow of my stubborn willful mind,
And in my heart a manger thou shalt find,
Surrounded by the bestial lusts I know.

I inter thee in myself, a wretched slave,
For so much grace a sepulchre too vile,
Unworthy all to hold thy body brave.
I cover thee in me, made out of soil,
Wherein I living worms of conscience have:
To cover thee, Oh make me marble whole!

Sor Juana Inés de la Cruz, "En que satisface un recelo con la retórica del llanto"

Esta tarde, mi bien, cuando te hablaba,
como en tu rostro y tus acciones vía
que con palabras no te persuadiá,
que el corazón me vieses deseaba.

y Amor, que mis intentos ayudaba,
venció lo que imposible parecía:
pues entre el llanto, que el dolor vertía,
el corazón deshecho destilaba.

Baste ya de rigores, mi bien, baste;
no te atormenten más celos tiranos,
ni el vil recelo tu quietud contraste
con sombras necias, con indicios vanos,
pues ya en líquido humor viste y tocaste
mi corazón deshecho entre tus manos.

Sor Juana Inés de la Cruz, "The Rhetoric of Tears"

Tonight, my dearest, when I spoke to thee,
I noted in thy bearing and thy face
That words of mine could not thy doubts erase,
Or prove I wanted thee my heart to see;

Then love, which my avowals came to prop,
Conquer'd, and the impossible occurr'd:
I fell to weeping tears which sorrow pour'd,
Which my melting heart distill'd in copious drop.

No more reproaches, ah my love, forbear;
Let doubt not hold thee in tormenting bonds,
Nor let vile jealousy thy peace impair
With foolish shades, with vain and useless wounds,
Since thou hast seen and touch'd a liquid rare—
My molten heart caught up between thy hands.

Sor Juana Inés de la Cruz,
"Que da medio para amor sin mucha pena"

Yo no puedo tenerte ni dejarte,
ni sé por qué, al dejarte o al tenerte,
se encuentra un no sé qué para quererte
y muchos sí sé qué para olvidarte.

Pues ni quieres dejarme ni enmendarte,
yo templaré mi corazón de suerte
que la mitad se incline a aborrecerte
aunque la otra mitad se incline a amarte.

Si ello es fuerza querernos, haya modo,
que es morir el estar siempre riñendo:
no se habla más en celo y en sospecha,
y quien da la mitad, no quiera el todo;
y cuando me las estás allá haciendo,
sabe que estoy haciendo la deshecha.

Sor Juana Inés de la Cruz, "A Method of Loving"

I cannot either keep you or reject you,
Nor know I why, should I depart or stay,
I-know-not-what my heart to love doth sway,
Though I-do-know-what doth urge me to forget you.

Since you will neither leave me nor amend,
I shall reform my heart in such a fashion
That half of it shall hate you with a passion
And half of it shall still to love you bend.

Let's find a way, if love must us control;
In constant quarreling we both do die:
Let's speak no more in jealousy or doubt.
Who gives but half should not desire the whole;
And when you do, deceiving, elsewhere lie,
Be sure that what I do you'll ne'er find out.

Sor Juana Inés de la Cruz,
"Verde embeleso de la vida humana"

Verde embeleso de la vida humana,
loca Esperanza, frenesí dorado,
sueño de los despiertos intrincado
como de sueños, de tesoros vana;

alma del mundo, senectud lozana,
decrépito verdor imaginado;
el hoy de los dichosos esperado
y de los desdichados el mañana:

sigan tu sombra en busca de tu día
los que, con verdes vidrios por anteojos,
todo lo ven pintado a su deseo;
que yo más cuerdo en la fortuna mía,
tengo en entrambas manos ambos ojos
y solamente lo que toco veo.

Sor Juana Inés de la Cruz,
"Green Fascination of Our Human Life"

Green fascination of our human life,
Mad Hope, thou frenzy gilded all with gold,
Dream of the waking, in which we behold
A tissue of dreams with empty treasures rife;

Soul of the world, senility in flower,
Decrepit greenness which our fancies feign,
The desir'd today the fortunate attain,
And for the desperate tomorrow's hour:

Let them thy shade pursue in hope to find
Thy promis'd day, who green eyeglasses wear,
And see the world with their desire painted;
Let me, more prudent, seek in different kind;
In both my hands my two eyes let me bear,
Only with what I touch my sight acquainted.

ITALIAN POEMS

Tommaso Campanella, "Del mondo e sue parti"

Il mondo è un animal grande e perfetto,
statua di Dio, che Dio lauda e simiglia:
noi siam vermi imperfetti e vil famiglia,
ch'intra il suo ventre abbiam vita e ricetto.

Se ignoriamo il suo amor e 'l suo intelletto,
né il verme del mio ventre s'assottiglia
a saper me, ma a farmi mal s'appiglia:
dunque bisogna andar con gran rispetto.

Siam poi alla terra, ch'è un grande animale
dentro al massimo, noi come pidocchi
al corpo nostro; e però ci fan male.
Superba gente, meco alzate gli occhi,
e misurate quanto ogn'ente vale:
quinci imparate che parte a voi tocchi.

Tommaso Campanella, "The World and its Parts"

A great and perfect animal is the world,
God's statue, which doth ever give him praise:
Vile worms are we, in our imperfect ways,
And make our life within this body curl'd.

We know nought of his love or intellect,
No more than doth the worm within my frame
Concern himself to know me, but to harm;
Therefore we ought to live in great respect.

Thus are we in this earth, great animal
Within the greatest; we are like to lice
On our own bodies, ignorant and foul.
Proud race of man, I bid you raise your eyes,
And measure what you're worth against the all:
Then learn your true position and be wise.

Giambattista Marino, "Durante il bagno"

Sovra basi d'argento in conca d'oro
io vidi due colonne alabastrine
dentro linfe odorate e cristalline
franger di perle un candido tesoro.

—O—dissi—del mio mal posa e ristoro,
di natura e d'amor mète divine,
stabilite per l'ultimo confine
ne l'océan de le dolcezze loro;

fossi Alcide novel, ché i miei trofei
dove mai non giungesse uman desio,
traspiantandovi in braccio erger vorrei;
o stringer, qual Sanson, vi potess'io,
che col vostro cader, dolce darei
tomba a la Morte, e morte al dolor mio!

Giambattista Marino, "During the Bath"

On a silver base, within a shell of gold,
I saw two alabaster pillars rise,
While perfum'd crystal floods reveal'd the prize
Of purest pearl, a treasure manifold.

I said, "Oh destin'd solace of my pain,
Object divine of nature and of love,
From the ocean of your sweetness do not move,
As its final limits still you must remain.

Were I a new Alcides I should show
Erect my standard where until this morrow
No man's desire has reach'd; or could I borrow
The strength of Samson, I should overthrow
Those columns, which in falling would bestow
A fragrant tomb to death, death to my sorrow.

Giambattista Marino, "Mentre la sua donna si pettina"

Onde dorate, e l'onde eran capelli,
navicella d'avorio un di fendea;
una man pur d'avorio la reggea
per questi errori preziosi e quelli;

e, mentre i flutti tremolanti e belli
con drittissimo solco dividea,
l'or de le rotte fila Amor cogliea,
per formarne catene a' suoi rubelli.

Per l'aureo mar, che rincrespando apria
il procelloso suo biondo tesoro,
agitato il mio core a morte gia.
Ricco naufragio, in cui sommerso io moro,
poich'almen fur, ne la tempesta mia,
di diamante lo scoglio e 'l golfo d'oro!

Giambattista Marino, "While his Lady Combs her Hair"

Through waves of gold, the waves which were her hair,
A little ship of ivory sailed one day,
A hand of ivory steered it on its way
Through precious undulations here and there.

And while along the tremulous surge of beauty
She drove a straight and never-ending furrow,
From the rows of tumbled gold Love sought to borrow
Chains to reduce a rebel to his duty.

My shipwrecked heart veers down to death so fast
In this stormy, blond and gilded sea that I
Am caught forever in its waves at last.
In golden gulfs, at least, I come to my
Tempestuous end, on rocks of diamond press'd,
—O rich disaster in which submerged I die.

Giuseppe Artale, "La donna con gli occhiali"

Non per temprar l'altrui crescente ardore
sugli occhi usa costei nevi addensate,
ma per ferir da piú lontano un core
rinforza col cristal le luci amate.

Se co' riflessi il Sol nutre il calore,
questa, per far piú fervide le occhiate,
l'oppon due vetri, acciò che 'l suo folgore
vibri, in vece di rai, vampe adirate.

Ella, quasi Archimede, arder noi vuole,
ché sa che cagionò fiamme e feretri
per dïafane vie passando il sole;
o i petti tutti acciò ferire impetri,
ed a gli strali suoi cor non s'invole,
vie piú scaltra d'Amor, benda ha di vetri.

Giuseppe Artale, "The Lady with Glasses"

'Tis not to quench her lovers' ardent flames
That she places on her eyes these sheets of snow;
Nay, 'tis that from a distance she may throw,
Strengthen'd with crystal, lovely wounding beams.

If with his rays the sun doth heat inspire,
She but to make incendiary her looks,
Puts on these glasses that her lightning-strokes
May shoot instead of rays a raging fire.

Like Archimedes, she's on arson bent,
For she knows the sun through glass in subtle ways
Is cause of fire and agoniz'd lament;
Or she turns to stone the better to harass,
And no heart can escape her burning rays;
She, wiser far than Love, hath bonds of glass.

Giuseppe Artale, "Il buon ladrone—a Pietro Valeri"

Qui sagace l'ingegno e 'l saldo amore
e di Cristo e del ladro oggi si mira;
questo del primo ardir perde il vigore,
quei del giusto rigor depone or l'ira.

Questi l'empio furor cangia in fervore
e quei fervor ne l'altrui petto inspira;
quei vuol, quei dona, e in quell e in questo core
l'industria, o Pietro, e la pietá s'ammira.

Cristo, ai martir giunto di morte in atto,
dá glorie a quello e con pietoso zelo
ne la sua povertá prodigo è fatto.
Rapace è l'altro, e dal corporeo velo
pria che l'anima uscisse, egli ad un tratto
ruba a costui con un sospiro il cielo.

Giuseppe Artale, "The Good Thief"

Behold this day the wisdom and the love
Of Christ and of this thief who here expire;
The one his former boldness doth remove,
The other doth cast off his righteous ire.

The one his impious rage doth change to fervor,
The other doth that gracious flame inspire;
One steals, one gives, and in both hearts the savour
Of wit and pity let us both admire.

Christ in the very moment of his dying
Gives glory to this man, with pitying zeal
In poverty his gracious gifts displaying.
Rapacious is the thief, before his soul
Can leave its fleshly veil, he turns and, sighing,
Doth all at once the heavens from him steal.

Brief Lives

GIUSEPPE ARTALE (1628–79). Of the innumerable Italian poets of the seventeenth century who followed the literary fashion established by G. B. Marino, Artale is one of the best as well as one of the most nearly original. His lyrics, whether amorous or devotional, usually show the coldness and triviality which are the besetting sins of *marinismo*, but his ingenuity occasionally kindles into passion, and his wit is employed more structurally than that of many of his countrymen. His works include, in addition to lyrics, a tragicomedy and a *dramma per musica*. His life has a certain dramatic interest: noted as one of the great duelists of his age, he traveled widely, distinguished himself in battle against the Turks, and ultimately lived in Germany, where he was known as "der blutgierige Ritter" ("the bloodthirsty knight"). He died in Naples.

JEAN BERTAUT (1552–1611). Bertaut was born at Caen in Normandy. Entering the priesthood early in life, he embarked on a career full of public honors—councilor of the Parliament at Grenoble, secretary to King Henry III, almoner to Marie de Medici, and finally, in 1606, Bishop of Sées. After his elevation to the bishopric he abandoned amorous verse and confined himself to the writing of frigid and solemn occasional pieces. He did not, however, reject the work of his earlier years; in 1606, in fact, he personally saw to the revision of his *Recueil de quelques vers amoureux* of 1602. It is this volume which gives Bertaut his poetic reputation, as well as his position as a minor Metaphysical poet. Like that of his contemporary Desportes, Bertaut's work is essentially court poetry and essentially trivial; its distinction lies in its author's fondness for *pointes*—witty or paradoxical turns of phrase which often recall the conceits of the English Metaphysicals.

✳ TOMMASO CAMPANELLA (1568–1639), The philosopher Campanella was born in Stilo, Calabria, and at an early age entered the Dominican order. Influenced by Telesio's *De rerum natura*, with its appeal to nature and its rejection of Aristotle, he aroused the hostility of his ecclesiastical superiors and fled from Naples to Florence, where he tried unsuccessfully to obtain an academic post. Returning to Naples, he was implicated in a conspiracy against the Spanish rulers of that city, and spent the next twenty-eight years in prison. During this time he wrote his sonnets as well as most of his philosophical works. After his release he went to Rome and then to Paris, where, after launching publication of his works, he died. Campanella's works, of which the Utopian *City of the Sun* (1623) is the best known, show a consistent concern with the achievement of a unified vision of human experience. His poems are distinguished by a combination of philosophical complexity and rugged personal honesty.

✳ JEAN DE LA CEPPÈDE (1550?–1622). Although praised in his own time by Malherbe, La Ceppède has had to wait until our century for recognition as an important poet. A variety of the same shift in sensibility which brought about the revival of the Metaphysicals in England led to the rediscovery of La Ceppède, since which time his reputation has established itself ever more firmly. La Ceppède, who was distantly related to Teresa of Ávila, was born in Marseille and died in Avignon; he spent most of his life in the south of France, where he was first counselor to the parliament of Aix and later president of the Chambre des Comptes of Provence. He found time, first in 1613 and then in 1621, to publish the two volumes of his *Théorèmes*, intricate and profound devotional sonnets accompanied by prose commentaries. *Les Théorèmes* constitute one of the finest examples of the application of the methods of formal meditation to the composition of poetry, and they rank with the best religious poems of the author's age.

✳ JEAN-BAPTISTE CHASSIGNET (1578?–1635?). Almost nothing is known of Chassignet's life, beyond the fact that he was born in Besançon, studied there, and took a degree in law. In addition to his devotional sonnets (*Le Mespris de la vie et consolation contre la mort*, 1594), he wrote paraphrases of the psalms. His work, like that of La Ceppède and Sponde, underwent some three centuries of almost complete obscurity, to be rediscovered with considerable enthusiasm by readers of our own century.

✳ AGRIPPA D'AUBIGNÉ (1552–1630). Soldier, lover, historian, theologian, and artist, D'Aubigné combines the energy and versatility of the Renaissance with the haunted intensity of the age which followed it. His epic, *Les Tragiques*, is one of the monuments of the French Renaissance, but it has often been cited as a characteristic Baroque work; the lyrics inspired by his love for Diane Salviati are in the Petrarchan mold but are touched with some of the analytic quality of Donne. D'Aubigné was born near Pons in Saintonge, into a Huguenot family, and came to know at an early age the bitterness of the French wars of religion. He fought bravely for the Protestant cause and was seriously wounded in 1577, at which time he began *Les Tragiques*, his apocalyptic vision of the religious conflict. He served as equerry to Henry of Navarre, but left his service when that prince, making his famous decision that Paris was worth a mass, adopted the Catholic faith. D'Aubigné died in Geneva, an appropriate resting-place for a Protestant champion.

✳ LAURENT DRELINCOURT (1626?–81). The son of the noted theologian Charles Drelincourt, this poet led a quiet life as a Protestant pastor in the Huguenot stronghold of La Rochelle. His *Sonnets Chrétiens* (1680) had great popularity among his co-religionists in the latter part of the seventeenth century, but they subsequently shared the neglect of most French Metaphysical poetry. Even at the present time Drelincourt remains less well-known than Sponde or La Ceppède. Despite the narrowness of his emotional range, his poetry deserves more attention, for it frequently displays an admirable blend of theological subtlety and passionate force.

✳ HEIMAN DULLAERT (1636–84). Born in Rotterdam, Dullaert studied painting under Rembrandt and practiced that art in his native city throughout his life. His master's influence remained always dominant in his painting, and it is perhaps not too fanciful to find something Rembrandtesque in the dark profundity of Dullaert's best religious poems. His poetic production, small but of consistently high quality, did not see print until 1714, by which time the taste for Baroque literature had passed. As a result, Dullaert's poetry, like that of so many of his French contemporaries, remained largely unknown until he was rediscovered in the later nineteenth century by the distinguished modern Dutch poet Albert Verwey. His position in Dutch literary history is now secure, and his recent reputation has been high indeed.

✳ ETIENNE DURAND (1590–1618). A member of a rich bourgeois family with aristocratic connections, Durand was marked by social and political ambitions which were to prove fatal to him. His modern editor, M. Lachèvre, has rather fancifully suggested that his motive was a desire to elevate himself socially because of his passionate love for his well-born cousin, Marie de Fourcy. However that may be, the fact is that Durand made himself useful in court entertainments, obtained the protection of Marie de Medici, and incurred the enmity of the king's favorite, the Comte de Luynes. Ultimately he became involved in the Concini intrigue, directed against Luynes by the Medici faction, and collaborated on a scurrilous pamphlet libeling Louis XIII. He paid for it with his life in 1618, being broken on the wheel and burned to death. The sole enduring achievement of his short life was the publication in 1610 of his *Méditations*, a collection of love lyrics which, with their fresh diction, striking figures, and perceptive psychology, give new life to the Petrarchan tradition.

PAUL FLEMING (1609–40). Born the son of a Lutheran pastor at Hartenstein in the Erzgebirge of Saxony, Fleming studied at Leipzig, where he became acquainted with Martin Opitz, and he then accompanied diplomatic missions to Moscow and to Persia. In the course of his wanderings he met, at Reval in Estonia, the sisters Elsabe and Anna Niehusen, who managed between them to inspire many of his love poems. The most important of the disciples of Opitz, Fleming differs from his master in the more immediate and personal quality of his lyricism and in his more consistent intellectuality. The Petrarchanism of his early love lyrics yields ultimately to a more individualized kind of expression, and his devotional poems are notable for their fusion of theological paradox and passionate feeling. Like so many German poets of his time, Fleming finally studied at Leiden, where he received his medical degree in 1640. Immediately thereafter he settled in Hamburg, where he met his early death through the plague. With him died one of the most promising lyric talents of pre-eighteenth-century Germany.

CATHARINA REGINA VON GREIFFENBERG (1633–94). Born of a noble family in Seyssenegg in Upper Austria, Catharina was obliged by her Protestant religion to flee to Regensburg, where she associated with a group of Austrian religious exiles. She came in contact with the Nuremberg poetic group and became a friend of the poets Birken and Zesen. The passionate directness of her language, her adherence to strict poetic forms, and her primarily devotional subject matter all underline a distinct kinship with Andreas Gryphius. The critic Lemcke, indulging a taste for paradox, has called her "the most manly character among the poets of her time," and a reading of her work will partially justify his observation.

✳ ANDREAS GRYPHIUS (1616–64). The greatest German poet of the seventeenth century was born in Glogau, Silesia, the son of a clergyman. Orphaned and driven from his home by the fortunes of the Thirty Years' War, he ultimately traveled to Holland, where he studied at Leiden and came under the influence of the great Dutch writers of the age, particularly Vondel. After working as a teacher in Leiden, he traveled further in France and Italy and then, in 1650, returned to Glogau, where he became "syndicus" of the town. Gryphius' dramas—the tragedies *Leo Arminius, Cardenio und Celinde*, and *Carolus Stuardus;* the comedies *Herr Peter Squentz* and *Horribilicribrifax*—have considerable importance in German literary history. The former show the influence of Seneca and Vondel, and *Squentz* is based partly on Shakespeare's *Midsummer Night's Dream.* But the great religious lyrics, with their tense interplay of a fierce love for earthly beauty and a rejection of it as vanity, are the source of the poet's immortality.

CHRISTIAN HOFFMANN VON HOFMANNSWALDAU (1617–79). Another protegé of Opitz, Hofmannswaldau was one of the most cosmopolitan men of letters produced by seventeenth-century Germany. He was born in Breslau in Silesia, native province of so many German poets of the time, and traveled widely in France, England, and Italy, after which he returned to Breslau to take up a post as a government official, a post in which he distinguished himself for his sensitivity and kindliness. Although Hofmannswaldau, as the chief member of the "Second Silesian School," which introduced *marinismo* into German literature, is usually regarded as a typical exponent of the High Baroque style, of that overblown manner to which the Germans apply the term *Schwulst*, his work is actually very versatile: he wrote "heroical epistles" in the manner of Drayton, translated Guarini's *Pastor fido* (1678), and reacted to the influence of Maynard, Racan, and Théophile de Viau, as well as to that of Marino. At their best, Hofmannswaldau's lyrics manifest a dynamic tension between erotically charged sensuality and a deeply Christian sense of the transience of earthly things. For all their differences, his vision of life is not ultimately opposed to that of Gryphius.

CONSTANTIJN HUYGENS (1596–1687). The offspring of one of the great Dutch families, Huygens was born in The Hague and educated at Leiden. In 1619 he went to London as the guest of the Dutch ambassador to the English court. Here, in addition to meeting King James I and Ben Jonson, he probably first became acquainted with the poetry of John Donne. Donne himself he probably met first in 1621, during his second trip to England as secretary to the embassy. In 1627 he married a beautiful blue-stocking named Susanna van Baerle; his love for her evoked some of the finest of his lyrics, and her death ten years later inspired some of his most moving. More than any other of the important poets of Holland's "golden century," Huygens typifies the prosperous, cultivated, and cosmopolitan ruling class. He knew English, French, German, Italian, Spanish, Latin, and Greek well enough to compose original verse in all these languages, he was active in public life, and his scientific interests were worthy of a man whose son, Christiaan Huygens, was to be one of the great scientists of his age.

SAN JUAN DE LA CRUZ (1542–91). Juan de Yepes y Álvarez was born in Fontiveros, Ávila. He became a member of the Carmelite order and attempted to introduce monastic reforms similar to those established for female monastics by his good friend Santa Teresa of Ávila. His attempts in this direction met with little success; at one point he was imprisoned and mistreated for several years by his opponents, the unreformed Carmelite monks of Toledo. St. John of the Cross is a giant figure in the history of mysticism, and the lyrics in which he attempts to communicate his experience of divinity give him a place among the greatest of all Spanish lyric poets. These poems (not published until a generation after his death) have continued to maintain their vital importance in our own time, which has seen translations of them into all the major European languages. Juan was canonized a century after his death.

✳ SOR JUANA INÉS DE LA CRUZ (1651–95). Juana de Asbaje y Ramírez de Cantillana was born in the village of San Miguel Nepantla near the foot of Popocatapetl. As a child she was a prodigy of learning and at an early age she became lady-in-waiting to the vicereine of Mexico. The motive for her entering the convent at the age of eighteen is not definitely known, but there has been the inevitable assumption of an unhappy love affair. Some experience, at any rate, gave her a knowledge of the nature of sexual passion, which combined with her intellectual and subtle nature to create lyric poetry of extraordinary power and insight. In the convent she continued her intellectual pursuits—mathematics, music, and theological speculation, in addition to the composition of poetry and drama. Rebuked for worldliness in a pseudonymous letter from the Bishop of Puebla, she replied in the *Respuesta a Sor Filotea*, a noble and witty defense of woman's right to learning. She died nursing plague victims, having given up her studies.

QUIRINUS KUHLMANN (1651–89). Even in an age of fanatics and eccentrics, Kuhlmann was very much an oddity. Born in Breslau, he studied there as well as at Jena and Leiden. Most of his life was taken up in travel—England, Scotland, France, Holland, Switzerland, Turkey, Russia—and everywhere he went he fervently preached his own private religion. It was a faith which owed something to the mystical philosophy of Jacob Böhme but owed a good deal more to Kuhlmann's own strange personality. Deeply convinced of the imminent second coming of Christ, Kuhlmann regarded himself as the Messiah's appointed prophet, with the task of organizing both church and state under his own guidance to await the great event. Inevitably, the authoritarian Russian government viewed him with alarm, and he was burned at the stake in Moscow at the orders of the Patriarch. Kuhlmann's poetry, with its private symbolism, ejaculatory syntax, and unrestrained rhythms, is both a complete expression of his strange temperament and a curious anticipation of many currents in twentieth-century poetry.

GUY LE FÈVRE DE LA BODERIE (1541–84?/98?). The writing of poetry was a relatively minor activity in the life of this energetic scholar and linguist, who was born near Falaise, the offspring of a noble Norman family. He acted as secretary and interpreter to the Duc d'Alençon and labored on the great *Polyglot Bible* of Antwerp (1569–73), for which he edited the Syriac text. His poetry, as one might expect, is minor, but though almost totally without humor or polish, it displays occasional felicitous perceptions.

LOPE DE VEGA (1562–1635). The great achievement of Don Frey Lope Felix de Vega Carpio is, of course, the astounding body of dramatic writings with which he effectively created the theater of his nation and his language. Nevertheless, with a display of that incredible energy proverbially associated with the Renaissance personality, he managed also to write a pastoral romance, a romance epic modeled on Ariosto, a religious epic modeled on Tasso, prose novels, a "romance in dialogue" (*La Dorotea*, 1632), a vast number of amorous lyrics, and some of the finest religious poems in the Spanish language. These latter are of importance in terms of this volume, for they demonstrate amply that the "monstruo de la Naturaleza," as Cervantes called Lope, was capable also of a delicacy of feeling, a subtlety of thought, and a complexity of language which place him in the mainstream of European Metaphysical poetry. Lope's life is as full of variety as his work: born in Madrid, he showed as a young man his genius, his love of adventure, and his weakness for women. After serving with the invincible Armada, he returned to Spain, where he began writing for the stage. From 1590 to 1595 he was in the service of the Duke of Alva; he was married twice; and in 1614 he entered the priesthood, a step which did not, however, keep him from another love affair. But the passionate involvement with life which burns in his life as in his works co-existed with a deep religious feeling, of which the poems in this volume are ample evidence.

✳ JAN LUYKEN (1649–1712). Born of a humble Baptist family in Amsterdam, Luyken was trained as an etcher and engraver. His literary talent appeared first in the amorous and secular poems of his *Duytse Lier* (1671), which showed him to be the best poet of his generation. A reading of Böhme kindled his religious feelings into a kind of mystical pantheism, however, and his later poetry, reminiscent of Vaughan's in its feeling for nature, is far above his earlier attempts. After the death of his wife Luyken withdrew from Amsterdam to the village of Hoorn on the Zuyderzee, where he led a life of contemplation. His splendid etchings, which illustrate many of his later volumes, are in some ways equal to his poetry; together they achieve an effect much stronger than that of the "emblem-poetry" of earlier generations, possibly because Luyken treats the relation between text and picture more freely and flexibly than any of his predecessors.

✳ GIAMBATTISTA MARINO (1569–1625). Marino was born in Naples, later lived in Rome and Turin, and in 1615 went to Paris, where he was immensely popular with various circles at the court of Louis XIII. Already well-known for the shorter lyrics published in his *Rime* at the turn of the century, Marino achieved European fame with his long narrative poem *Adone*, which he wrote during his Paris years. In 1623 he returned to Italy, and he died in his native city a few years later. A great technician, a master of the effects of "meraviglia," or wonder, Marino suffers from an ultimate lack of artistic seriousness. His chief importance is historical—as a major influence in western European literature in countries ranging from Portugal to Sweden, as the chief exponent of the sensual, highly colored manner in High Baroque poetry, and as a poet who remained for several generations the chief model for the poets of his own country. The modern reader can still, however, be charmed by Marino's wit, fluency, and ebullience.

PIERRE MOTIN (1550?–1615). Condemned by Boileau for breaches of neoclassical taste but cited by the Académie Française, praised by his friend the satirist Regnier as "the only poet who isn't mad," Motin is a distant and minor figure who nevertheless exerts a certain attraction. Born at Bourges sometime around the middle of the sixteenth century, he later lived in Paris, where the wit and polish of his verses won him considerable admiration. Unlike his contemporary Desportes, even more unlike the poets of the Pléiade, Motin ranks with Bertaut as an early representative of secular Metaphysical poetry in France.

MARTIN OPITZ (1597–1639). First in the succession of important Silesian poets of the seventeenth century, Opitz is more important for his work as a theorist than for his actual artistic accomplishment. His *Buch von der deutschen Poëterey* had an incalculable influence, not only through its introduction of the Renaissance poetic theories of Ronsard and Scaliger into Germany, but also through its definitive establishment of the accentual principle in German metrics. He was born of a Protestant family in Bunzlau, studied in Frankfurt-an-der-Oder and Heidelberg, traveled in Holland (where he met the poet and critic Heinsius), Denmark, and Transylvania. In 1635 he became historiographer to the king of Poland, whose fiefs at that time included Danzig, and in that city he spent the rest of his life. Opitz' accomplishments include the writing of the libretto for the first German opera (Heinrich Schütz' *Dafne*, 1627), and his generous encouragement of younger poetic talent. His own more ambitious works seem stiff, but a handful of delicate lyrics make his memory secure.

✻ FRANCISCO DE QUEVEDO (1580–1634). Francisco Gómez de Quevedo y Villegas was born in Madrid and studied theology at Valladolid and Alcalá. Much of his life was spent in the service of the Duke of Osuna, for whom he undertook missions in Naples and elsewhere; banished to his estates at the fall from favor of his noble master (1620), Quevedo returned to court in 1623, became royal secretary in 1632, but fell into disgrace again in 1639, after which he was imprisoned for four years. His remaining years were spent in retirement. The exigencies of a busy and troubled public life did not prevent Quevedo from creating an amazing body of art which stands almost with Lope's as a manifestation of the vigor of Spanish culture in its great period. His picaresque novel, *El Buscón*, ranks with the finest examples of the genre; his *Sueños* are among the world's great satires; and his miscellaneous prose works reveal a master stylist and a perceptive thinker. The steady flow of lyric poetry —amorous, devotional, and occasional—which accompanied his life was long underestimated because of the disfavor into which his type of *conceptismo* had fallen, but his lyrics are now generally regarded as among the best in the language.

✳ JACOB REVIUS (1586–1658). Born in Deventer in the eastern part of the Netherlands, Revius studied theology at the universities of Leiden and Franeker. After several years as a minister, he became a member of the faculty at Leiden, where he worked on the official translation of the Bible. A confirmed Calvinist, he fought the theology of Arminius and the philosophy of Descartes with equal fervor. Revius was more concerned with religious doctrine and controversy than with art as such, and as a result his poetry shows few traces of contact with the fashions of the day in his country. Nevertheless, it is poetry of rare formal perfection and great emotional impact, frequently suggestive of George Herbert in its immediacy, its ingenious and often homely metaphors, and its skillful matching of form and vision.

✳ MARC-ANTOINE DE SAINT-AMANT (1594–1661). Antoine Girard, or, to give him the full glory of the pseudonym which he was to assume, Marc-Antoine de Gérard, Sieur de Saint-Amant, was born in the market town of Rouen. A *libertin* and free-thinker like his friend Théophile de Viau, Saint-Amant led a restless life but managed to avoid his friend's painful conflicts with authority. Led by some obscure impulse, he traveled incessantly—Madrid, Rome, London, Warsaw, perhaps even in America and Africa—but produced poems in varied genres and styles. His most ambitious effort, the religious epic *Moïse sauvé*, is not a success, but descriptive pieces such as "La Solitude" and "Le Melon" seem the work of a dilute Marvell, and his wonderful burlesques have a naturalness which frequently becomes naturalism.

MAURICE SCÈVE (1500?–64). Born in or near Lyon, Scève is the greatest product of the cultural blossoming which occurred in that city in the early sixteenth century. The importance of Lyon in the French Renaissance is due to many factors—its commercial and cultural links to Italy; its importance as a printing center; its schools, which were under the direct control of neither church nor state and hence encouraged a high degree of intellectual freedom. Scève is the characteristic poet of this civilization—in his learned subtlety, his habit of speculation, and his absorption of Italian influences. But although Petrarchanism and Platonism are important elements in his greatest work, *Délie* (1544), the profound psychology of passion which has made that work so admired in our century is to be attributed more to Scève's individual genius than to any particular literary tradition. His chief disciples were the "learned ladies" Louise Labé and Pernette du Guillet, and the latter was, in the view of some scholars, the inspiration for *Délie*. Scève's other works include *La Saulsaye* and the encyclopedic *Microcosme*.

JOHANN SCHEFFLER (1624–77). Scheffler, best known to literary history under his pseudonym "Angelus Silesius," was born in Breslau, Silesia, the son of Protestant refugees from Poland. He studied medicine in Strasbourg and Leiden and took degrees in philosophy and medicine at Padua. At some point he encountered the writings of the ubiquitous Jacob Böhme, who was to have a lasting effect on his view of experience. Böhme's mystical pantheism retained its force in Scheffler's thought even after the poet became converted to Catholicism (1653) and was ordained a priest (1661). His masterpiece, *Der Cherubinische Wandersmann*, is at once a set of moral apothegms and a consistently presented vision of the immanence of God in nature and man.

DAVID SCHIRMER (1623?–83). The few known facts of Schirmer's life can be briefly summarized: he was born in Pappendorf near Freiberg in Saxony, studied in Leipzig, was employed by the court of the Elector of Saxony in Dresden as a writer of opera librettos (1650), became Royal Librarian in 1656, and continued to live in Dresden until his death in 1683. Schirmer's lyric poetry is in the spirit of Fleming, but it bears the stamp of a gay, perhaps shallow, but charming individual personality.

✳ FRIEDRICH VON SPEE (1591–1635). Spee, the first truly important poet to appear in seventeenth-century Germany, was born in Kaiserwörth in the Rhineland. He became a member of the Jesuit order in 1610, and in 1627 he was given the ghastly assignment of being confessor to all those condemned for witchcraft in the diocese of Würzburg. He was compelled to assist at the last agonies of some 200 people, of whose innocence he, as an intelligent man, was wholly convinced. The result was his anonymously presented *Cautio criminalis* (1631), a fervent argument against the witchcraft persecutions, which did, in fact, bring about some lessening of the frenzy. Spee's religious poetry is contained in his *Trutznachtigall* (1649), not published until after his death. Spee's one subject is the love of God, and few poets have sung it with more passion and splendor; the sensuous texture and naive pose of Spee's lyrics mask a fine theological intelligence. He is one of the most attractive figures of the German Baroque.

✳ JEAN DE SPONDE (1557–95). Sponde is, like La Ceppède, a discovery of the twentieth century, specifically of the British scholar Alan Boase. The author of some felicitous and highly original amorous verses, Sponde poured his poetic energy primarily into his *Sonnets de la mort* and *Stances de la mort*, powerful and macabre meditations on the fact of death which have something of the accent of Villon. Noted in his own time as a humanist scholar, the editor of Aristotle and Hesiod, Sponde was born in Mauléon, near the Pyrenees, and died in Bordeaux. He was a Protestant in his youth but was converted to Catholicism in his maturity.

✳ THÉOPHILE DE VIAU (1590–1626). One of the most fascinating figures of his time, Théophile, as he is usually called, was born in Clairac. His father was a Huguenot, but the poet seems at no point to have concerned himself unduly with matters of faith. First in the service of the Comte de Candale, then in that of the powerful Duc de Montmorency, Théophile seems to have been torn between a desire for security and an unfortunate tendency to say shocking things in public. The latter habit gained him a reputation as the greatest *libertin* of his time and made it inevitable that any shocking or subversive pamphlet which appeared should be attributed to him. Banished in 1623, then condemned to death *in absentia* for atheism, Théophile probably owed his life to the influence of Montmorency, an influence which did not, however, preserve him from later imprisonment and further banishment. He died with his great talents not fully exploited. Théophile's poetry, which is distinguished by an individuality of tone strongly opposed to the classicism of Malherbe, falls into three periods—an early period of idyllic descriptive poetry, a middle period of elegies and sonnets in the Metaphysical manner, a late period of ornate, sometimes almost surrealistic work in an extreme High Baroque style. In each of these periods Théophile shows himself to be a master of tone and implication.

❋ Joost van den Vondel (1587–1679). The greatest poet of the Dutch language was born in Cologne, the son of Mennonite parents who had fled from Antwerp because of religious persecution. While still a young man, he settled in Amsterdam, a city with which his memory is indissolubly linked. His poetic development was slow but consistent; his satirical poems *Roskam* and *Rommelpot* won him the friendship of P. C. Hooft, at that time the dominant figure in Dutch letters, and his allegorical attack on the extreme Calvinists in the drama *Palamedes* won him fame as well as notoriety. The patriotic play *Gijsbrecht van Aemstel*, Vondel's contribution to the opening of the Amsterdam municipal theater in 1637, disturbed some of his fellow citizens with its sympathetic use of Catholic imagery, and it was not completely surprising when, in 1640, the poet embraced the Roman faith with a devotion and an intensity which were never thenceforth to diminish. In the 1650's Vondel's dramatic genius achieved its heights with *Lucifer* (1654) and *Jephta* (1659), dramatic poems in which the impact of the classical heritage on a mind essentially medieval and a temperament essentially bourgeois manages somehow to produce poetry of the highest order. Vondel himself conceived of the drama as his chief field, but it is for their poetic rather than their dramatic qualities that his masterpieces in that genre are now chiefly valued. The lyrics which he produced with such careless abundance throughout his long life are now an equal source of his fame.

Bibliography

Sources for Texts

BERTAUT, JEAN, *Oeuvres poétiques*, ed. A. Chenevière, Paris, 1891.

CAMPANELLA, TOMMASO, *Poesie*, ed. G. Gentile, Bari, 1951.

CEPPÈDE, JEAN DE LA, *Les Théorèmes*, 2 vols. Toulouse, vol. 1 in 1613, vol. 2 in 1621.

CHASSIGNET, JEAN-BAPTISTE, *Le Mespris de la vie et consolation contre la mort*, ed. A. Müller, Geneva and Lille, 1953.

CRASHAW, RICHARD, *Poetical Works*, ed. L. C. Martin, Oxford, 1927.

CROCE, B., ed., *Lirici Marinisti*, Bari, 1910 (for Giuseppe Artale).

CRUZ, SAN JUAN DE LA, *Obras*, ed. Padre Silverio de Santa Teresa, C. D., Burgos, 1929–31.

CRUZ, SOR JUANA INÉS DE LA, *Obras completas*, ed. A. Mendez Plancarte, 4 vols. Mexico City, 1952–55.

D'AUBIGNÉ, AGRIPPA, *Le Printemps*, ed. F. Desonay, Geneva and Lille, 1952.

DONNE, JOHN, *Poetical Works*, ed. H. J. C. Grierson, 2 vols. Oxford, 1912.

DRELINCOURT, LAURENT, *Sonnets Chrétiens*, Amsterdam, 1766.

DURAND, ETIENNE, *Méditations*, ed. F. Lachèvre, Paris, 1907.

FLEMING, PAUL, *Teutsche Poemata*, Lübeck, 1642.

FLETCHER, GILES AND PHINEAS, *Poetical Works*, ed. F. S. Boas, 2 vols. Cambridge, 1908–09.

GREIFFENBERG, CATHARINA REGINA VON, *Geistliche Sonnette, Lieder und Gedichte*, Nuremberg, 1662.

GRYPHIUS, ANDREAS, *Deutscher Gedichte*, Breslau, 1657.

HERBERT, GEORGE, *Works*, ed. F. E. Hutchinson, Oxford, 1941.

EDWARD, LORD HERBERT of Cherbury, *Poems*, ed. G. C. Moore Smith, Oxford, 1923.

Herrn von Hofmannswaldau und andrer Deutschen auserlesener und biszher ungedruckter Gedichte erster theil . . . , ed. Benjamin Neukirch, Leipzig, 1697 (for Christian Hofmann von Hofmannswaldau).

HUYGENS, CONSTANTIJN, *Gedichten*, ed. J. A. Worp, 8 vols. Groningen, 1894.

LE FÈVRE DE LA BODERIE, GUY, *Encyclie des secrets de l'éternité*, Antwerp, 1571.

Bibliography

Lope de Vega y Carpio, Felix, *Coleccion de las obras sueltas*, ed. F. Cerdá y Rico, 21 vols. Madrid, 1776–79.

Marino, Giambattista, *Poesie varie*, ed. B. Croce, Bari, 1915.

Marvell, Andrew, *Poems and Letters*, ed. H. M. Margoliouth, 2d ed. 2 vols. Oxford, 1952.

Milch, W., ed., *Deutsche Gedichte des 16. und 17. Jahrhunderts*, Heidelberg, 1954. (For Quirinus Kuhlmann.)

Motin, Pierre, *Oeuvres inédites*, ed. P. d'Estrée, Paris, 1882.

Opitz, Martin, *Deutsche Poemata*, Breslau, 1625.

Quevedo y Villegas, Francisco de, *Obras completas*, 11 vols. Madrid, 1790–94.

——— *Obras completas*, ed. L. Marin, 2 vols. Madrid, 1945.

Revius, Jacob, *Over-Ysselsche Sangen en Dichten*, ed. W. A. P. Smit, 2 vols. Amsterdam, 1930.

Saint-Amant, Marc Antoine de, *Oeuvres*, Paris, 1661.

Scève, Maurice, *Oeuvres poétiques complètes*, ed. B. Guégan, Paris, 1927.

Scheffler, Johann (Angelus Silesius), *Sämtliche poetische Werke*, ed. G. Ellinger, Berlin, 1924.

Schirmer, David, *Poetische Rosengepüsche*, Dresden, 1657.

Spee, Friedrich von, *Trutz-Nachtigall, Oder Geistlichs-Poetisch Lust-Waldlein* . . . Cologne, 1649.

Sponde, Jean de, *Poésies*, ed. F. Ruchon and A. Boase, Geneva, 1949.

Viau, Théophile de, *Oeuvres poétiques*, ed. J. Streicher, 2 vols. Geneva, 1951–58.

Vriesland, V. van, ed., *Spiegel van de Nederlandsche poëzie door alle eeuwen*, Amsterdam, 1939 (For Dullaert and Luyken).

Vaughan, Henry, *Works*, ed. L. C. Martin, 2d ed. Oxford, 1957.

Vondel, Joost van den, *Werken*, ed. J. F. M. Sterck, *et al.*, 10 vols. Amsterdam, 1927–37.

References

Adam, A., *Théophile de Viau et la libre pensée française en 1620*, Paris, 1935.

Bennett, J., *Four Metaphysical Poets*, Cambridge, 1934.

Boase, A., "Jean de Sponde, un poète inconnu," *Mesures*, 5 (1939), 129–51.

306

———— "Poètes anglais et français de l'époque baroque," *Revue des sciences humaines,* new ser. *55–56* (1949), 155–84.

———— "Then Malherbe Came," *Criterion, 10* (1931), 287–306.

BOCK, C. V., *Quirinus Kuhlmann als Dichter,* Basel, 1957.

BORINSKI, K., *Die Poetik der Renaissance und die Anfänge der Literarischen Kritik in Deutschland,* Berlin, 1886.

BRAY, R., *La Préciosité et les Précieux, de Thibaut de Champagne à Jean Giraudoux,* Paris, 1948.

BREDVOLD, L., "The Naturalism of Donne in Relation to Some Renaissance Traditions," *JEGP, 22* (1923), 471–502.

BRENAN, G., *The Literature of the Spanish People,* Meridian ed., New York, 1957.

BRINK, BERNHARD TEN, *Schets eener Geschiedenis der Nederlandsche Letterkunde,* Leeuwarden, 1867.

BUFFUM, I., *Agrippa D'Aubigné's Les Tragiques: a Study of the Baroque Style in Poetry,* New Haven, 1951.

———— *Studies in the Baroque from Montaigne to Rotrou,* New Haven, 1957.

BUSH, D., *English Literature in the Earlier Seventeenth Century,* Oxford, 1945.

CLARK, R. T., "Gryphius and the Night of Time," in *Wächter und Hüter: Festschrift für Hermann Weigand,* ed. C. von Faber du Faur, K. Reichardt, and H. Bluhm, New Haven, 1957.

COLIE, R. L., "Constantijn Huygens and the Metaphysical Mode," *GR, 34* (Feb. 1959), 59–73.

———— *Some Thankfulness to Constantine,* The Hague, 1956.

CURTIUS, E. R., *European Literature and the Latin Middle Ages,* Bollingen Series *36,* Eng. tr. of *Europäische Literatur und Lateinisches Mittelalter,* New York, 1953.

DE BACKER, F., "De zogezegde Invloed van John Donne op Constantijn Huygens," in *Album opgedragen aan Prof. Dr. J. Vercoullie,* 2 vols. Brussels, 1927, *1,* 93–105.

DE MOURGUES, O., *Metaphysical, Baroque and Précieux Poetry,* Oxford, 1953.

DE SANCTIS, F., *Storia della letteratura italiana,* 5 vols. Milan, 1950.

D'ORS, E., *Du Baroque,* Fr. vers. Mme. Agathe Rouardt-Valéry, Paris, 1936.

DRYDEN, J., *Essays,* ed. W. P. Ker, 2 vols. Oxford, 1926.

ELIOT, T. S., *Selected Essays,* New York, 1950.

Bibliography

ELIOT, T. S. "Deux attitudes mystiques: Dante et Donne," *Chroniques, 3* (1927), 149–73.

EYMAEL, H. J., "John Donne's Invloed op Constantijn Huygens," *De Gids*, 4th ser., *9* (1891), 344–66.

FABER DU FAUR, C. VON, *German Baroque Literature*, New Haven, 1958.

FRICKE, G., *Die Bildlichkeit in der Dichtung des Andreas Gryphius*, Berlin, 1933.

GOSSE, E., *Seventeenth Century Studies*, 4th ed., London, 1913.

HOLMES, E., *Henry Vaughan and the Hermetic Philosophy*, Oxford, 1932.

HUIZINGA, J., *Nederland's Beschaving in de 17de Eeuw*, 2d ed., Haarlem, 1956.

JOHNSON, S., *Lives of the English Poets*, Everyman's Library ed., 2 vols., London, 1925.

JORISSEN, T., "John Donne en Constantine Huiygens," *Nederland, 3* (1870), 62–84.

KEMP, F., ed., *Deutsche Geistliche Dichtung aus Tausend Jahren*, Munich, 1958.

LEAVIS, F. R., *Revaluation*, Cambridge, 1936.

MARTZ, L. L., *The Poetry of Meditation*, New Haven, 1954.

MEEUWESSE, A. C. M., *Jan Luyken als Dichter van de Duytse Lier*, Groningen, 1952.

NEWALD, R., *Die Deutsche Literatur vom Späthumanismus bis zur Empfindsamkeit*, Vol. 5 of H. de Boor and R. Newald, *Geschichte der Deutschen Literatur*, 6 vols. Munich, 1957.

POWELL, H., ed., *Andreas Gryphius' Carolus Stuardus*, Leicester, 1955.

PRAZ, M., "Poesia metafisica inglese del seicento," *Poesia, 3–4* (1946), 232–312.

——— *Secentismo e marinismo in Inghilterra*, Florence, 1925.

SAYCE, R. A., "The Use of the Term Baroque in French Literary History," *Comp. Lit., 10* (1958), 246–53.

SMITH, J., "On Metaphysical Poetry," *Scrutiny, 2* (Dec. 1933), 222–39.

SONNENBERG, W., *Studien zur Lyrik David Schirmers*, Göttingen, 1932.

STRUCK, W., *Der Einfluss Jacob Boehmens auf die Englische Literatur des 17. Jahrhunderts*, Berlin, 1936.

TORTEL, J., ed., *Le Préclassicisme Français*, Paris, 1952.

WALLERSTEIN, R., *Studies in 17th-Century Poetic,* Madison, Wisc., 1950.

WARNKE, F. J., "Jan Luyken: a Dutch Metaphysical Poet," *Comp. Lit., 10* (1958), 45–54.

—— "Marino and the English Metaphysicals," *Studies in the Renaissance, 2* (1955), 160–75.

WARREN, A., *Richard Crashaw: a Study in Baroque Sensibility,* Baton Rouge, La., 1939.

WEDGEWOOD, C. V., *The Thirty Years War,* Penguin ed., London, 1957.

WELLEK, R., "The Concept of Baroque in Literary Scholarship," *JA, 5* (1946), 77–108.

WELLEK, R., and WARREN, A., *Theory of Literature,* New York, 1949.

WHITE, H. C., *The Metaphysical Poets,* New York, 1936.

WILLIAMSON, G., *The Donne Tradition,* Cambridge, Mass., 1930.

WILSON, E. M., "A Key to Calderón's *Psalle et Sile,*" in *Hispanic Studies in Honour of I. González Llubera,* Oxford, 1959.

—— "Spanish and English Religious Poetry of the Seventeenth Century," *Journ. Eccl. Hist., 9* (1958), 38–53.

WÖLFFLIN, H., *Kunsthistorische Grundbegriffe,* 9th ed., Munich, 1948.

Index to Introduction

Achillini, Claudio, 58
Allegory, 12, 23
Ambiguity, 3, 43, 44
Angelus Silesius. *See* Scheffler
Antithesis, 3, 20, 23, 57
Aquilano, Serafino, 77 n.
Argensola, Bartolomé de, 60
Ariosto, Ludovico, 50
Artale, Giuseppe, 7 n., 52, 64 n.

Baerle, Susanne van, 27
Baroque, 1–4, 6, 7, 11, 14, 19, 20, 21, 26, 30, 41, 42, 43, 44, 45, 46, 47, 50–51, 52, 55, 57, 58, 59, 61, 62, 66, 67, 72, 76–77, 78 n., 79, 81, 83. *See also* High Baroque, Renaissance
Baudelaire, Charles, 77, 78, 83
Bernini, Giovanni, 81
Bertaut, Jean, 31–34, 39
Boehme, Jacob, 75, 76
Bredero, Gerbrand Adriaenszoon, 28
Bruno, Giordano, 34
Buchner, August, 49

Calderón de la Barca, Pedro, 57 n., 60 n., 81
Campanella, Tommaso, 52, 78, 81
Caravaggio, Michelangelo da, 81
Carew, Thomas, 12, 26, 34, 45, 48
Cariteo (Gareth, Benedetto), 6, 77 n.
Catachresis, 23
Cats, Jacob, 54
Catullus, 44
Cavalcanti, Guido, 77
Ceppède, Jean de la, 21, 24, 58, 63–64, 65, 68, 69, 70–71, 79
Chapman, George, 52
Character-books, 26
Chassignet, Jean-Baptiste, 21, 56, 57, 62
Chiabrera, Gabriele, 50

Cino da Pistoia, 77
Cleveland, John, 12
Conceit, 2, 5–6, 7, 14, 23, 29–30, 45, 47, 52, 53, 55, 60, 65, 68, 69, 71
Conceptismo, 53
Counter-Reformation, 2, 22, 80
Cowley, Abraham, 12, 54
Crashaw, Richard, 1, 6, 12, 15–16, 20, 21, 22, 23, 24, 43, 55, 58, 61, 65, 74, 82
Culteranismo, 53
Cusa, Nicholas of, 8 n.
Czepko, Daniel von, 72–73

D'Annunzio, Gabriele, 77 n.
Dante Alighieri, 23, 54, 81, 83
D'Aubigné, Agrippa, 3, 22, 30–31, 32, 51, 52, 54, 57, 82
Denham, Sir John, 26
Desportes, Philippe, 31, 32
Devotional poetry, 54–76
Donne, John, 1, 2, 4, 5–12, 13, 14, 15, 16, 17, 18, 19, 21, 22, 23, 24, 25, 26, 27, 28, 29, 30 n., 31, 34, 35, 37, 38, 39, 40, 43, 44, 45, 46, 47, 48, 52, 53, 55, 56, 58, 60, 62, 66, 68, 69, 71, 74, 75, 77, 79, 81, 82, 83
Drelincourt, Laurent, 66, 68, 73
Dryden, John, 5, 10, 24
Du Bartas, Guillaume, 4, 22, 32
Dürer, Albrecht, 43
Dullaert, Heiman, 21, 63–64, 65, 66, 68
Durand, Etienne, 24, 34–36, 37, 79

Eliot, T. S., 1, 5, 10–11, 78
Emblem, 26, 54

Fleming, Paul, 21, 24, 46–47, 48, 49, 60, 61, 66, 68, 71–72, 79
Fletcher, Giles, 3, 15, 16, 22, 58, 63, 64 n.
Fletcher, Phineas, 64 n.

Index to Introduction

Galileo Galilei, 81
Gerhardt, Paul, 63 n., 72
Goethe, Johann Wolfgang von, 83
Goliardic verse, 44
Góngora, Luis de, 3, 51, 52–53, 59
Greiffenberg, Catharina Regina von, 72
Grévin, Jacques, 73
Gryphius, Andreas, 3, 20, 22, 23, 43, 56–57, 58, 61, 62, 64, 72
Guarini, Giambattista, 43
Günther, Johann Christian, 49
Guillet, Pernette du, 30
Guinicelli, Guido, 78

Hadewych, 55
Herbert, Edward, 1st Baron Herbert of Cherbury, 12, 13, 18 n.
Herbert, George, 1, 3, 6, 11–12, 13–15, 16–17, 20, 21, 26, 30 n., 45, 54, 60, 65, 66–67, 68, 70, 74, 75, 79, 81, 82
Hermeticism, 16 n., 75
Herrick, Robert, 45
High Baroque, 3, 6, 7, 10, 11, 15, 16, 19, 20, 21, 23, 24, 28, 30, 32, 34, 37, 41, 46, 47, 49, 51, 56, 57–58, 60, 63, 65, 77, 79, 82. See also Baroque
Hofmannswaldau, Christian Hofmann von, 49, 72
Hooft, Pieter Corneliszoon, 28, 74
Huygens, Constantijn, 20, 25–29, 60, 66, 68–71, 72, 79, 81

Iacopone da Todi, 55
Irony, 3, 7, 23, 57, 69

Johnson, Samuel, 5, 10
Juana Inés de la Cruz, Sor, 53, 81 n.
Juan de la Cruz, San, 54–55, 59

King, Henry, 12
Kuhlmann, Quirinus, 59, 68, 74–76

Labé, Louise, 30
Laforgue, Jules, 78
Le Fèvre de la Boderie, Guy, 73
Leon, Luis de, 59
Leopardi, Giacomo, 4, 83
Libertins, 34, 39, 40, 41, 47
Lope de Vega y Carpio, Felix, 52, 60, 64 n.
Luyken, Jan, 24, 68, 74–76, 81

Malherbe, François de, 32, 57
Marino, Giambattista, 2, 3, 4, 6, 7 n., 15, 20, 27, 28, 33, 42, 45, 47, 49, 50–52, 53, 54, 57, 58–59, 61
Marvell, Andrew, 1, 6, 11, 13, 15, 19, 20–21, 24, 29, 37, 39–40, 43, 47, 73–74
Meditation, 8 n., 55–56, 59
Meistersinger, 42
Middle Ages, 11, 58. See also Renaissance
Milton, John, 1, 18 n., 83
Minnesinger, 42
Monteverdi, Claudio, 81
Motin, Pierre, 31, 34, 39
Mysticism, 17–18, 55, 73

Naturalism, 38–41
Neoclassical poetry, 2, 3, 32, 50
Nicholas of Cusa, 8 n.

Opitz, Martin, 43–45, 46, 47, 49, 72
Oxymoron, 23

Paradox, 3, 7, 9, 10, 12, 20, 22, 23, 41, 45, 46, 47, 52, 53, 57, 59, 65, 67–68, 69, 70, 71, 73, 76
Parody, 60
Petrarch, Francesco, 8, 29, 30, 31, 32, 33, 46, 48
Platonism, 8, 10, 20, 75
Pléiade, 31
Poetry. See Devotional, Goliardic, Neoclassical, Romantic
Poliziano, Angelo, 50

Préciosité, 3, 12, 27, 31, 32, 41, 42, 47, 51–52, 58

Quarles, Francis, 54
Quevedo y Villegas, Francisco de, 52–53, 59, 60, 64 n., 66, 68, 79, 81

Reformation, 2, 22
Renaissance, 2, 3, 11, 19, 23, 32, 36, 38, 40, 42, 43, 44, 45, 50, 51, 58, 59, 60–61, 75, 81. *See also* Baroque, Middle Ages
Revius, Jacob, 21, 24, 66–68, 81, 82
Richelieu, Armand, Cardinal, 82
Rilke, Rainer Maria, 78
Romantic poetry, 1, 83
Ronsard, Pierre de, 23, 31, 32, 43, 44
Rotrou, Jean de, 57 n.
Rubén Darío, 77 n.

Saint-Amant, Marc-Antoine de, 21, 34, 38–39, 40, 52, 54
Scève, Maurice, 29–30, 31, 37, 77
Scheffler, Johann ("Angelus Silesius"), 24, 72–73, 74
Schirmer, David, 21, 47–49, 72, 79, 82
Schwartz, Sybilla, 49
Shelley, Percy Bysshe, 83
Silesius, Angelus. *See* Scheffler
Simile, 12, 23
Southwell, Robert, 56, 61
Spee, Friedrich von, 21, 43, 56, 59, 61–62, 72

Spenser, Edmund, 23
Sponde, Jean de, 4, 24, 31, 64–66, 68, 82
Sprachgesellschaften, 27, 51
Steen, Jan, 26
Stevens, Wallace, 78
Stilnovisti, 29, 77–78
Suckling, Sir John, 12
Swinburne, Algernon Charles, 77 n.
Symbolists, French, 77

Tasso, Torquato, 28, 50, 59, 81, 83
Taylor, Edward, 21, 53, 70
Tebaldeo, Antonio, 6, 77 n.
Thirty Years' War, 42, 49, 72
Traherne, Thomas, 73–76, 81
Tristan L'Hermite, 34, 41, 42

Valdivielso, José de, 60
Vaughan, Henry, 1, 11, 12, 15, 16–18, 19, 20, 21, 24, 54, 55, 58, 66, 73–75, 81
Viau, Théophile de, 21, 34, 36–38, 40, 43, 47, 82
Villon, François, 66
Visscher, Tesselschade, 28
Voiture, Vincent, 42
Vondel, Joost van den, 3, 15, 20, 28, 51, 56, 57–58, 62

Wordsworth, William, 4

Yeats, William Butler, 75

Index of Titles

Ach Liebste, lass uns eilen, 166

Aen myne uitbrandende kaerse, 244

Ah, Dearest, Let Us Haste Us, 167

Alas, but Count Your Days, 119

All Do Protest the Cruel Enmity, 121

A Love Constant beyond Death, 259

Als sie gestorben, 196

A Method of Loving, 271

Amor constante mas allá de la muerte, 258

An Basilenen, 174

Andacht, 182

An meinen Erlöser, 180

An seine neue Buhlschafft, 200

An sich selbst, 186

Asses plus long, qu'un Siecle Platonique, 90

Assies toy sur le bort d'une ondante riviere, 126

Auff ihr Abwesen, 172

Au moins ay'je songé, 140

Aus naturalistes et mécreans, 96

Beside a Flowing River, 127

Canciones del alma en la íntima comunicación de unión de amor de Dios, 274

Cette rouge sueur, 98

Christ Dying, 241

Christus stervende, 240

Come, Let Us Go A-Strolling, 169

Creation, 213

De bekeerde moorder, 242

Delie: dizain cxxix, 89

Delie: diszain cclxxii, 93

Delie: dizain ccclxvii, 91

Delie: dizain ccclxxviii, 95

Del mondo e sue parti, 278

Der Cherubinische Wandersmann (excerpts), 190

Der XXIII. Liebeskuss: die Geburtsnacht des Herrn, 208

Devotion, 183

De Ziel betracht den Schepper uit de Schepselen, 248

De Ziele betracht de nabijheid Gods, 246

De Ziele in aandacht over de nieuwe Creatuur, 250

Die gespons Jesu klaget ihren hertzen brand, 162

Durante il bagno, 280

During the Bath, 281

Easter, 237

Ecce Homo, 101

Elégie à Cloris, 142

Elegy to Cloris, 143

En que satisface un recelo con la retórica del llanto, 268

Entrer dans le bordel, 154

Er hat Vergünstigung, 202

From the Moment of My Waking, 231

Gods Besluyt, 216

Gods Evenbeelt, 220

Gods Kennisse, 218

God's Likeness, 221

God's Virtues, 217

Goede Vrijdagh, 234

Go in the Whorehouse, 155

Good Friday, 235

Grant That I May Receive Thee, 103

Green Fascination of Our Human Life, 273

Helas! contez vos jours, 118
How Much Can Touch Thy Heart, O Christ, 105

If on the Waters Earth Hath Its Support, 115
Il buon ladrone—a Pietro Valeri, 286
In Her Absence, 173
In Time of Rejection, 179
I've Just Received a Very Pretty Letter, 151

Je viens de recevoir une belle missive, 150
J'ouvre mon estommac, une tumbe sanglante, 106

Kommerlick Ontwaken, 228
Kompt, lasst uns ausspatzieren, 168

La blanche Aurore a peine finyssoit, 94
La donna con gli occhiali, 284
Lágrimas de un Penitente: Psalmo IV, 262
Lágrimas de un Penitente: Psalmo X, 264
Le feu devers le Ciel s'eslève incessament, 130
Le jour passé de ta doulce presence, 88
Lorsque fâché, ta cruaulté j'accuse, 122

Mais, ô combien, mon Christ, 104
Mais si faut-il mourir, 116
Maria's Journey, 225
Mentre la sua donna si pettina, 282
Me voyant plus frisé, 152

Ne vous offensez point, belle ame de mon ame, 108
New Year's Day, 233
Nieuwe Jaer, 232

O Croix, qui de la croix ton beau surnom retire, 124
On God's Gracious Providence, 207
On Her Death, 197
On His Dream, 171
On His Oath, 199
On My Candle Burning Out, 245
On Precious Stones, 157
On the Birth of Jesus, 185
On the Birth of Our Saviour, 159
On the Same (God's Likeness), 223
On the Supreme Grace of Creation, 205
Our Life One May to Servitude Compare, 129

Paeschen, 236
Pastor, que con tus silvos amorosos, 256
Persevera en la exâgeracion de su afecto amoroso, y en el exceso de su padecer, 260
Prayer before Communion, 267

Que da medio para amor sin mucha pena, 270
Quel lieu vous tient cachez, 132
¿Que tengo yo, que mi amistad procuras?, 254

Reconocimiento propio, y ruego piadoso antes de comulgar, 266
Renewal, 215

Scheppinge, 212
Seeing Me Spruce as Some Fat German Count, 153
Shepherd Who Did Me from the Depths of Sleep, 257
Si c'est dessus les eaux, 114
Sie Quället Ihn, 194
Soit que je vo' reçoive, 102
Sondagh, 238

Song of the Soul in Union with God, 275
Sonnet to Mlle. La Croix, 125
Soul of my Soul, Take No Offense, 109
Stances à l'Inconstance, 136
Stanzas to Diane, 107
Sunday, 239
Sur la Naissance de Notre Seigneur, 158
Sur les Pierres précieuses, 156

Tears of a Penitent: Psalm IV, 263
Tears of a Penitent: Psalm X, 265
The Cherubic Wanderer (excerpts), 191
The Dream, 141
The Excess of Amorous Suffering, 261
The Fire Rises Ever to the Sky, 131
The Good Thief (by Artale), 287
The Good Thief (by Dullaert), 243
The Knowledge of God, 219
The Lady with Glasses, 285
The Nativity of the Lord, 209
The Permission, 203
The Rhetoric of Tears, 269
The Soul Considers Its Nearness to God, 247
The Soul Contemplates the Creator in the Creation, 249
The Soul's Devotion at the Rebirth of Life, 251
The Spouse of Jesus Bewails Her Passion, 163
The Transience of Beauty, 189
The World and Its Parts, 279
This Red Sweat Slowly Falling, 99
To Basilene, 175
To Himself, 187
To his New Love, 201

To Inconstancy, 137
To Materialists and Unbelievers, 97
To My Redeemer, 181
To My Tormentor, 195
Tout le cœur de nos jours au service est semblable, 128
Tout le monde se plaint de la cruelle envie, 120
Troubled Awakening, 229
T' Selve (Gods Evenbeelt), 222
Tu m'es le Cedre encontre le venin, 92

Über die Geburt Jesu, 184
Über Gottes gnadige Vorsorge, 206
Über seinen Eyd, 198
Über seinen Traum, 170
Uitvaert van Maria van den Vondel, 224

Van d'ure dat ick waeck, 230
Verde embeleso de la vida humana, 272
Vergänglichkeit der Schönheit, 188
Vernieuwinge, 214
Voicy-l'Homme, 100
Von der hohen Erschaffungs Gnade, 204

What Interest, My Jesus, Drives You Thus?, 255
Whenever I Rage and Blame Your Cruelty, 123
Where Are You Hidden, 133
While His Lady Combs Her Hair, 283

Yes, So We All Must Die, 117

Zur Zeit seiner Verstossung, 178